Russian Spirituality & Other Essays

Mysteries of Our Time
Seen Through the Eyes of a
Russian Esotericist

VALENTIN TOMBERG

RUSSIAN SPIRITUALITY
AND OTHER ESSAYS

⊕

Mysteries of Our Time
seen through the eyes of a
Russian Esotericist

⊕

Logo Sophia
San Rafael Ca

First published in the USA
by LogoSophia
an imprint of Sophia Perennis
© Robert Powell 2010

Series editor: James R. Wetmore

For information, address:
LogoSophia, P.O. Box 151011
San Rafael, CA 94915

Library of Congress Cataloging-in-Publication Data

Tomberg, Valentin.
[Aufsätze aus der Zeit von 1930 bis 1938 über
östliche und westliche Geistigkeit. English]
Russian spirituality and other essays:
mysteries of our time seen through the eyes of a
Russian esotericist/Valentin Tomberg.— 1st American pbk. ed.

p. cm.
Includes bibliographic references.
ISBN 978 1 59731 502 9 (pbk: alk. paper)
1. Anthroposophy. 2. Christianity—Miscellanea. I. Title
BP595.T6513 2006
299'.935—dc22   2009052189

Cover image: 'The Holy Trinity',
icon painted by Andrei Rublev (c. 1411),
Moscow Tretyakov Gallery

CONTENTS

PART ONE

Early Essays

INTRODUCTION

by Robert Powell

THESE ESSAYS BY VALENTIN TOMBERG from the 1930s not only provide extraordinarily profound insights into Russian spirituality, but are also strikingly relevant to our present time. For example, the remarkable renaissance of the Russian Orthodox Church since the collapse of the Soviet Union can be viewed in light of the author's statement, regarding the organic relationship of the East European people with the Christ Impulse, that 'the significance of the Christ Impulse is for them a motivation for living. When it is alive in the soul, then life has value. But now [at that time in the Soviet Union] there arises a terrible void—the void of an absence of motivation for living.'

These words apply in our time just as much as they did in 1931 when they were written. For modern Western humanity also suffers from a terrible void, a void that, as we shall see, is destined to be filled either from the heavens (enlightenment) or from the interior of the earth (demonic possession). Even though Soviet communism has died, its spirit lives on in a variety of contemporary manifestations— for example in a draconian apparatus for control over the populace on a scale now undreamt of in the Soviet Union. Aided by modern technology, it is more possible than ever for 'big brother' to keep a large portion of humanity under constant surveillance.

Another such example is revealed in the essay on the 'Secret Motto of Bolshevism', where the inversion of the human being's thought process is discussed. This inversion is just as much a phenomenon relevant to modern Western humanity as it was during the era of Soviet communism. In order to understand this inversion, we must first grasp that the normal mode of decision-making for modern human beings is to analyze a situation with one's own powers of thought and conscience and then make a decision based on the clear light of insight. And this decision must be supported by moral considerations relevant to it, including consideration of the consequences for others of the decision made. An inversion of this mode of decision-making occurs when, instead of proceeding from the light of thought and conscience, decisions are prompted by the wish for fulfillment of the will, which rises up and shapes the thought process. Tomberg refers to this as 'metabolic thinking', representing a complete reversal of the normal mode of decision-making.

Instead of moral intuition lighting up in thought and conscience, guiding the will from above to perform deeds in freedom, dark currents of the will, motivated by sympathy or antipathy, arise from below and commandeer thinking, providing clever 'justifications' for deeds altogether lacking in moral content. The thoughts and deeds of Adolf Hitler and Joseph Stalin were of just such a nature: all that counted for them was the brutal, ruthless implementation of their will. Contrast such a will-shaping process, effected through the cunning of a serpent-like intelligence bent on fulfilling the will, with the thoughts and deeds of Rudolf Steiner (1861–1925), author of *The Philosophy of Freedom*, who practiced moral intuition as his path of decision-making, thus informing his deeds with the pure light of spirit-filled, conscientious thinking imbued with moral substance. The 'secret motto of Bolshevism', whereby normal thinking is inverted and 'the human heart becomes a mere organ of the metabolism,' in fact provides a key to understanding the crisis of modern civilization. As in the era of Soviet communism, Western society today shows a remarkable lack of moral fiber. An inversion of thinking has taken place here too, but in a more subtle way than in Nazi Germany or in the Soviet Union. Money, sex, power, and the longing for fame ('stardom') are primary driving forces in our time, manipulating a morally-drained thinking oriented solely toward attaining these ends.

In contrast, the quality of thinking Tomberg offers here demonstrates a remarkable clarity, that of the light of conscience—a profoundly awakened conscience able to survey a multiplicity of phenomena belonging to the modern era. It is this kind of thinking, permeated with morality, that is so needful in our time in order that we may navigate the present crisis and create a world sustained by moral values.

And it must be said that it is precisely the inversion of this quality of thinking that is symptomatic of a force traditionally identified by the word 'Antichrist': a shaping force totally devoid of morality. The Antichrist (who is the focus of several articles in this volume) is here seen not just as a force at work in the world but as an incarnated being whose endeavor is to become world ruler—a master of deception whose plan to achieve this goal is masked by a beguiling appearance. Tomberg describes the encounter with the Antichrist as the greatest trial facing modern humanity. The Antichrist's mask of deception becomes apparent in the author's description of a personality perfectly attuned to the feelings and judgments of the age, a great philanthropist leading an irreproachable life who is an outstanding figure in the realm of thought and whose works, read with enthusiasm by all, proclaim universal peace.

This characterization of the Antichrist is drawn largely from the prophetic vision of the Russian philosopher Vladimir Solovyov. In Tomberg's own words, the goal of the Antichrist is 'to produce a new human being: a human being whose thinking reflects, not heaven, but the interior of the earth. . . . Now one might think that no reasonable person could ever willingly surrender to being possessed, as this indeed implies a darkening of self-consciousness and an annihilation of human freedom. But the opposite of this is true, for there are actually many who yearn to be possessed.'

Thus the choice facing modern human beings, as mentioned earlier, is that between enlightenment and possession. Most of us today are neither enlightened nor possessed, but in Tomberg's words 'amoral-neutral'. However, the coming of the Antichrist now forces us to make this choice. The cultivation of thinking based on moral intuition, characterized above as 'thinking permeated by morality', is the starting-point on the path leading to enlightenment, for it represents an opening to the light of the spirit from the heavens. Enlightenment is the attainment, as a permanent condition, of complete permeation by the heavenly light of the spirit. By contrast, what was alluded to above as 'metabolic thinking' is the starting-point for demonic possession by forces arising from the interior of the earth. Both Hitler and Stalin were possessed by forces arising in this way. Their condition of possession was the opposite of enlightenment.

The Austrian spiritual teacher Rudolf Steiner and the Russian esotericist Valentin Tomberg were enlightened human beings whose thinking was grounded in moral intuition and who represented in the world the antithesis or antidote to what came to manifestation through the Austrian-born Hitler (who became Germany's *Führer*), and the Georgian-born Stalin (who became dictator of Russia). Fortunately, the works of Rudolf Steiner have for the most part long been available in English translation and so have been able to work upon the minds and hearts of many in the Anglophone world throughout much of the troubled second half of the twentieth century up to the present; but those of Valentin Tomberg have only recently begun to be made available in English translation to a larger audience (see further reading at the end of this book), and so the publication of this volume of Tomberg's early articles by LogoSophia is a welcome event indeed. May it serve as a stimulus toward the development of thinking permeated with morality, and as a source of profound insight into the challenges of our time.

THE GOSPEL OF ST JOHN AS A WAY
TOWARD UNDERSTANDING THE
SPIRITUAL HIERARCHIES

Emptiness and Fullness

WITHIN THEIR LIFE OF SOUL, human beings ordinarily experience the universe as an immense void in which certain spaces are 'filled'. About this various speculations can be made, but it remains a fact that *in the first instance*, the universe presents itself to our sensation as a tremendous void having within it filled-out-spaces that are the cosmic bodies: planets, stars, comets, cloud formations, etc. Now this basic sensation of emptiness did not always exist. There were times when interplanetary space was felt to be just as substantial as the ground underfoot. The space of heaven was felt to be *filled out* with substance. The earth swam in this substance like a fish in water, and people felt themselves, together with the earth, supported by it. This support—the *ether*—was not only experienced dynamically, but also morally, so that it was actually for them the dwelling place of gods.

In still more ancient times, the basic feeling of emptiness and fullness was again different. At that time universal space was felt as not just filled out—as the earth is—but was experienced as the plenitude surrounding the 'void' of the earth and all earthly things. World space was activity and reality; the concrete formations of matter were holes in this reality. As the impress of a seal in wax consists of meaningful signs, so for people's feeling in these ancient times the realms of nature consisted of meaningful impressions: of imprints made by a universal realm filled with gods into the world ether. Thus the three realms of nature that surround human beings were regarded as divine 'seal' impressions. This feeling is the root out of which sprang, for instance, the *Tabula Smaragdina* (Emerald Table) of Hermes Trismegistus. For the basic principle of the *Tabula Smaragdina*—'that which is above is *like to* that which is below, and that which is below is *like to* that which is above'—expresses in thought the ancient feeling that the One speaks in two languages: first in that of the fullness (*pleroma*) in which is its essence; and secondly in that of the emptiness (*kenoma*) into which, through a hollowing out, its essence is given *contour*. There in the *Tabula Smaragdina* we find formulated the ancient instinctive insight that knowledge 'as in a glass darkly' [*in dunklen Konturen*] corresponds to knowledge 'face to face'.

The gradual emptying of cosmic space for the experience of human feeling was simultaneously accompanied by profound changes in humanity's actual inner soul-life. For in the same way as those who look out through the body finds around them the outer world that can be experienced as we have described, so do those who look out through the soul likewise find around them an outer world that can be experienced as full or empty. For the human being, the relationship to this inner space of the soul has changed as radically as has the relationship of the body to its outer space. Also the fullness of light of the myth-making consciousness has withdrawn from here, and into its place has entered darkness, the void. Previously, the actual plenitude of inner life was productive cosmic activity of wakeful dreaming; while one's own ideas, opinions, etc. were felt to be mere shells — that is, empty. Later, a new relationship asserted itself. On the one hand, the visible world bodies — previously empty shells in etheric space — became 'bodies' in 'empty' space; on the other, abstract thoughts and ideas became the content of the inner 'heavenly' space of the now empty soul.

So it happened, according to the decree of world destiny, that the human soul was deserted by the fullness, both outwardly and inwardly. It became surrounded by fields of emptiness where the material and the abstract confronted it as pale reality.

The desertion of the soul by the plenitude of spirit caused loneliness. The emptiness surrounding the soul gave it the impulse to seek for *that* place in the world where a portion of fullness, where something alive, could still be found. That place is the soul *itself*. For here is alive that which is neither material nor abstract. This is the striving for *self-awareness* that arises in the soul out of its perception of loneliness.

The soul thus thrown back upon itself now has the choice: either to remain passive in the experience of the fact of its own existence; or to *replenish the world emptiness* out of its *own* reality, its own fullness. This would require an inner unfolding of power by the soul: the courage to say: Emptiness surrounds me on all sides. Neither truth nor goodness are there. But I will ray out truth and goodness *from myself* into a world empty of truth, empty of goodness.

Such a decision on the part of the soul would, however, be utopian unless the real power to carry it out were available; that is, *unless there existed in the human 'I' the potential to unfold the same fullness as that of old*—that fullness which filled starry space and soul space. This power—as divine plenitude of the *human soul*—had first to manifest within one human being in order that confidence in the inner power of the 'I' could arise in human beings. This necessary and yearned-for revelation of the divine plenitude *in one human being* is the historical life of Christ Jesus. The earthly work of Christ Jesus is the beginning of a refilling of existence with truth and goodness (*aletheia kai charis*) from out of the *human being*.

Thus, contemplation of the plenitude and void of existence lead us to the necessary recognition of the reality of the Christ Impulse, preceded by the reality of John the Baptist; that is, the human soul becoming aware of itself in the void of existence—'the voice of one crying in the wilderness.'

The Plenitude of the Hierarchies and Christ

To the Gospel of John is given the task of describing the working of the plenitude through the body of Jesus; that is, of showing the process of filling the emptiness by essential being on three levels of soul: the moral ('sin'), the bodily ('sickness'), the karmic ('death'). In other words, St John's Gospel describes how the divine plenitude of 'I' power fills out the void of 'corporeality' in its threefold form of astral body, life body, and physical body. For: 'in Him the plenitude of the Godhead became bodily.'

Now in Greek, the concept 'plenitude' bears not only the meaning of the opposite of a void, but also of a *working together*: the joint *activity* of a community of beings. So, for instance, the crew of a ship, as the active group who together filled and directed it, was called 'pleroma'. 'Pleroma' in the cosmic sense, in the sense of St John's Gospel, means the crew of the world ship. So it is important to note that 'pleroma' is not simply substance, a substance that fills out, but rather means an effective *working*, a joint working together of many. Thus 'pleroma' means not only the opposite of emptiness, but also the opposite of inertia, of passivity, of disunity, of divergence. In order to translate the ancient concept into a modern thought, we would have to say that 'pleroma' is the unity of cosmic beings in activity. This definition *in abstracto* corresponds *in concreto* to the reality of the spiritual hierarchies. Regarded Anthroposophically, 'pleroma' means the working together of the spiritual hierarchies.

The intention of the writer of St John's Gospel is to describe the working together of the spiritual hierarchies through the body of Jesus, the Nazarene, during the period when the Christ Being, whose consciousness comprised the hierarchic consciousness, was incorporated into it. In our present considerations it will be a question of splitting the white sunlight of the plenitude as described in St John's Gospel into its component colors, in order to distinguish the activity of the individual hierarchies within their cooperating whole. First, however, it will be a question of sketching roughly the working of the individual hierarchies in the earthly life-work of Christ as described by John. We shall start from the picture of Christ's Being as John portrays it, for the plenitude of the periphery, the working together of the spiritual hierarchies, gathers into this center of the circle, into this focal point, the Christ Being. And from this focal point outward, proceeding from the center point outward, we will then consider the workings of the periphery in order to comprehend this periphery of heavenly hierarchies.

The consciousness of the beings of the third hierarchy (Angels, Archangels, Archai), as characterized by Rudolf Steiner, differs from human consciousness. Instead of *individual* inner life, these beings have a 'spirit-fulfillment' out of *cosmic* heights. And instead of having an outer world that is *independent* of the inner life, they have an outer world created by their inner life. So the outer world of these beings has absolutely the character of inwardness—that is, it is morally revealing; while their inner life has the quality of objective necessity—that is, it works cosmically. Human beings, on the other hand, have around them an amoral world of given facts and *in* them a subjective world of their own ideas, feelings, wishes, and so on.

Holding on now to this fundamental difference, when we turn to St John's Gospel we confront the fact that the portrayal of the working of the Word in a human body begins with the Baptism in the

Jordan. What does the evangelist actually tell us through this fact?

The writer of St John's Gospel tells us the following: I set myself the task of describing the working of the Word in the body. All that took place before the Jordan Baptism in the man Jesus—all that happened in his outer destiny up to that point of time—is not for me to consider. For before that, in the soul of Jesus there were individual thoughts, experiences, and so on. These belong to his *own* being, and so do not come into the sphere of my task. However, at the Baptism in the Jordan, the *cosmic* spirit descended upon him, *filling* his soul. Instead of *his own* views, ideas, and so on, from this point onward he has *spirit-fulfillment*. What works in him is cosmic spirituality. For this reason, from this moment on we no longer have a *man* to consider, but rather, a divine being.

What then follows the Baptism in the Jordan is the beginning of the miracle-working of the Baptized One. There unfolds within him the power to create *Signs*. St John's Gospel describes seven such Signs.

What do they actually convey to us?

It is possible to read the language of the seven Signs in the following way: To begin with, human beings are surrounded by the facts of the natural realms—stones, plants, and animals. These facts are there without our cooperation; they are quite independent of human beings and of the human element. In itself, this realm is amoral. There is no 'goodness' (morality) to be found in nature herself. Natural laws are not moral laws. Morality, however, is bounded within the breast of the human being, it does not have the power of natural law. Facts of nature are amoral; moral impulses do not have the power of natural happenings. However, there once existed a Being on earth whose morality possessed the power that nature has, who could place before humanity *morality as powerful as nature*. The Christ Being added to the given world of outer facts a created world of 'signs'.

Thus in the first part of his Gospel (up to the twelfth chapter) St John describes for us the *first* great teaching of the Word made flesh, the *first* stage of His revelation in the human body; namely, the replacement of His own inner life by *spirit-fulfillment* (Baptism in the Jordan) and the juxtaposition to the given world of nature by the self-created world of moral facts—the world of the seven 'signs'.

And thus, from the manner of the description of the Christ Being in the first part of St John's Gospel, what we are shown is that He reveals the characteristic of consciousness of the *third* hierarchy—in human circumstances.

The Washing of the Feet (John 13) introduces a new stage in the revelation of the Word. There begins a sequence of Sayings (John 13–17). In place of 'signs' enters the spoken Word. *Speech* now becomes the means for Christ's revelation. While previously (up to John 12) speech related to miracles or Signs, supplementing and explaining them, it now becomes (John 13–17) an independent *direct* revelation: it becomes *itself a Sign*.

After repeatedly immersing oneself in the so-called 'Farewell Discourses' of Christ (particularly in the original Greek text), one gradually experiences their extraordinarily profound effect. They are not actually *communications* of insights or facts, nor are they sermons. They are, rather, a direct stream of *life-stimulation* flowing in a characteristic rhythm in the heart. It is *direct* speech; it does not pass through the head, but also it does not exert a forceful influence upon the will. It spreads out in concentric circles as a spiritual substance, streaming forth from Christ. The forces of His life body are given to the disciples. For instance, there is not much value in saying anything about loving one another from out of the point of consciousness and motivation where ordinary human speech generally arises. Yet speaking of such things can be of the greatest value when not only the astral body of the speaker is brought into motion, but also the *ether body*. Then things are not only spoken about, but the *things themselves* are spoken, and this discourse of Christ is a pouring forth of his life body. It is, in the most eminent sense, *living* speech. Every sentence is a stream that penetrates directly into the heart of the listener, and there *creates* life. The listener is not only a receiver, but is in a process of becoming. The inner life is not only enriched, but also transformed. The listener becomes a different person. The discourses of Christ to his disciples are a process through which *creative 'being'* is produced.

The Last Supper as described by the other Gospel writers is seen from the point of view of imaginative consciousness, whereas the Farewell Discourses are the Last Supper described from the point of view of inspired consciousness. For this reason, the effect of these discourses is that through their rhythm, powerful inner articulation, and potency of verbal formulation, the same effect is produced as by the taking of bread and wine as Body and Blood of Christ at the Last Supper. It penetrates into the ether body.

On the other hand is the fact, which must here be considered, that the *deeper* the effect works down into the body, the *higher* must be the level of consciousness from which the power emanates. The source of consciousness, the Imagination-creating Being (He who doeth Signs), who not merely *beholds* imaginations but *enables others to behold* them, comes from the consciousness level of the Third Hierarchy (spirit messenger, folk mission fulfiller, and time spirit revealer). The source of consciousness of the Inspiration-creating Being, who not only receives Inspirations but enables others to receive them, comes from a still higher level of consciousness. The Last-Supper-like communications of the Farewell Discourses of Christ are in fact a creating of Inspirations, just as the 'miracle-working' in the first thirteen chapters was a creating of Imaginations. For in what other way than through a directly *inspiring* speaking could the communication be made to which the disciples replied: 'Lo, now speakest Thou plainly and speakest no parables. Now are we sure that Thou knowest all things and needest not that any man should ask Thee: by this we believe that Thou camest forth from God' (John 16:29–30). This not only inspired, but also inspiring speaking, streams forth from a state of consciousness that differs as much from one's own spirit-fulfillment as the latter does from human objective consciousness; it is no longer just the spirit-fulfillment of *one* person, but rather the *spirit-fulfilling* of *others*. Inwardly, it can be perceived that a stream flows directly from the Father *through* the person and is conveyed to other people, giving form to their 'being'. This process is powerfully expressed in the words: 'And the glory which thou gavest me I have given them: *that they may be one, even as we are one: I in them and thou in me. . . .*' (John 17:22–23). Here, in monumental manner, is expressed the process of Christ conveying Inspiration to the disciples—this is the *creative formative* power of the Father Being's *life-creating* stream, pouring forth *through* Christ upon the disciples.

Now the state of consciousness characterized above is that which belongs to the beings of the *Second* Hierarchy. The consciousness of the beings of the Second Hierarchy is on the one hand outwardly creative;

it has the power to create beings in their own image, beings that are alive (but alive only until they have taken effect). On the other hand, it is inwardly more devoted to the cosmic spirit than the consciousness of the beings of the Third Hierarchy. They are not only 'spirit-filled' but also the 'spirit flows through them'. A life-generating stream goes *through* their inner being and becomes an essence-transforming activity—an activity working creatively on the essence of another being. Thus the consciousness of the Second Hierarchy could be characterized as: an essence-transforming life-generation.

The Farewell Discourses of Christ are such an essence-transforming life-generation carried down into human existence. With wisdom impulsated power (where Kyriotetes, Dynamis, and Exusiai, as 'fullness', work together), the speech of Christ, proceeding from the Father, flows forth and transforms the disciples for a time. *Later on* they must receive understanding ('the Spirit of truth He shall teach you. . . .') of what is actually *happening* to them through these Farewell Discourses. Only in the future will the disciples, as individuals, be mature enough to comprehend what is *happening* through this speaking. In order that the transformation could remain *permanent*, a still higher power, descending from a still higher level of consciousness, would have to intervene. This necessity was indicated by Christ when He said that He is going to the Father, who is greater than He.

For the *permanent* transformation of beings, the working of forces from the *First* Hierarchy—the plenitude of Thrones, Cherubim, and Seraphim—is necessary. The Second Hierarchy can create living beings, but cannot give them an *independent* existence. This remains within the power of the *First* Hierarchy.

In the third part of St John's Gospel, which begins with the eighteenth chapter, a still further stage of revelation of the Word made flesh is described. Here the power no longer works through Imagination-creating power that from within Christ projects outwardly toward others (miracle-working); neither does it any longer work through bringing forth Inspirations that go forth *into* others; rather, it now works through the force that creates *events of destiny* from outside; that is, through the force that creates *Intuition*.

The following schematic drawings can serve to illustrate the three kinds of effective activity of Christ Jesus.

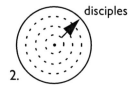

We can represent Christ's power of creating Imaginations as follows: let the spirit-filled inner life of Jesus be the center point *out of which*, through the imagination-projecting power of Christ, Signs were made for the disciples and the people—*the center works on the periphery* (1).

Then in the case of the Inspiration-creating work of the Christ Being, the center grows outward and becomes periphery. *The center becomes the periphery* (2); that is, the inner life of Christ flows into the inner life of the disciples, they become one.

Then in the case of the Intuition-creating work of Christ, the action comes from outside, from people and events, toward Christ Jesus; *from the periphery back to the center* (3)—the periphery acts on the center.

Thus we have in the third stage the action of destiny-forming powers, for destiny works on human beings *from without*. With this we enter into the realm of the *First Hierarchy*.

In recounting the threefold activity of the 'fullness' through Christ Jesus, we must have clearly in view the difference between the levels of consciousness of the three hierarchies and the levels of consciousness possible to human beings. The human initiate *has* Imaginations, Inspirations, Intuitions. So human beings *perceive* these Imaginations, Inspirations, and Intuitions of the spirit world through their developed organs, whereas the spirit beings of the higher hierarchies are their *Creators*.

This is also the incisive distinction between Christ Jesus and a human initiate—Christ was not a mere beholder of the spirit world, but also its Creator. And this fact alone should suffice to convince anyone of the Divinity of the Christ Being, for only a God can unfold the creative activity described in its stages of development by the writer of St John's Gospel.

The Miracles and Discourses, as well as the events in the last chapters of St John's Gospel, are to be comprehended as *deeds* of Christ. Yet the *active consciousness* is to be sought on another level than before; for not only does it live in things and beings of the outer world, but it also works *out* of the things and beings of the outer world. It becomes karmic. Without Himself being *subject* to Karma, the Christ Being works in the *manner* of and with the power of Karma. Thereby the Karma of humanity and of the earth was changed. In the same depths of existence out of which work the destiny-forming powers, works the Doer of the Deed of the Mystery of Golgotha. These depths, however, are also in the innermost being of humankind. And into this innermost being reaches the effect of the Mystery of Golgotha.

While the effect of the living Word of the Last Supper was that the listeners *temporarily* were inwardly transformed, the effect following after the Mystery of Golgotha was a gradual process of *permanent* transformation. This, the *birth* of the 'New Adam', was just as real as that of 'old Adam'. It is an effect that reaches from the *other side* of existence into the human 'I', inwardly filling it so that it receives the power to work ever more strongly on its surrounding bodily sheaths. It is a process of the objective *giving* of essential reality to the human 'I', whereby what is given is not something temporary or on loan, but rather an *actual* growth in humanity. One *becomes* more human through the effect of the Mystery of Golgotha.

We can say, then, that the Mystery of Golgotha (as portrayed by St John) is a process of the new creation of the human core of being through a power of the same nature as destiny. Now it is the *First Hierarchy* that is able to create beings (differing therein from the *Second Hierarchy*, which cannot create independent beings), so that they are able to leave those beings *independent*. They give the gift of being. And this activity of bestowing existence issues from the 'fullness' of the Word made flesh in the third stage of His earthly working. It is the fullness of the *First Hierarchy* with which we are met in the description of the Passion according to St John's Gospel.

So, if we would understand the working of the fullness of the hierarchies with the help of St John's Gospel, we have in the description of the seven signs a schooling that can educate us to a comprehension of how the *Third Hierarchy* holds sway through Christ Jesus. The seven signs are keys to understanding the message of the time spirits

(Archai) working in fulfillment of the mission of the Jewish folk spirit. These signs are the result of the cooperation of Angels (messengers), Archangels (folk spirits), and Archai (time spirits) in Christ Jesus. The awaited messiah of the Jewish People, proclaiming the spiritual message (the Gospel) which is for all humankind—that is the *first* stage of revelation of the Word.

In the second stage, Christ moves from an *instructing* to an *enlivening* activity. The directly streaming Word creates Inspirations. The Imaginator becomes Inspirator. And this Inspiration is a wisdom-borne stirring formation of the inner life of those inspired. It is a working in cooperation of the *Second Hierarchy*—the Spirits of Wisdom, the Spirits of Movement, and the Spirits of Form—in the living Word of Christ Jesus.

On the third stage of the revelation of the Word, we behold the power of the *First Hierarchy* working through events. They work the destiny-forming world power of love. The mystery of the Seraphim reveals itself as an event of world destiny through the might of the Thrones in the Crucified One.

Thereafter follows Death, Entombment, and Resurrection. The three days of Death; the dark, silent cleft of the Tomb—they are the *fourth* language of the Word.

And in this language is 'revealed' something still higher: *in the three days of deathly silence in the darkness of the Tomb, we confront the unspeakable Mystery of the Trinity of Father, Son, and Holy Spirit.*

And from this depth the powers of Resurrection were drawn—which overcame Death. 'The deeper the effect, the *higher* the cause,' is a principle that is fully verified in what we have described. The Baptism in the Jordan was related to the 'I' of an individual *human being*. The Signs that follow it were related to the Imagination-creating power of the *astral body* of Christ Jesus through the *Third Hierarchy*. The living Speech was an Inspiring activity of the *Second Hierarchy* through the *life body* of Christ Jesus. The power of the *First Hierarchy* revealed itself through the Event of the Crucifixion of the *physical body* of Christ Jesus. Then the highest power of the Godhead became manifest in the *sub-sensible* realm of death, in hell, where death was conquered.

After the 'descent into hell'—or rather *through* it—it can be said of the Christ Being: 'He sitteth at the right hand of God, from whence he shall come to judge the living and the dead,' for He has become Lord of Karma.

The stages characterized above are the degrees of fulfillment of the emptiness of existence (*kenoma*) by the fullness of spirit (*pleroma*). And the fullness penetrates through the 'I' into the astral body, then into the etheric body, then through the physical body down into hell. The Body of the Risen One is an absolutely *filled-out part of existence*. Thereby the cosmic activity of the 'filling' of the earthly void began.

From the above account it can be seen that the writer of St John's Gospel *actually* describes the gradual revelation of the *Fullness*; that is, of the working together of the spiritual hierarchies in the human body.

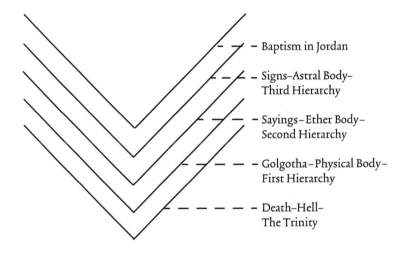

THE METAMORPHOSES OF LOGIC: THE LOGIC OF THE MATERIAL, SOUL, AND SPIRITUAL WORLDS

THE MINERAL WORLD is the region where the logical axiom, 'a part is less than the whole', has full and unlimited validity, for in this region everything can be expressed in numbers having *quantitative* significance. It is the realm of the quantitative *per se*. In the case of anything that is regarded *quantitatively* (that is, in its most material aspect) it is true that the whole is greater than its parts. A brick is more than the piece of a brick, and one million votes in favor of the socialists is more than a single vote.

However, when we move from the mineral to the realm of life, the organic, the validity of this axiom becomes significantly weaker. Here we find the *functional* added to the quantitative. An organism is a unity of functions, of living forces. These forces make up not only a unity, but still more a *union* because an organism is a *system* of functions. In this union it is no longer right to speak of 'lesser' or 'greater', but rather of the *significance* of individual forces for the whole. But the significance of individual forces in the organism can be very different. Thus the axiom 'the part is less than the whole', used not in relation to the quantitative, but now applied in relation to the significance of function (that is, the qualitative), is unable to retain its full validity. It should here be expressed more like this: 'The significance of the part can be less than, or equal to, the whole.'

Let us take a step further and proceed to the sphere of soul-morality, without losing sight of the axiom relating part to whole. Here we meet with a radical metamorphosis of this axiom.

In order that this metamorphosis not become too abstractly characterized, we must approach it with the help of an example. The ideologists of the group who seized power through the Bolshevist revolution justify (and this argument applies more or less to every revolution) the necessity for their atrocities with the axiom: 'the benefit of the whole demands the annihilation of a *part*.' 'Chop wood and the chips will fly'—this Russian proverb was heard innumerable times by the present author as an excuse for the terror.

The whole method of Lenin's social thinking was consistent with the proverb 'chop wood and the chips will fly.'

Now it must be frankly admitted that this mode of thinking (and the mode of action arising from it) would be entirely correct if the axiom 'the part is less than the whole' were valid also within the realm of *human* social life. If this axiom were valid where soul meets soul, then two people would have the full right to put a third forcibly out of the way if that person was a hindrance to the intention of the other two. When this axiom is applied to the realm of soul, there springs from it inhuman, *anti-soul* or *sub-soul cruelty*; that is, an element comes in that is of a nature foreign to the soul as such. Therefore this axiom is not fitting to the soul realm, where it is invalid, *false*.

The soul has its own logic, and this logic of the heart knows no calculation. For it, the pain and joy of one person are of equal value with the pain and joy of thousands. To the logic of the heart every single soul is of equal value. Never will the heart admit that it is right to stamp on one soul for the benefit of others; never will it be in harmony with true heart-sense to recognize the right to violence. For the *true* logic of the soul is *compassion*. And for *this* logic, the axiom we are considering should be formulated: *the part is equal to the whole*.

The attitude of mind that demands the sacrifice of a part for the benefit of the whole is just as fundamentally false in the *soul realm* as 'a part is greater than the whole' would be false in the *material realm*.

By establishing this point, we have not yet exhausted the metamorphosis of our logical axiom. We have merely ascended from root to stem and from stem to leaf—the fruit formation in the blossom we have not yet pursued. This however does take place. The logical axiom of part and whole is subject to a further metamorphosis, and rises thereby into the realm of the beauty of blossoming.

We now approach the task of considering the application of our axiom in the sphere that extends up beyond the human—the sphere of spirit. We now have to picture to ourselves an axiom of *divine* logic in the same way as we have tried to imagine axioms of human and sub-human logic.

This axiom of divine logic already had been characterized thousands of years ago—not, indeed, as a thought formulation, but in a *picture*. The description of the axiom of part and whole as it lives when lifted up into the divine, we find in the *Gospels*. What is found there is the parable of the Good Shepherd who leaves ninety-nine sheep behind to go in search of *one* lost sheep. And when he had found it, there was more joy among the *angels in heaven* than there was over the ninety-nine.

In this picture the axiom is shown in relation to 'the angels in heaven'; that is, as an axiom of *divine logic*. This logic is oriented toward the *individual*. Human beings live within the individual; with effort they learn to cognize the whole. Their cognition is oriented toward the whole. The gods *live within the whole*—their vision is directed toward the individual. Schematically, we could show the difference as follows:

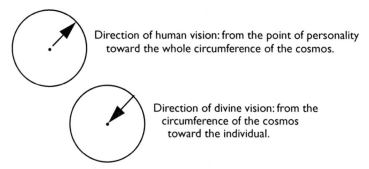

Direction of human vision: from the point of personality toward the whole circumference of the cosmos.

Direction of divine vision: from the circumference of the cosmos toward the individual.

Actually, the same is expressed more beautifully by Rudolf Steiner: 'The gods are the religion of human beings; human beings are the religion of the gods.'

The gods look down from the cosmic whole upon the wonder of the *free personality* who has the choice between good and evil. And this personality is *a part* of the cosmic whole. Yet the gods orient the activity of the whole *cosmos* toward this part. For that is the nature of *their* logic, *the logic of divine love.*

For divine logic, *the part is greater than the whole.*

Thus we can summarize the process of the metamorphosis of the logical axiom concerning the relation of the part to the whole as follows:

The part is less than the whole—logic of the material realm.
The part is less than or equal to the whole—logic of the living realm.
The part is equal to the whole—logic of the soul realm.
The part is greater than the whole—logic of the spirit realm.

In developing the above thoughts we have overcome *formal* logic (merely formal thinking) and have moved on into living, *mobile* thinking. In other words, we have proceeded with our thoughts out of the sphere of activity of the Spirits of Form into that of the Spirits of Movement. In order to be able to go a further step, to rise into the realm of the Spirits of Wisdom (that is, to enable the *wisdom* of these concepts that have been made mobile to emerge), we have to be able to *apply* them. Only thus can we come to an inner conviction that they contain *objectively active* wisdom; that is, truth borne by the Spirits of Wisdom—and not just the truth of the Spirits of Form and Movement.

So we put the question: in what realm of life does the above sequence of metamorphoses of the axiom relating the part to the whole prove itself?

The realm of life where the most mobile and *realistic* thinking is essential is the social realm. Here the above must either prove true or fail. For this reason we will choose *this* realm, and try *freely* to apply the above to it.

Social life is—as is the life of the human organism—threefold. It is an interaction of economic life, rights (political) life, and true cultural (spiritual) life. (Why this is so, and what is meant exactly by these designations, can be learned from some works of Rudolf Steiner—for instance, *Towards Social Renewal*.[†] Here it can only be our task to *think further* along the lines of what is conveyed there.) Each of these three life realms of the social organism has its own laws. One ought not to think about cultural life in the same terms as about the economic life. Each of these realms requires a different kind of thinking. One ought not, for instance, to think juristically about religion, or economically about rights. In the sphere of *economic life*, the relation of the part to the whole is of a kind that the part must be 'subservient' to the whole. Here the principle of equally valid claims holds good, and the sum of the equally valid claimants is greater than a part. The whole must be the determining factor. The interests of the whole, not of the individual, are here decisive. A healthy economic life is run according to the principle *a part is less than the whole*.

If we were to apply the same principle to the *life of rights*, we would meet with absurdities. If, for instance, in legal proceedings the majority were always in the right as opposed to the minority, then no *justice* would exist at all. The meaning of justice is equality before the law, regardless of number or power. For the *life of rights, the part is equal to the*

---

† Rudolf Steiner Press, London, 1977; also under title *Threefold Social Order*, in earlier editions from 1920. German original entitled *Die Kernpunkte der sozialen Frage in den Lebensnotwendigkeiten der Gegenwart und Zukunft*, 1919. ED

whole. The life of rights is only true to itself when the rights of the individual, even when in opposition to a whole nation, can be recognized.

In the *cultural life* it is different again. There everything depends on the individual, the one who is 'productive'. In the realm of the purely 'productive', for example in the realm of *art*, the 'producer' is everything. The *creative personality* is the very basis of all cultural life. Therefore, the axiom valid for the cultural life is: *the part is greater than the whole*.

Only *that* culture has *spiritual* stature, which makes possible the existence and work of great personalities. Only *that* state is a just one, where the rights of the individual are secured against all others by the law. Only *that* nation is economically sound, not where there are multi-millionaires, but where there are no beggars.

The part is less than the whole—economic life.
The part is equal to the whole—life of rights.
The part is greater than the whole—cultural life.

THE METAMORPHOSIS OF THINKING
THROUGH THE STUDY OF SPIRITUAL SCIENCE

THE STUDY OF SPIRITUAL SCIENCE is the first stage, or more precisely, the first level of work on the path of initiation. Here, the essential thing is to conceptually grasp and understand spiritual-scientific communications. Rudolf Steiner repeatedly mentioned that such comprehension is *possible*; but everyone who has attempted it has experienced that it is not *easy*. It is a task that thinking, as such, is capable of carrying out; but the difficulty is that the *kind* of thinking we are generally accustomed to using is not capable of mastering it. The customary way of thinking—that to which we have immediate access—has first to re-educate itself. It must first go through a process of metamorphosis in a sequence of 'deaths and regenerations'.

The necessity for a 'death and regeneration' first asserts itself for thinking when it is faced with a description of the etheric—for instance, the human etheric body. A reality has to be considered whose nature should not be imagined as either material or as psychic. The ether body is neither a 'concept' nor a 'cloud of steam'—neither is it an 'emotion'. Here thinking stands before a necessary inner jolt. It has to brace itself for an effort that is essentially new. The formative force of the organism has now to enter into the thinking process, just as matter has already entered into it. To make this possible, the tendency of thinking to fixate, to immobilize, must be given up. Thinking ordinarily feels satisfied when it has succeeded in bringing a process to a standstill and attaching a fixed thought to it. But now thinking should strive not to feel satisfied until it has succeeded in setting itself in motion in unison with the process it is considering. Through cognitively participating in the motion, there then enters into thinking the reality of the formative force. Thinking thus becomes *organic*. The characteristic of organic thinking is its faculty for thinking in processes. Concepts (vor-*stellungen*) become processes (vor-*gängen*); what was stationary is set in motion.

For this cognition that thinks in processes, the spiritual-scientific description of cosmic metamorphosis from the Old Moon existence to the Earth state becomes comprehensible. The formation of races and cultures in human history can also be comprehended by this thinking. However, with regard to Sun and Saturn states, one would have to admit that this thinking is not really able to reach the unique essence of their cosmic conditions. It can indeed call forth the Saturn and Sun processes with satisfactory clarity, yet this calling forth takes place in 'Moon-like' concepts. By means of this thinking, only *that* in those earlier cosmic states which resembles the metamorphosis from the Moon to the Earth condition can be comprehended. The result is that to this thinking the Sun and Saturn states seem to be mere 'youthful Moon' states. This very important difference is often—very often—not considered.

What we have here is this: thinking that thinks solely in processes meets yet another boundary—namely, the reality of reincarnations. It is called upon not only to acknowledge them, but also to have knowledge of them. Reincarnation is not simply a transformative process; more than that, it is an objective moral process. In order to comprehend this moral process, it does not suffice to have mere mobility of concepts; this must give way to the ascendancy of *moral* mobility of concepts. Here the morality of *deeds* takes over the determining role in the process of metamorphosis. Thinking faces the task now of understanding objective events not only in thoughts, not only in processes, but also in *deeds*.

The thinking of Oswald Spengler,† which rises only as far as a metamorphic process, can only follow the organic flow of historical happenings. Moral initiatives that enter into them, free deeds that change these organic lines of direction, remain beyond the scope of his thinking. But the fact is, history can as little be understood from a merely organic approach as can human destiny from consideration of the human organism alone.

The characteristic quality of *moral* thinking is *spontaneity*. It does not move in consciously pursued flowing lines like organic thinking; rather, it has a raying-out character. Schematically we could show the difference thus:

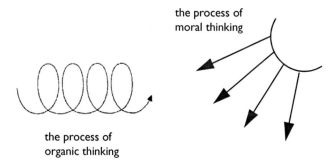

the process of
moral thinking

the process of
organic thinking

These diagrams indicate that 'continuity' is essentially different in moral thinking than in organic. In organic thinking one thing *follows* from another. In moral thinking each thought has to be followed back to its source, in order *from there* to go on to the next thought. This process of thinking is not a flowing but a raying-out.

At this point we may allude to the fact that for human beings in the West it is natural to think in ideas or concepts, whereas Middle-Europeans think organically, and East-Europeans—for instance, nearly all Russian thinkers—tend to think morally.

This last-mentioned radiant (raying-out) thinking, this thinking

† Oswald Spengler (1880–1936), German cultural historian and philosopher best known for his book *The Decline of the West* (1919), in which he puts forth a cyclical theory of the rise and decline of civilizations. ED

that conceives in deeds, is capable of comprehending the Sun state. The ancient Sun existence cannot be grasped by fluid thinking alone; here the thinking itself must ray forth in unison with the Old Sun. For this thinking, the world—and also human history—becomes a history of deeds: of divine deeds and of human deeds.

Yet deeds proceed from Beings. Now a deed is only *one* manifestation of a Being. In the *Being* lies the secret of the *continuity* of deeds, for it is the Being itself that connects the deeds together. In order to comprehend the unity of deeds in the Cosmos, thinking must not only move in deeds, but must also *raise* itself up to *Beings*. It must itself take on the nature of *Being*.

The moral unity of human history can only reveal itself to a thinking that thinks in Beings—that has become essential being itself. Thus the Mystery of Golgotha cannot really be understood when it is thought of only as a *deed* of the Christ Being. It can only be comprehended when thought of as a deed of the *Christ Being*. The Christ Being himself is the deepest secret of the Mystery of Golgotha. In him the unity of human history is comprehended.

For *this* thinking, the sentence 'Christ is the meaning of the Earth' is a mighty, shattering revelation. And for *this* thinking, a real and complete answer is given when spiritual science communicates to it that through their working the spiritual Hierarchies cause this or that cosmic happening. If at first one thought materialistically or abstractly, then later this developed into a mobilized thinking, and further, one's thoughts were spiritualized into a moral comprehension of deeds—then at this last stage of one's thinking's development, *Hierarchies* are thought. The world becomes a great *community* (the Gnostic *Ecclesia*) of Beings who in their essential being stand in graded ranks. And their unison must be sought on a still higher stage of thinking's evolution—to which we can only allude.

In Eastern Christian thought there lives a remarkable figure. This figure is Mary, the Mother of God, who is at the same time Sophia, the Holy Wisdom. She is also the 'Church', the principle of the *community* of all humanity, and is therewith of the same essence with Christ. This principle is therefore the principle of community (*ecclesia*); that is, that which unifies Beings. It provides the possibility and manner of the unison of the graded ranks of hierarchical Beings.

At this point our thinking is faced with a still higher challenge—the challenge to think in 'communities', to think 'sophianically'.

What in essence can be seen from the foregoing is that the study of spiritual science presents us with the task of the threefold re-education of our thinking.

First we must make our thinking flow, and thereby capable of comprehending how the Earth evolved from the Old Moon, and how the human being evolved out of a higher world.

Then, through enabling our thinking to ray out morally, we become able to comprehend the Old Sun as a divinely-wrought deed of Gods, and the destiny of man as the consequence of human deeds.

Finally, through the fire of a thinking that has itself become essential being, by knowing the Beings of the cosmic Hierarchies, we can have knowledge of Saturn existence; and in Earth history, of what is revealed to us in the Mystery of Golgotha.

So the thinking of one who with devotion and reverence studies Anthroposophy goes through a dramatic metamorphosis:

Within the flowing stream of the etheric, it transforms itself;
In the light of the astral, it rays forth;
In the fire of the spirit, it glows.

Thus, through the 'study of spiritual science' as the first stage on the path of initiation, one acquires the capacities not only to grasp fixed matter with fixed concepts, but to grasp liquidity with flowing thoughts, the radiant with radiant ideas, and the fiery with fiery ideals.

THE FORMULATION OF
MEDITATION IN EAST AND WEST

THE life OF ANTHROPOSOPHY works in two directions: in an outward direction, where it is culturally creative and streams out into the general spiritual life of humanity; and in an inward direction, where it works in the intimate depths of individual human beings as a force that forms them. That Anthroposophical life as it moves outward takes on varying colors and forms according to the region and nation in which it lives is a general experience that requires no elaboration.

But the fact that the inner side of Anthroposophical life is also dependent to a certain degree on place and language is a reality not often seen as such, or perhaps only theoretically accepted. For this reason it is often the case that Anthroposophical speakers handle questions connected with the *meditative life* as if no differences existed in this realm. It is true that meditation, when it is consistent with Rudolf Steiner's spiritual science, is, in its inner principles, always the same; yet the *relationship* of the person in question to meditation can vary according to whether that person belongs to the Eastern, Western, or Central European cultural sphere. For the difference in the soul attitude of people, for instance in East and West, reaches right into the intimate realm of meditative life.

In order to quite clearly present this divergence in soul attitude so as to pursue it into this more intimate realm, let us first take an example from a sphere where the facts are more 'robust' than in the sphere of meditation. For instance, when giving a lecture before a Russian audience, it is possible to achieve success—yes, even win adherents— when one can convey to the audience that the *ideals motivating* the speaker are noble and unselfish. One can for instance successfully spread an idea or outlook solely by bringing forward the moral quality of its *motivating impulse*. A theory will only find acceptance because of the good intentions that lie behind it. On the other hand, a teaching will meet with little echo—even if objectively correct—when it is not brought forth out of moral intentions.

With Central European audiences the case is quite different. There it does not suffice to interest people in one's motivations: *ways* must be shown *how* these motivating impulses can be brought to realization. A European audience has little interest for ideals in themselves, but becomes interested when their realization is possible; that is, in ideals for which *methods* of realization have been worked out. The audience in Europe demands a description of the actual *steps* to be taken in order to realize the ideals.

Again the relationship of the audience to the speaker is different in the far West. There people are neither satisfied by ideals nor with methods. They demand to see something that has been achieved. They do not become enthusiastic for the content of a lecture unless to a certain extent *results* can be presented to them.

From this (somewhat crass) example it can be seen that East Europeans are focused on the *intention*, whereas its realization in the future is of less interest than is the *content*. They can be made enthusiastic for an ideal without knowing the method by which it can be realized.

The people of the Center do not become enthusiastic over the ideal: their focus is on the *method*. They get enthusiastic for *plans and ways*, often arduous and tedious, but which can be practiced.

In contrast, Westerners are only open and enthusiastic for the new when what is presented is not only an ideal and a plan, but also something *already achieved* of this ideal by means of this plan. They are oriented toward results.

That this is true can be seen, for instance, in the history of the spiritualistic movement. While spiritualism, which is entirely directed toward observable results, was hardly more than a party game in Russia, it took on forms of an almost religious or ecclesiastical nature in the West. To the Russian mentality, the *motivations* behind the spiritualistic activities appeared too insignificant and superficial. In the West, on the other hand, the *results* of the spiritualistic activities roused a storm of enthusiasm that moved millions of people. In the Center (Europe), however, so-called *scientific* spiritualism arose, which strove to build up spiritualism as a scientific *method*.

The above-characterized differences in attitudes of soul also hold sway in relation to meditation. Russians, for instance, could hardly have any enthusiasm for meditation if it were presented to them as a mere *exercise*. The soul-life is for them too holy, too sacred, for mere 'exercises' to be practiced there. They would feel it to be an importation of something foreign, even mechanical, into the life of soul. It could drown out the inner angel voice. The soul is a wonderland where wonders still take place. East Europeans never lose the feeling that something unexpected can happen in the soul: a great repentance, a great conversion, or perhaps a revelation. They believe in the *miracle in the human being*. So, therefore, many believe for instance that the future of Bolshevism does not lie in the form of a reaction to it, or in the realization of its aims, but rather in the form of a mighty *transformation of soul attitude*: a grandiose penitence.

The feeling that human beings *can* unexpectedly rise above themselves in insight and deed—this belief in the miraculous in the human being is actually an instinctive consciousness of the presence of the angel in the depths of human inner life—whence an intervention can always be counted upon. This consciousness is at the same time a hindrance for the working of the 'I' as the systematic educator of inner life, for it is feared that thereby something greater could be displaced by something lesser.

For these reasons, the motivation of meditation as a mere exercise is not only insufficient for the East European, but also antipathetic. Still, they can rouse much energy and enthusiasm for meditative work when they are presented with *another* motivation for it.

Now the actual significance of *fasting* consists in the fact that, through abstinence and reduction to the level of necessity, forces are freed from lower members of the organism which can then be put at the disposal of the higher activity of upper members. This 'making available' of the lower forces to the higher activity is in Eastern Europe one of the most important aspects of spiritual life. And there can be found there—in contrast to the Catholic asceticism for merit or reward—the general, partly subconscious conviction that all of the 'lower' *can* be transformed into something 'higher'. This transformation takes place through *fasting* during periods of spiritual effort.

Now thinking is not the highest faculty for which the human being has potential. It can be transformed into a still higher faculty—that of *vision*. For this it is necessary for thinking to be just as much internalized as speaking has become internalized into thinking. As we are silent while thinking, so must we silence our thinking for inner vision to take place. We must proceed from *thinking* to the *thought* (a formulation of Rudolf Steiner's) and then proceed further to let go of the thought. This process is the spiritual equivalent to *fasting*; that is, transformation of thinking forces into *higher* forces of vision. And so, meditation understood as *fasting* is the sacrifice of lower forces for the benefit of higher, future faculties. This is the Eastern attitude toward meditation. And for the East European, meditation is not an exercise, it is a sacrifice, a continuous, repeated sacrifice called *fasting*.

If East Europeans have problems in the realm of motivations that they have to resolve *before* meditation, so Westerners have difficulties in the realm of results, of successes in meditation. They are focused on the achievement of results. Here the problem arises that at first these results are imagined to be other than they really are. For the fruits of meditative work are to be sought on another level than the one where the work has begun. The special quality of this work lies in the fact that through it something *new* arises. Now Westerners have the tendency to visualize this new thing in an old way, that is to say, it is actually visualized as being on the same level as where their ordinary consciousness exists. Results are expected which are visualized materialistically. Thereby arises a grave hindrance; there enters in a 'haste', a *desire* for success. Instead of remaining quietly steady and with loving devotion in the clarity of meditation, there enters a mechanical 'let's get on with it.' Through the pursuit of a goal that has been projected down into a material plane, the meditation becomes *mechanized*.

This hindrance can be eliminated by taking up, before and alongside the meditative work, a comprehensive *cognitive effort* to penetrate the concepts communicated by spiritual science. Through this effort, thinking is released from its materialistic tendency. It is gradually trained to think of spiritual and intimate things in a spiritual and intimate manner. Thus it becomes capable of envisioning the results of meditation in advance in such a way that instead of arousing desire, it brings forth sacrifice and renunciation in the soul.

So we see that people of the East, through permeating their motives with *morality*, clear away the hindrances that block their way to meditation, while people of the West achieve the same through the *labor of thought*. Now morality is the most effective weapon against the *Luciferic*, while thinking is the best antidote to the *Ahrimanic*. Had Easterners not concerned themselves with motivating ideals before they went in for meditation, they would have fallen into a voluptuousness: a self-seeking enjoyment of the inner life. Had Westerners decided to save themselves the effort of the labor of thought and tried to achieve higher faculties only through meditation, their meditation would have degenerated into mechanical 'gymnastic' exercises. In other words, the Easterner would have succumbed to Lucifer, the Westerner to Ahriman.

People of the Center have the fortunate predisposition to foster the *way* as such. For them there is comparatively little difficulty in pursuing *meditation for its own sake*. They work with the feeling: Meditation is something by means of which I increase my value as a human being. *Because* of the presence of this predisposition, the stream of modern meditative life, the living Anthroposophy of Rudolf Steiner, was able to—and had to—arise in the Center.

For the people of the Center, meditation is more an 'aesthetic' than a moral-religious or practically correct activity. They labor at the work-of-art, 'Human Being'. They sculpt themselves and experience a deep satisfaction in the process of formation.

This fortunate predisposition must, however, be wrought with effort, for it appears only in the state of balance between the moral and the practical. This balance is not always present, nor is it easily established. The contrasting tendencies in the conceptions of medita-tion in East and West struggle here against each other in the souls of prospective meditators. They have to make their way through *doubt*.

The way through doubt—until the emergence of the inner faculty—is described in an excellent manner in the book *Meetings with Rudolf Steiner* by Friedrich Rittelmeyer.† This book, highly instructive from several other points of view also, contains a description of the intimate experiences in meditation of a *Central European*. It is only nec-essary to read a few things between the lines.

In order to summarize the above, and to answer the question which doubtless many a reader has come to—How may the characterized trinity in meditative life be brought into unison?—we need no more pregnant a formulation than that given in St John's Gospel: *I am the Way, the Truth, and the Life.*

In these words the solution suited to meditative consciousness for the problem 'East, Center, West' may be found, right into its most intimate consequences within the sphere of meditative life. The true 'I', the 'I am', is that which unites the tendencies to *morality, reality,* and *method* into a higher unity. This solution of the problem can be visualized in the following picture:

† English title: *Rudolf Steiner Enters My Life,* Floris Books, Edinburgh, 1982.

THE STUDY OF SPIRITUAL SCIENCE
AS AN ESOTERIC SCHOOLING

RUDOLF STEINER often indicated that his books are so written that the mere reading of them is itself a sequence of exercises. A book such as *Theosophy*, for example, is so formed that it not only conveys a certain body of information, but also induces a series of *effects*. Not only the content of the book, but also its style is a gift from the author. Indeed, the content is a help for one who seeks knowledge, while the style is a help for the person engaged in self-development. For as the 'what' of the book enriches the 'I' of the reader, so the 'how' of the book gives the 'I' strength to work upon the soul body. And an organizing effect on the soul body is an occult exercise when it proceeds from the activity of the 'I'; that is, when this activity is fully conscious.

The devoted reader of *Theosophy* will have the experience that during reading, something like a contraction of forces to a central point takes place in the head. The sharply outlined concepts *relating to* something essentially *new* demand an effort in thinking that is similar to the effort made when one wishes to see more clearly. It is not only through the perceptual quality of the examples and comparisons, but also through the manner in which thoughts are placed before the reader, that the book causes one to exert oneself to 'see' with one's thinking. The book is written in such a way that thinking develops into a *seeing-thinking*.

In the course of this effort the thinking concentrates itself, as it were, and gathers itself around a powerful central point. There streams out from this center a ray of clear thought-light that makes the objects under consideration visible. And as the sunlight falling on objects produces colors, so does concentrated thought-light color the objects of cognition. Thinking becomes not only clear, but also colorful. And for this colorful seeing-thinking, the chapter in *Theosophy* about the human aura, for example, is just as stimulating and edifying as is the treatise of a classical philosopher for abstract thinking. As abstract thinking acquires new concepts through the process of formal reasoning, so seeing-thinking is able to comprehend through colors. Colors are, to this thinking, just as much answers to its questions as reasoned explanations are answers to abstract thinking.

The theme of the book has just as sharply defined contours as do the concepts that form its content. In it everything is avoided which could bring about a dizziness in the perceptual thinking (seeing-thinking) that we have characterized. The destiny of *the human being* through life and death in the three worlds—this is essentially the theme of the book. Cosmic evolution, the history of humankind, the spiritual hierarchies—these themes are not dealt with. A cross section of that part of the world which at first most directly concerns human beings is here described. Answers are given to a complex of questions within which modern people do not become powerless in their thinking—here they can unfold and maintain the clarity of thought of which we have spoken.

As regards the book *An Outline of Esoteric Science*—originally intended as a continuation of *Theosophy* but appearing finally as an independent work—the case is different. Here readers are placed before a task with which they cannot cope if they apply the same measure and type of thinking effort that sufficed for the study of *Theosophy*. In the first chapters there is a repetition of a great part of the theme of the book *Theosophy*, in which the reader can use the concentrated seeing-think-ing centered in the head. Then all of a sudden the theme is widened to such an extent that consciousness, wanting to maintain the same clar-ity as previously developed, falls into a mild faint. The complexity of the different spiritual hierarchies working together on the various members of the human being during the seven cycles of each embodi-ment of the earth is so immense that the sharply contoured thinking begins to get dizzy. The head becomes giddy when faced with the mighty tableau of interweaving cosmic beings who, in a surging-up-and-down-activity, work in the forming of humanity. If conscious-ness wants to maintain its clarity without dissolving in the wide expanses of semi-obscure vagueness, if it wants to retain the full savor of experience of firmly grasped and clearly envisioned knowledge, then it has to proceed to a new way of handling the material. Previ-ously it had concentrated itself in the thought life of the head. From this center it had projected itself out toward the intended object of cognition, aiming to strongly illuminate it so that it became inwardly visible. Now it has to direct its effort, not toward seeing an object in front of it as a picture, but to becoming conscious of a surging web of deeds in a process of interweaving. This becoming conscious is however only possible when the consciousness proceeds from a 'seeing' to a 'listening' effort. The thinking must take on a listening quality if it would understand cosmic development as described in *An Outline of Esoteric Science*. Here, thinking's will-to-accurate-vision does not suffice—here the inner musical structure of world events must be listened to. Thinking must become rhythmical; it must learn to hear the cosmic symphony.

If consciousness re-orients itself this way, that is, if it awakens in the human rhythmic system, then what had seemed impossible becomes possible. What had previously appeared to be wholly closed to real insight, and seemed graspable at best as a superficial schematic system, becomes knowable to a thinking no longer centered in the head, but which descends, with full consciousness, into the surging waves of the rhythmic system.

Cosmic evolution cannot be merely 'studied'; it has to be grasped by a thinking that works out of artistic sensitivity. Those who are not capable of grasping world evolution as a grandiose work of art will hardly progress further than to a schematic system in their comprehension of it. For *listening-thinking*, it is not a mere 'assertion' that human evolution occurs in seven stages; rather, the sevenfoldness of world evolution is as inwardly evident to it as is the twofoldness of eyes, ears, hands, etc. And just as a human being with one eye, one arm, would be a cripple, so world evolution, were it not sevenfold, would also be incomplete. A thinking that apprehends the world through rhythms knows it not as a mere system but rather as an interplay of rhythms. And within this interplay it knows false and true rhythms which, as *rhythms*, can be false or true just as ordinary thinking perceives logical conclusions as being true or false. To this thinking the sevenfold rhythm reveals itself as true.

After this description of cosmic evolution and human history in *An Outline of Esoteric Science*, there follows the chapter on the path of initiation. It contains practical guidance for those who not only want to understand evolution—but would take part in it. To this theme, however, a whole other book is devoted, namely, the book *Knowledge of the Higher Worlds and its Attainment*. It is written solely for practical purposes. It has little value for theorists who seek to know the world with those faculties that they already possess. It has, however, the greatest conceivable value for those who seek to attain not only new knowledge but also new faculties of cognition. The book directs itself to the will of the reader, it describes exercises that can actually be understood only by doing them. A large part of the book is only comprehensible to the practitioner: it appeals to comprehension through doing.

Just as *Theosophy* is directed toward the 'head person' thinking in sharply defined concepts, and *An Outline of Esoteric Science* is directed toward the 'rhythmic person' centered in the breast, so *Knowledge of the Higher Worlds* is directed toward the 'will person', the person of deeds.

If through work on *Theosophy* a perceptual, living thinking is exercised which in working through *An Outline of Esoteric Science* becomes rhythmic (i.e., when the feeling, concealed behind thinking, becomes conscious), so through the study of *Knowledge of the Higher Worlds* an activity is fostered that amounts to an awakening of the will.

The first reading of the book *Knowledge of the Higher Worlds* requires a different approach toward its theme than do the descriptions of cosmic and human destiny contained in the two other works. Instead of the 'seeing' approach to *Theosophy* and the 'listening' approach to *An Outline of Esoteric Science*, what is necessary now is a 'tactile' approach. Here direct experience is constantly being called for—a trying-out, a living-into, an approach whereby the soul of the reader comes as close as possible to the object of study. Most of what is said in this book must be inwardly touched with invisible soul-arms, must be much more concretely, surely, and closely known than the panorama of world evolution—for it is there to be practiced.

Thus we see that the three basic works of Rudolf Steiner stand as an inwardly related whole, a whole that corresponds to the threefold human being. At the same time, however, it is to be noted that this correspondence is a real one: that is, just as each member of the human being is interpenetrated by the other two members, so each of these three works contains elements of the other two. *Theosophy*, then, corresponds to the head person, *An Outline of Esoteric Science* to the breast person, and *Knowledge of the Higher Worlds* to the limb person. Not only do the three works accord with the three parts of the human being, but they are at the same time a three-stage school for the threefold human being. They contain three kinds of exercises—not only in their content, but also in their style — for the whole human being. Together they form a system of practice that corresponds exactly to the makeup of the human being. In other words, the three works as a whole can be of significance for the earnest reader not only as reading material but also as an esoteric schooling on a fundamental level, for three steps can be taken by the consciousness of the reader (albeit in elementary fashion) by studying the three books. These three steps are characterized in *Knowledge of the Higher Worlds* somewhat as follows: first, a preliminary center is formed in the head of the student; it is then transposed to the region of the larynx; and finally, it is carried over from there to the heart region.

Now the course of the earnest study of the three basic works of Rudolf Steiner is exactly the same: a center is formed in the head through the study of Theosophy. This center is transposed to the larynx-region through a study of *An Outline of Esoteric Science*. It is transplanted into the heart through work on the book *Knowledge of the Higher Worlds*.

And so, in conclusion, we can confirm the truth of this frequent indication of Rudolf Steiner's: that his works are so written that they comprise inner exercises.

H. P. BLAVATSKY'S *Secret Doctrine* AND RUDOLF STEINER'S *Esoteric Science*

TWO COMPREHENSIVE WORKS that deal with the whole occult world-conception have appeared in modern times within Western culture: the *Secret Doctrine* by H. P. Blavatsky and *An Outline of Esoteric Science* by Rudolf Steiner. These are the only two works containing communications of a cosmological nature that are of value for their true revelations. These two works—in the midst of a large number of writings with symbolic content containing semi-obscure half-truths (either theoretical kabbalistic expositions or mystic-lyrical effusions)— contain more or less complete pictures of a world-conception entirely unknown to the public. The truth of the matter, one would have to admit, is that not one of the well-known Theosophical or kabbalistic writings can be compared in *objective value* with them, for not one of the works of occult literature *offers* the reader so much as they do.

If fundamental significance has to be conceded to these two writings, the question then arises: How do the two relate to each other? Is there a difference—or even contradiction—between them in principle; or can *An Outline of Esoteric Science* be regarded merely as a supplement to or completion of the earlier *Secret Doctrine*?

Let us consider first the *Secret Doctrine*. This is a two-volume work (the third volume appeared after the author's death) that describes the coming into existence of the world and humankind, and discusses the prevailing philosophical, religious, and scientific theories on the subject. It contains a wealth of insights into the secrets of creation and the primal history of humankind. And although these insights are described in an erratic and chaotic style, still their content has value. The coming into being of the cosmos is pictured there as a breathing process of the primal Being. Inbreathing and outbreathing of Beings—these are the two fundamental tendencies present in all cosmic events. In the outbreathing, matter arises; in the inbreathing, the spirit reveals itself.

Accordingly, there also exists a twofold cosmic 'ideology': that of the creators who affirm cosmic evolution, and that of the beings who reject the material creation. The battle of these 'ideologies' takes place as much on earth as in heaven. In heaven it is the battle between the affirming and denying gods; on earth, the battle between souls following 'the path of the Moon' (*Chandravancha*) and souls following 'the path of the Sun' (*Suryavancha*). The Moon is the cosmic 'headquarters' of the materializing world-stream; the Sun that of the spiritualizing stream. Now, it became necessary for these two streams to unite at a particular point of cosmic evolution. This event, its causes and effects, form a profound *mystery*. And the whole work of H.P. Blavatsky is oriented toward this mystery. Everything that is communicated in detail in the *Secret Doctrine* has, in the last analysis, the purpose of shedding light on the *Mystery of the Fall into Sin*. The *Secret Doctrine*, in spite of having an unclear style and erratic train of thought, is a strongly centered work. It is oriented toward one point: *the event of human incarnation and division of the sexes, which took place in the middle of the Lemurian period.* For through this event, the opposition of Sun and Moon was incorporated into humanity. On the one hand, therewith arose human intellectuality, the Sun nature in us; on the other hand, human beings thereby became subject to the curse of sex, the Moon nature in us. Recognition of this fact leads to the practical conclusion: the purpose of human existence is to achieve victory of the Sun over the Moon nature. The physical procreation of human beings must cease. Humanity must return again to a spiritualized state, such as was its condition before the Fall—preserving, however, the intellect that was achieved through the Fall.

Thus the attitude of soul that follows from the world picture presented in the *Secret Doctrine* is *single-poled*. Human beings recognize a duality in the cosmos and in themselves, and place themselves decisively on one side of the recognized polarity. The whole inner attitude of the author herself is also of this nature. For her, not only is sex something that has to be fought by the spirit, but also the *West* is the lower pole of human culture that has to be fought by the East. For when there are only two tendencies—upward to the spirit and downward to matter—then the West is where the darkening stream prevails, and the East where the light-filled stream predominates. And the significance of cultural evolution is that Western darkness is to be overcome by the Eastern light—preserving in the process, however, the Western intellectuality.

From this one-sidedness there follows a quite definite moral attitude. Because the *Secret Doctrine* discerns only the opposition between above and below, the concepts of good (what is worthy of pursuit) and evil (what is to be fought against) become synonymous with the concepts of spiritual striving and earthly striving respectively. That which frees human beings from earth is to be striven after; that which binds them to earth is to be combatted. But the moral questions: Can there be an element of evil in spiritual striving, or can there be some good in earthly striving? is an attitude foreign to the *Secret Doctrine*. And so it is, indeed, understandable that the *Secret Doctrine* regards Lucifer as a leader of humanity, and Jehovah, the Moon God, as the dark power of the drive to procreate. The *Secret Doctrine* sees only the antithesis of *Lucifer* and *Ahriman*. The author definitely adopts the standpoint of the Luciferic principle, while combatting with all her passionate energy the Ahrimanic. Yet the traditional ideas of Jehovah on the one side, and Christ on the other, hardly fit into this polarity. Jehovah would have to be viewed as an Ahrimanic being and Christ as Luciferic. But thereby the Mystery of the Blood, the central mystery of the Old Testament, remains uncomprehended. Also the Mystery of Golgotha, the central Mystery of the New Testament, has remained beyond the comprehension of Madame Blavatsky. For the love principle, working out of human sub-consciousness and combatting individual egoism through the love for one's parents, children, and siblings, cannot be explained by the idea of an Ahrimanic Jehovah. Nor can the depths of the Mystery of Golgotha as *earthly* mystery be fathomed when the Christ Being is envisioned as Luciferic. If one comprehends Christ Jesus merely as a witness and proclaimer of a higher world, one cannot from *that* standpoint understand the mystery of the *bringing down of* spiritual life *into* earth existence. The *magic* significance—the most vitally important aspect—of the Mystery of Golgotha remains hidden to this manner of comprehension. Madame Blavatsky sees the Christ only as an upward-bearer; that he is also the greatest of downward-bearers remains hidden to her. She has no understanding for what is essential in Christianity. She does indeed speak of Christian esotericism, but only about the *old* esotericism that exists in it. About that in it which is *new*, which came into the world through Christianity 'as mystical fact', the *Secret Doctrine* has nothing to relate.

And that which is new as a *cosmic* event stands as the central point in Rudolf Steiner's *An Outline of Esoteric Science*. For just as the *Secret Doctrine* is oriented toward *one* central point, namely, the 'Fall into Sin', so does *An Outline of Esoteric Science* have the Mystery of Golgotha as its central point, toward which all is oriented. The *Secret Doctrine* aims to be an instrument through which people can learn about the event of the separation of the sexes (in the middle of the Lemurian Epoch) and what followed after it, and then draw certain conclusions from that knowledge. *An Outline of Esoteric Science* has the task of being a similar instrument in relation to the Mystery of Golgotha, which took place in the middle of the fifth Epoch.

From this fact follows something quite significant: the *effect* of *An Outline of Esoteric Science*, first on the thinking and then on the will of the reader (for all thinking becomes sooner or later willing), is very different from the effect of the *Secret Doctrine*. The latter places the reader before the choice: either spirit or matter. The practical consequences of this choice are contradictory to the disposition of European people, for they do not actually have a tendency toward one-sidedness. Madame Blavatsky knows this. She warns on various occasions against *practical occultism*. For Europeans the *theory* must suffice, because they are little disposed to what she views as *true practical occultism*; that is, to an occultism consistent with the theory of the *Secret Doctrine*. Only in Asia would it be possible to put into practice the above-mentioned 'either–or' to a satisfactory extent.

For this reason the *Secret Doctrine* contains no description of a path of initiation intended to be put into practice. And in other places on this subject, Madame Blavatsky tries to show European readers how it is actually hopeless for them to take up the path of Eastern occultism. For that, they would, *as a first step*, have to give up their whole European nature, because it is, as such, a hindrance.

Because the *Secret Doctrine* contains beside a theoretical Monism, a practical Dualism, it cannot offer a *path* to Europeans. *An Outline of Esoteric Science*, however, contains not only a theoretical, but also a *practical* Monism. Therefore its practical consequences can be realized by European people. The book contains a detailed description of the conditions, means, and trials of Initiation. This path can be followed by anyone of good will, for it is *suited* to the nature of European people.

'Practical Monism'—the practice of the monistic 'not only–but also' instead of the dualistic 'either–or'—is actually the *Christ impulse*, the central significance of *An Outline of Esoteric Science*. To bring the cosmic working of the Christ impulse *before* and *after* the Mystery of Golgotha to the comprehension of the present time—that is the chief task of this book. In *An Outline of Esoteric Science*, readers are not confronted with a *duality*, but with a *threefoldness*. They gradually learn to understand that, apart from the Mystery of Light and the Mystery of Death, there exists a third and greater Mystery—*the Mystery of the Life of that Light who passed through Death*. And they learn, too, to understand that just as striving for the spirit can be egoistic, so also can a descent into the earthly realm be selfless. They learn to see not only evil below and good above, but also evil above and good below. He learns to distinguish within the light the fullness of the *Elohim* from the brilliance of *Lucifer*; in the darkness to distinguish the cold, deathly breath of *Ahriman* from the silvery glow of *Jehovah*. And, like a rainbow, the seven-colored, radiant Christ impulse bridges over the abyss between light and darkness.

This 'seven-colored rainbow' is the impulse and the possibility for that standpoint which we have designated as 'practical Monism'. It joins the two opposites of light and darkness together into a third element. Knowledge and action are joined together by the cosmic love principle—making possible the transformation of knowledge into action. Through this, the publication of the description of the path of Initiation in *An Outline of Esoteric Science* becomes understandable. If in *An Outline of Esoteric Science* the central place had not been conceded to the Christ impulse, then the book could not offer people of modern culture a practicable path. It would have to, like the *Secret Doctrine*, contain only aspects of a world-conception. For it would be senseless to offer the public a path that could only be taken by individuals with particular tendencies: people as one-sidedly gifted for the spiritual life as, say, a wholesale merchant is gifted for material life. However, the path described in *An Outline of Esoteric Science* can be trodden by anyone, for it appeals to that in a human being which strives after the *transformation* of the 'lower', the darkness, into the 'higher', the light-filled. On this path both poles of human nature are taken into account: what is still to be transformed is here just as valuable as what is already transformed.

So we see that the *Rosicrucian* path of Transformation, is a direct result of knowledge about the cosmic working of the Christ impulse, whereas the absence of knowledge of the Christ impulse in an occult stream—however holy and ancient—makes it impossible for European people to take a practical path, a path that could lead to real progress.

In occult writings, such as the two we have here compared, we must ask not only about the *truth* told therein, but also about the *completeness of that truth*. For incomplete truths can lead the whole practical striving of a human being down a blind alley. Therefore, when considering occult writings we must ask: what follows from this for *life*? Asking this question, one reaches certain answers with regard to the books just considered: namely, that Europeans can only to a small degree bring the *Secret Doctrine* into their lives, whereas through *An Outline of Esoteric Science*, *life goals* open up for them.

WESTERN OCCULTISM,
VEDANTA, AND ANTHROPOSOPHY

ALL THROUGH THE MIDDLE AGES right on down to the present, an unbroken stream of occult tradition has flowed in the West. This occult tradition has branched out and taken many directions; yet all show a certain relation to each other. One branch of this tradition, the one pre-eminently characteristic of Western occult tradition, is the occult stream which usually calls itself *Templar*.

The content of this Templar tradition passed down through time contains both a theory and a practice; but before one comes to the stage of practice, it is necessary to have acquired at least part of the theory. Now access to the theory is not an easy matter; for it is not brought forth openly as a system of thought, but is hidden in a comprehensive symbolic system. This symbolic system is, in turn, stratified into four layers: first there is the picture; this then corresponds to a geometric figure; this figure in turn corresponds to a speech sound, or to a letter of the Hebrew alphabet; and lastly, the sound corresponds to a number. Thus if we wish to understand a symbol, we first immerse ourselves in a colored picture in which color and form are intended to express an occult 'configuration', that is, a group of facts. Here we have to exert all our capacity for keen discernment, all our inventiveness, in order to 'extract' content out of the picture.

In principle students should do this without aid, but in reality they will be helped. It is intended, though, to limit this help to a minimum.

After we have penetrated to a certain degree into the meaning of the picture, we are then introduced to the corresponding geometric figure that expresses the 'same idea'. After this—a more difficult part of the work—has been accomplished, one learns a 'letter' or a speech-sound, and a 'number'. The process here of 'penetrating' to these three 'levels' has to be accomplished twenty-two times in order to learn the 'alphabet'. After having thus mastered the 'alphabet', we then learn to 'read'—which means, arranging the letters and joining them together. Now the so-called 'higher instruction' begins. It is as follows: When the 'script' is learnt, one receives a 'book' to read; that is, it is then understood what the script was intended for. This book consists of fifty-six symbols arranged according to a certain system that corresponds to the manner in which a human being traverses the four worlds.

Now these two stages of instruction—the stage of learning the 'script' and of 'reading the book'—correspond to a practical teaching. This practical teaching is divided also into grades: 'lower' and 'higher'. Now the content of this teaching is magic, which is also divided into lower or ceremonial magic and 'higher magic'. Ceremonial magic is used for two kinds of purposes. On the one hand it is used to affect outer events by means of invisible forces; on the other hand, to receive answers to questions put to the supersensible realm. This latter use is very characteristic. Through performing ceremonial magic, communications from the supersensible are made sense-perceptible. Here it is not that consciousness is raised to an experience of the supersensible, but rather that the supersensible is brought down and made sense-perceptible. Thus one is in a position to experience imaginations—yet these are imaginations made perceptible through being materialized in smoke or steam.

Higher magic is primarily centered on the use of the relation of the four elements *in* the human being to the four elements *outside* the human being. The forces of the Man, the Eagle, the Lion, and the Bull are brought into movement by the human 'I' with the aid of thinking, feeling, and willing, so that in the 'fire', 'air', 'water', and 'earth' of the objective elemental kingdom, appropriate effects are called forth.

Therefore we can characterize the essential aspects of the Templar occult tradition somewhat as follows: it is a grandiose system of symbolism, containing within it theoretical knowledge of the supersensible worlds and their deeper laws. This theoretical knowledge is applied in magic. The supersensible worlds are not *seen*, rather they become theoretically known. But if one wishes to experience the *reality* of the supersensible that corresponds to theory, then one turns to magic which, however, does not present the supersensible itself, but only its *effects*. Yet these effects are of such a kind that they enable us to feel the reality of the supersensible hidden behind them. Thereby the 'theory' is confirmed by the 'experiment'—which may well suffice for a typical European.

Typical Asian occultists would certainly reject, with a shrug of the shoulders, this method of coming into contact with the supersensible realm (and they really do this). They turn to the supersensible with quite different demands than those of the European. Europeans wish to *know* the supersensible, but to know it in a way that suits their frame of mind; namely, through knowledge of 'objective things' outside themselves, in the same way as the outer world is known to them by means of the senses and through scientific theory. They must have it *before* them as an object so that they may master it with their 'I'. They are in the strongest measure careful of their 'I'. The supersensible may not enter into their 'I' as an overwhelming power, it may only enter in the form of theory. For with 'theory', the 'I' remains free. But theory alone is too bloodless, it is not reality. So reality of the supersensible as a *force* is presented to them by magic—in this way it cannot *flow* directly into their 'I' as *content*.

Asians, on the contrary, do not at all strive toward objective knowledge. They yearn instead for a particular *inner condition* of their 'I'. What the European wishes to avoid—the penetration into the 'I' of supersensible reality—the Asian yearns for. Asians have hardly any interest in objective things. They await nothing salutary from 'without'. But there is, in the subjectivity of their 'I', what for them is worth striving for in the world. There, reality of cosmic spirituality can be experienced in its *content*, as it were, *from within*. The Asian yearns not for *objective knowledge*, but for *subjective experience*. To raise themselves out of their present to a higher state of existence in their inner life—that is their striving. The goal for the *self* is another inner condition. And the stream of Asian (Indian) spiritual life, in which this attitude appears very clearly and is philosophically founded, is the *Vedanta stream*.

The Vedanta stream is in fact as characteristically representative of Eastern occultism as the modern Templar stream is characteristically representative of Western occultism. It, too, is the bearer of a tradition. But this tradition, in its essential qualities, is very different from the Western tradition we described. It is not a system of symbolism bearing within it theoretical knowledge, but is a 'naked' theory, a logical system of abstract concepts. And as students of the Western school must work their way through a system of symbolism in order to reach the theory, so students of the Vedanta must work their way through the logic of the enormously enlightening thought system of the Vedanta.

Where the student arrives through this work, and what it actually consists of—this 'working his way through' the Vedanta —is in fact the requirement that he reach a *simple synthesis*; that is, that he begin with a *plurality* of thoughts and come to *one thought* at the end. This *one thought*, as the final synthesis within which the whole Vedanta philosophy is contained, is the well known basic maxim: Atman and Brahman are one.

In this condensation of the whole system into *one* point, the student passes over into yoga, into praxis. 'Yoga is bringing to rest the movements of thought formation' (*Yoga citta vritti nirodha*)—as it is formulated in the monumental definition of Pantanjali. From many thoughts we proceed—through synthesis—to one thought, which we then let fall also. This concentration on the one thought, and then the subsequent dropping of this thought, is *practical* Vedanta, *Jñana yoga*. In order to facilitate this process, breathing exercises are used (which in modern Vedanta are regarded merely as a secondary aid). Furthermore, in order to help in this letting go of the thought, mantra are used; and the most 'Vedantic' of such mantra is the syllable 'om' (*aum*). Thus, in speech-sounds is embraced the above basic maxim of essential identity between inner and outer being.

Yet the concentration is carried further, moving to the resonance— the soft reverberation in the heart—of the 'm' sound with which the syllable 'om' ends. Then comes a stillness, a void. In this stillness, in this emptiness, the inner sun of the self rises. This is experienced in unspeakable bliss. This is the Vedanta, the 'end of knowledge', no longer as theory, but as experience. This experience has three qualities: it is a *higher existence* than the usual; it is a spiritual *light experience* in greatest clarity; and it is an experience of deepest *bliss*. Sat, Chit, Ananda—these are the states of thinking, feeling, and willing striven for in the Vedanta stream. Questions, sufferings, and desires melt like snow in the light of this state. The human being is at peace.

What is going on in the world and the preoccupations of humanity do not concern such people. They care neither for magic nor science; for everything exists solely so this state of 'liberation' can be attained.

Swami Vivekananda, at present [1930] the most significant representative of the Vedanta stream, once made a rather drastic, but highly convincing, remark about his relation to the world: 'The world is like a dog's curly tail—however often one uncurls it, it always rolls itself up again.' For him the world is only there as a school for the *inner life.* When one has learned from life what it can teach, one then turns his back to it. The world is there for humankind. The enlightened one has as little responsibility toward it as one who wakes in the morning has toward his dreams of the night.

Whereas the Western occultist strives to transform theoretic knowledge of the spirit world into magical operations on the outer world, the enlightened Vedantist, in contrast, actually has nothing to do with what 'remains' of the outer world. Another difference, highly characteristic of the two streams, is that while Westerners have a comprehensive theoretic *knowledge* of a manifold spiritual world with its nine hierarchies, Easterners have the *experience* of a unified world of World Spirit, of Brahman, with whom they become one. Easterners experience the spiritual world *subjectively*—they *enjoy* it in too large a measure to have *knowledge* of it. So it happens that this spirit world presents itself to them, as it were, as a unity, while in reality it comprises hosts of spirit beings. Although Westerners know the spirit world, because they do not *experience* it, their knowledge is merely theoretical.

Rudolf Steiner's Anthroposophy is a spiritual stream that can be described as neither 'Western' nor 'Eastern' in the sense of the above considerations, for what is characteristic of the Anthroposophical spiritual direction—what is conspicuous in it, if I may say so—is the striving toward a *cognitional experience of the spirit world*. It is neither just a philosophy that leads over into mysticism, nor just a theory that leads over into magic. It is, rather, a way to an experience of the spirit world that is as real as the Vedantic experience, yet is as *objective* as are the *spiritual* phenomena brought down into the material realm by the Western magician.

The two paths that proceed out of theory—one into mysticism and the other into magic—are here *not* pursued; but theory itself, or more correctly *thinking*, is lifted up onto a higher level. Anthroposophy thereby becomes *the mysticism and magic of thinking*.

Inasmuch as thinking—through meditation—gains an *inner* power, it becomes creatively pictorial; but inasmuch as the picture-making thinking then gains the strength to disregard the pictures, it becomes a sensitive membrane for revelations from the spirit world. In *Imagination*, thinking becomes *magical*; in *Inspiration* it becomes *mystical*. Yet this 'magic' is not a case of making things sense-perceptible, rather it happens within the spirit world. And this new 'mysticism' is not egotistical, for it has freed itself from merely subjective experience—it is objective.

In Anthroposophy, the *egoism* of Eastern mysticism and the *materialism* of Western occultism are overcome. By this means the Anthroposophical spiritual researcher can experience the manifold spirit world, instead of the formless one of the Vedantist. Thereby he can learn to know this spirit world just as objectively and consciously as the sense world is known. Anthroposophy is the redemption of Western occultism from materialism, and of Eastern mysticism from egoism. It fulfills the profoundest inner yearning of East and West.

It seems to me to be extremely important that the *mood* which can stream through insight into the significance of Anthroposophy for humanity should increasingly and more strongly permeate the General Anthroposophical Society, especially those who publicly represent it. Thereby an intimate, deep note of conciliation would come into the whole 'lifestyle' of this Society—which could be a blessing not only for the spreading of the Society into the East and West, but also as a highly enriching attitude for every individual in his struggle to solve life's riddles. Such a conciliatory attitude in no way contradicts the necessary courage to stand as combatant for the truth against enemies (including 'occult' enemies) in the West and East. This should be obvious. Whoever has an open *heart* for spiritual movements foreign to him, will truly have an open *eye* also for opposing forces within those movements. We should not fear to delve into strange spiritual streams with our whole being, for in *this* way one becomes an Anthroposophist.

THE PHILOSOPHY OF
TAKING COUNSEL WITH OTHERS

THE *Philosophy of Spiritual Activity* by Rudolf Steiner bases the independence of the human being upon himself—both in cognition as well as in moral action. In this book, the reality of the 'I', working on the impulse for freedom, finds its expression in thought. It is a philosophy which is based neither on God, nor on nature, but on the human 'I'. It answers the question: How can I attain real knowledge? How can I act freely?

However, the human 'I' is not alone—it is only alone in the physical body. When it raises itself above the bounds of the physical body, it steps immediately into living *community* with other 'I's. There the question arises: How can *we* attain a true knowledge in common? How can we work together in freedom?

This question is answered through Rudolf Steiner's Mystery Dramas. There an answer to the question about the significance and the way of the *community* both in knowing and activity is dramatized. Gradually rising above mere experience in the physical body, the characters depicted flow one into another as soul-spiritual beings. *Within* each other, they *know*; *with* and *through* each other, they *act*.

We can see, therefore, an inner continuation of the *Philosophy* in the Mystery Dramas, for they provide an answer to the next question which arises. If the *Philosophy* answers the question of *individual* knowledge and *individual* action, then the Mystery Dramas can be an answer to questions of *community* in knowledge and action; that is, how *more* can be brought about in knowledge and action through the union of individuals than by the same individuals, each standing alone.

This difference becomes visible, too, in the *form* of the two works. While the *Philosophy* is intended for single readers who want to come to terms with themselves, the Mystery Dramas are intended for dramatic performance before an audience. The form here corresponds to the content: wisdom in community could only be expressed by means of community; that is, dramatically.

Through the *Philosophy*, the thinking consciousness frees itself from the physical organism and experiences itself in the life of pure thinking, the moral consciousness frees itself from tyrannical urges and from compulsive laws and experiences itself in the pure act of moral imagination.

Through the Mystery Dramas, the consciousness, free of the body, penetrates the soul-life of other people; the soul, as it frees itself, intimately unites with other souls to carry out deeds in common.

The work in powerful thoughts and sharply-defined concepts that can be stimulated by the Philosophy may free the soul from the physical body and lead it to experience in the etheric body. Working in dramatic pictures and word rhythms, the substance of the Mystery Dramas educates the soul to the *capacity for transforming* the body-free consciousness.

A soul that has achieved the above-mentioned capacity for transformation can, to a certain degree, no longer be alone. It lives in other people and bears others within its being. In a certain sense, it loses the right to private possession of knowledge. It becomes hard for it to distinguish between knowledge gained more by its own efforts and suffering and knowledge gained through inner relations with others.

The sentence, 'I know this—it is *my* knowledge,' increasingly loses its meaning. Gradually one can only speak of knowledge in the soul that has arisen through the *whole stream of life*.

Such persons inwardly 'takes counsel with others' who are connected to them. Every insight that comes to them is the result of a 'council'—a consulting 'together'. For before the knowledge ripens, a person must enter into various standpoints and cognitive levels. Not until one has identified selflessly with a series of different views and dispositions of mind does there arise out of these a *harmony*. This harmony *is itself* the newly gained insight.

The various standpoints and attitudes whose concordance provides a new insight cannot be merely thought out. They are real, represented by real people. It is through a living *experience* of the viewpoints in the souls of others that one comes to living insight.

Through an inner participation in the destinies and struggles of others, I can achieve wisdom which I cannot reach through *my own* striving, through struggling alone. Other people can make me wiser—if I meet them with love.

Only when we humbly strive for the *harmony* of various viewpoints—instead of stressing our *own* opinions and brandishing our own 'principles'—does esotericism begin. Only then does there begin a *life* free from the body. Our 'own' opinions, moreover, are concocted in the lower parts of our organism.

'By this shall all men know that ye are my disciples, if ye have love one for another,' said the loftiest Creator of a community. This attitude is necessary not merely to guarantee 'a peaceful atmosphere for study,' rather it is itself *the* means for developing higher knowledge. A school in the highest sense is not only a *place* where spiritual knowledge is taught; it is much more than that, it is a community that is enabled to form common insights by passing through trials together. Rudolf Steiner speaks in several places in his Mystery Dramas of the 'council of the brothers'. This 'council' must not be understood as if all the members of this brotherhood already know everything and only meet for discussion of a problem out of mere consideration for each other, nor must it be understood that they confer so that perhaps one of them may accept the opinion of another as being more correct.

A council of 'brothers in the temple', as described for instance in the *Portal of Initiation*, takes place neither out of politeness nor from uncertainty of decision; rather it is *in itself a cognitive act* through the harmonization of individual standpoints represented by the different personalities. If only *one* point of view (in various shades) were represented there, such a council would not be a spiritual community. A council with standpoints 'east, northeast, southeast' would not be complete—it would be *weak*—for not until the *polarities* of 'north' and 'south', of 'east' and 'west' are unified does it carry the possibility of higher knowledge and of stronger effect. It is important to bear in mind that the polarities working together in such a community can actually have the appearance of conflicting moral principles.

What, then, is a 'council' intended for spiritual knowledge and spiritual work? It is a new living being, an organism, whose life consists in the working together of polarities. Just as in the human body life consists on the one hand in a *struggle* between nervous system and digestive system, and on the other hand in the *working together* of these two polarities for the good of the whole organism in the rhythmic system, so the life of a spiritual council exists through the fact that opposite opinions are ever and again united on a higher level *after they have fully revealed themselves as opposites.*

Already this requirement is portrayed in Scene One of the first Mystery Drama. Here we are presented with a sequence of different— even conflicting—views which are, however, in themselves correct. The standpoints from which the views arose are entirely justified.

It is also characteristic that thinking gradually becomes ever more capable of unifying contradictions as it emerges from the physical body—when it lives in the life body. It acquires ever more strongly the capacity for *reconciliation.*

The schools of Western occult tradition in the culture-epoch preceding ours fostered the wisdom of the intellectual soul through teaching thinking in such a way that the student had to solve a sequence of problems which could, and can still be described as 'the neutralization of binaries'. Pupils were given a concept to which they had to find its antithesis. Then they had to discover a *third* concept with which they could bind together the two contradictory concepts into a higher unity. It was an exercise in 'ternary' thinking. Fabre d'Olivet's ternary about destiny can be cited as an example.[†] The concept 'freedom' was given for a start: the freedom of human personality. The antithesis to freedom is fate; fate which for human consciousness is, in the first instance, incomprehensible. The polarity between a fate that operates out of the past and a will that is directed solely toward the future finds its reconciliation in eternal providence (Divine direction). Thus:

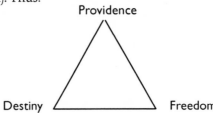

the whole figure equaling the idea of *Destiny.*

---

† See in particular d'Olivet's *Hermeneutic Interpretation of the Origin of the Social State of Man and of the Destiny of the Adamic Race.* In his *Golden Verses of Pythagoras* similar reflections are found on the same subject, though somewhat less clearly expressed. ED

This approach is not suitable to our times and can no longer be considered seriously. We feel it resembles a game, for we are living in the age of the consciousness soul. But to attain the *faculty* of reconciling antitheses by means of thinking is still required today—only it has to be done in another way.

One way of achieving this, one which is suited to modern consciousness, is the Philosophy. As a whole it is so constructed that a 'not only—but also' type of thinking must be exercised. The challenge is already there, even in the fundamental principle of epistemology in the Philosophy; namely, that it is the organization of the human being that divides the one total reality into the realm of ideas and the world of perception. And the task of cognition is to overcome the separating element in the human organization in order to establish the unity of idea and percept as *truth*. This fundamental thought presents a challenge to human cognition to bridge over a basic cleft in human consciousness. It is a challenge to create a 'ternary', not through intellectual speculation, but rather through mature thought activity of the consciousness soul.

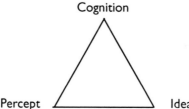

Actually, the content of the first part, the epistemological part of the Philosophy, is expressed by this diagram if it is imagined as being *in movement*. Then the bottom side of the triangle (the separating element of the organization) is gradually overcome as it rises upward until, arriving at the top of the triangle—where percept and idea are united in the act of cognition—it entirely disappears.

Thus the *Philosophy of Spiritual Activity* is a path toward overcoming the organization, a path of freeing the consciousness from the body.

The Mystery Dramas of Rudolf Steiner, however, contain the *life* of the body-freed consciousness. Here human beings become members of a community through which they can widen their knowledge by way of the harmonious accordance of the individual insights of a number of free personalities.

THE SIGNIFICANCE OF A
FREE ANTHROPOSOPHICAL GROUP

AN ANTHROPOSOPHICAL GROUP,[†] like every living organism, has its stages of maturity. These stages come to expression through the way members relate to their group, so that the significance the group has for its members is an indication of the level to which it has matured. For example, it could be that a group has significance for its members in being a place of study: people gather together to learn and to teach. A group can also have the significance of being a place for discussion: people gather together for the express purpose of exchanging points of view; here the element of conversation replaces that of the lecture. A group can, however, have a significance of yet a third kind: that of purposefully forming an organ of knowledge wherein knowledge not accessible to the single individual becomes possible. For there are things in spiritual life that are not meant for the individual, but are intended for the community. And these reveal themselves to individuals only when they inwardly represent a community. The important fact here is that such things belong to the higher aspects of life; that is, to matters which are spiritually-morally of greater consequence than those one seeks and finds by oneself and for oneself.

If in a group the mood predominates which develops out of the insight that its effort can mean a path of knowledge, then the group has reached a stage of maturation at which one may have reason to hope that it can become an organ of cognition, and an organism of knowledge. In this process of becoming, it is of fundamental importance that the elements of lecture and discussion undergo an inner transformation: a transformation in the sense that teaching (holding forth) and discussion evolve into a 'taking counsel' with one another. What matters is that a group meeting become more and more a conferring together, wherein not only practical things are spoken about, but also pure questions of knowledge. Such is the aim of a group: that it become a council of friends.

---

† *Arbeitsgruppe*: 'working group', study group, branch; here and throughout is simply translated as 'group'.

But meeting in 'counsel' means more than merely adding together what the individual members know. A 'counsel' is no mere summation of that which is already known; instead, it is an actual process of attaining knowledge, making it possible for entirely new ideas to come to light.

This 'coming to light' occurs in the center of a circle which the persons involved have to form. If they form a circle on a moral-spiritual basis, that is, in the spirit of mutual help, then a middle-point of this circle comes into being—like the sun within the zodiac. This center point, which can be viewed from all sides, begins to shine and to enliven. In other words, the fundamental principle of the John Gospel, 'Where two or three are gathered in my name, I am there among them,' also shows itself to be true on the more modest level of honest and free anthroposophical group work. Here, too, something appears between and above the individuals which goes beyond each of them. The spiritual being of a group becomes perceptible.

This appearance of the spiritual being of a group was also the reason why Rudolf Steiner gave names to groups: to bring to expression the connection of a group to a spiritual being. In this giving of names (which was always a very solemn affair, often carried out with great ceremony) it was not a matter of simply giving a group a title, a designation; the decisive thing was that a group recognize and seek its 'higher I'. The name of a group denoted at the same time its esoteric task in that it pointed to an 'I among them' to whom a conscious relationship was to be attained through the group's work. (For it was not a matter here of the individual karmic relationships of the members on their paths of destiny, but of the common endeavor to be together in the work of the group.) Thus the names—Luke Group, Benedict Group, Christian Rosenkeutz Group, etc.—indicated not merely titles, nor the directions of the particular sympathies of those involved, but rather the task of uniting themselves with a particular source of inspiration.

And when people have formed a circle in an honest, free and earnest disposition of soul, they indeed become united with a certain higher source of inspiration. Where there is such a circle, an illuminating center point also comes into being. But how is such a circle formed, and what human moral significance does it have?

When a number of free human beings come together for a task involving questions of knowledge, it is only natural that the points of view can be quite different. These different, often diverging, viewpoints offer just those elements which should bind together to form a circle; one built not on personal sympathies, but on a spiritual foundation.

Initially, however, the individual viewpoints by no means comprise this binding, uniting element. On the contrary, at first they have the effect of separating. And yet the task consists in having the viewpoints together produce a unifying substance, so that a circle comes into being. To attain this, we can try to bring the views together by attempting to unite them on the level of thoughts. But the result of this attempt (if we are totally honest) will unavoidably prove to be thoroughly unsatisfying. It will become clear that the views are thus combined, but not bound together in a real unity. This is due to the fact that there is always an abyss, an empty space, between the individual views. As a *pralaya* condition is interposed between the Old Saturn stage of existence and that of the Old Sun, so in a similar manner is a kind of 'thought-pralaya' interposed between one viewpoint and another. In order to bridge these abysses, we must avoid going about the task in such a way that we try to create a connection on the same level; that is, in the region of thought-life. To create this connection, we must actually descend from the head, from the level of thoughts, and immerse into the heart, and then from there rise again to the level of thoughts—in the head of the other person. Only in this way does one learn to understand the other. For when people confront each other with their heads, they cannot understand each other. But one understands the other person when their thought world is entered into by way of the heart. And when one has thus understood the other's world of thought, one will also have insight into that which is true and justified in the other's views. Then will also be found the missing links that unite viewpoint with viewpoint.

The inner activity of the forming of a circle is therefore not a surface movement such as this:

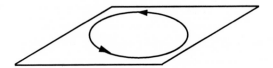

Instead, it is a rhythmic wave-like movement that occurs between the levels of the head and the heart:

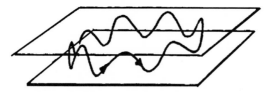

It is this kind of inner activity which forms a circle or a group of people united through the heart who are striving for knowledge. Hence the persons involved do not merely observe one another but have inwardly extended their hands to each other. And when a group of people have in this sense mutually reached out to each other, the circle is created. Then the illuminating center point comes into being—and a free anthroposophical group has come about, having a name that is also valid in the spiritual world. The work of this group will then be such that it sets itself in a vertical relationship to the higher world. Thus it will truly be 'in accord with the Christmas Foundation Meeting of 1923.'

Such groups are the backbone of the anthroposophical movement as well as the hope that there endure not only the anthroposophical treasure of knowledge, but—also—living anthroposophical endeavors. And when single groups of this kind find objective human contact with each other on matters of content, they will not only be preserved from the danger of 'spiritual provincialism', but they can also unite together, forming a moral-spiritual association that does not exist exclusively for its own well-being. To further this association is the worthiest tasks, since it would be a matter of cultivating what is most needed in the present situation of the anthroposophical movement.

RESURRECTION AS A PROCESS WITHIN THE HUMAN ORGANIZATION

IN MANY DIFFERENT WAYS, Rudolf Steiner has shown how the forces at work in the human organism present a living contradiction. The human organization, as such, is a contradiction become flesh; for constructive and destructive forces are continually at loggerheads there. And this struggle is—itself—human life.

In the philosophic language of Hegel we could say: the 'human being' is that place in the world where thesis and antithesis are *adjacent to each other*, and out of this adjacency arises a process that strives toward synthesis. This synthesis does not yet exist; but the demand for it is unavoidable, for the contradiction *is* there. The human organism, as such, is far from being a solution to the problem—on the contrary, it is a *concrete* illustration of the problem. Through its own make-up, the organism has within it demands for other conditions.

What we have here expressed abstractly can be made more vividly comprehensible by stating: the human organism is the arena for life-processes and consciousness processes. The life-processes are unconscious, the consciousness processes are lifeless.

For me, my activity of digestion is unconscious, whereas my activity of thinking is conscious. Further, through my digestive process my organism is built up, whereas through my thinking my organism is broken down. While I am thinking, a death process takes place in my organism. An effect takes place that works contrary to the life-processes. Every process of consciousness means the conquest of the life forces in an area in the organism—however small it may be. Where the life forces are inhibited so that a space empty of life is made in the organism, consciousness lights up.

So human beings, as long as they live, stand within this contradiction: Death-bringing consciousness and consciousness-extinguishing life. This contradiction between light of consciousness and darkness of life is described in a dramatic manner at the beginning of St John's Gospel: 'and the light shineth in darkness, and the darkness comprehended it not.' And all the words in this Gospel that follow contain a description of the solution to this contradiction of light and darkness.

The fact that St John's Gospel is oriented toward this contradiction is not surprising, because its existence has the greatest possible moral significance. It is to this contradiction in the moral life that St Paul spoke such fiery words in the Epistle to the Romans, stating there that the darkness in human beings has power of life, while the light in them, though it makes visible the evil in darkness, lacks the power to overcome it. 'The good that I would do, I do not; but the evil which I would not do, that I do,' said Paul, thus pointing to the archetypal problem of moral life; namely, the question: How can moral insight, once gained, work with the same natural force as the instinctive urges work? How can the *power* of the good be added to the *insight* into goodness?

This question has been asked by all striving people. Schiller's *Aesthetic Letters*, Goethe's *Tale of the Green Snake and the Beautiful Lily*, Dostoevsky's whole life-work, the drama, *Four Apocalyptic Beasts*, by Albert Steffen—all these works have as the central question: How can consciousness gain the power of life, and how can life shine with the clarity of consciousness?

What is actually meant by this question? An answer can be found if we consider certain results of Anthroposophical research into the human being. According to this knowledge, human beings can be viewed as a duality consisting of one part that withdraws during sleep, and one part that remains lying in bed. During sleep a division occurs: the 'I' and astral body separate from the life body and physical body. On awakening, both parts join together into a unity once more. But the polarity between the two parts is not reconciled through this unification. On the contrary, it actually gains a more intense reality, for the processes of consciousness of the astral body come right up against the life-processes of the life body. Thus within the awake human being, the contradiction arises which we have described above.

And when now the striving 'I' of the human being has gained moral insight so that it 'wants the good', then this insight is there, shining brightly and lighting up the initially independent life stream, which, nevertheless goes its own way. What *Paul* meant by the tragic contradiction between the 'law'—'the good, that I would do'—and the power of evil in human nature—'the evil, which I would not do'—is an experience of the fact that the human 'I' can work on the astral body, but that it has not the power to substantially transform the life body and physical body. The contradiction between the moral law that throws its light on evil (thereby making it visible) but is then powerless to overcome it, and the elemental power of the dark urges of evil—this is the contradiction carried over into the moral realm of the 'I' and astral body on the one hand and of the life body and physical body on the other.

What is it, then, that gives the good, once seen, the power to be not only a *process of consciousness*, but also to become a *life process*? What is this power, capable of carrying moral qualities over into the biological realm so that it may work with a vital strength? Or, in other words, what is it that can give the 'I' the power to work not only on the astral body, but also deeper, into the life body; yes, and even right down into the physical body?

The answer given by Paul is: Christ Jesus. Christ Jesus is that power who can give strength to the good in human beings, enabling it to work in that region of human beings where life and death battle each other.

But this working of Christ Jesus should not be thought of as coming from without, like the working of natural forces. Although the Christ-power in human beings works with elemental force, it does not work in the same way as nature forces, for it works *through the human 'I'*—whereas nature processes take place outside the human 'I'. Natural processes compel the human being; the Christ force does not compel, but works without infringing upon human freedom in the slightest degree.

In order to understand how this is possible, we have to imagine that the human 'I' has a 'front' and a 'back'. In *front* of the human 'I' is spread the whole world of appearances that the 'I' beholds and also influences. *Behind* the human 'I' is a background that is at first unknown to it. Out of this background the 'I' receives promptings, just as from the foreground percepts impress themselves on the 'I'. The effects of nature proceed from the foreground, while the effects of the Christ-power stream from the other side of existence, from the background.

The Christ-power streams from the *background* fundaments of existence into the human 'I', fills it, and thus bestows on it a strength that it does not have of itself—namely, the strength to bring the good, as an elemental force, down into the being of the world. This working of the Christ-power—offered to the human 'I' as a gift, *inwardly fulfilling*, leaving it free—was called by Paul 'grace' (*charis*). Thus grace is a process through which the 'I' in its strivings toward goodness receives the strength to achieve *more* than it could with its own forces alone.

To make this operation of grace possible, the 'I' must open itself to it. The 'I' must become permeable. This happens when the 'I' is *active*. An 'I' that streams out forces, sending them out forwards, creates the possibility for a streaming-in of forces out of its background. An 'I' that shuts itself off selfishly from the outer world does not make possible the working of grace from above. It congests in itself.

This opening of oneself to the influence of grace working into the 'I' from the background Paul called 'faith' (*pistis*). And in contrasting 'righteousness through faith' to 'righteousness through works', he meant to say that the 'works' (the actions stemming from a human 'I' not streamed through by the Christ) extend their *essential* influence only to the astral body. In the physical and etheric bodies they operate only *formally*. On the other hand, the working of 'faith', that is, the Christ-power acting through the human 'I' which has opened itself to it, penetrates right down to the profoundest depths of human corporeality, not formally but *essentially*.

And this 'faith' is also contrasted by Paul with the 'wisdom of this world'. For the 'wisdom of this world' is that which forces itself as *given facts* or natural law upon the human 'I' from without, from the foreground—while 'faith' is a free deed of the 'I' itself, in opening itself to the influence of Christ. We can show the difference between 'faith' and the 'wisdom of this world' more clearly in the following manner:

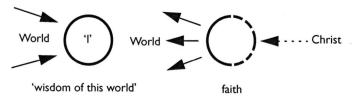

Now nowhere is the difference between the 'wisdom of this world' (a consciousness busy stating facts or reflecting on events) and 'faith' (a consciousness creating out of its own being something new, not yet existent in the world)—nowhere is the difference between them so clearly to be seen as in the problem of the Resurrection. The 'wisdom of this world' (the world of what is given) teaches that according to its laws every individual existence ends with death.

However, Resurrection cannot be established as a fact, nor accepted as an ordinary event. The Resurrection is not something that could happen without human cooperation, and it cannot happen without 'faith'. It is humanity's task for the future, the fulfillment of which cannot be expected of the *world*, but only of the human 'I', through which the creative power of grace works from above downwards into the finished world of facts.

The Resurrection is the goal of the work of the human 'I' on the organism. This organism is—as we attempted to show above—a living contradiction. All consciousness unfolds in it on the basis of death processes; all life unfolds in it by pushing back consciousness. This organism, being thus constituted, puts this question to the future: Is it possible to develop a consciousness that is not death-producing, and to have a life that is conscious?

Now the effect of Christ's power on the human organism consists in this: that there *consciousness processes begin which are at the same time life processes*. And what we call 'Christianity' is not a system of dogmas, or of rituals, but the coming into existence of essentially new processes in the human organism that gradually wrest the ground from the disintegrating processes of consciousness and from the upbuilding processes of life. Within the organism—where consciousness is only possible through death, and life only through unconsciousness—there comes into existence a new organism that consists of *life-giving* consciousness. There, where the life body holding together the mineral substances penetrates the physical body, arises a new body: the body of love.

Love is that cosmic essence which inwardly binds together consciousness *and* life into a unity. This love body is still small and weak—it is as yet hardly perceptible behind the processes of death-giving consciousness and of unconscious life. But it will grow and gradually conquer ever more territory within the ordinary organism, the 'old Adam'.

On through the millennia, humanity will gradually array itself in the 'new Adam', the love body, the Resurrection body. It is happening, but not of itself. It requires the working together of 'faith' and 'grace' inasmuch as people freely open themselves up to the Christ-power, which then streams into them, so reorganizing them that in the future a body will be theirs which has been won from death.

JOHN DEE OF LONDON

TWO BOOK REVIEWS

Review of *The Angel of the Western Window*, by Gustav Meyrink
(current English edition, Dedalus, Ltd., 1990)

THIS BOOK offers an astonishing abundance of concrete detail regarding the tragic history of an occult stream represented here by John Dee. For it can be said that the figure of Dee, astrologer and alchemist to the Queen of England, is thoroughly representative. Although an historical personality—or better, precisely *because* this is so—John Dee is the *representative* of this particular occult stream.

Dee was an occultist. But in his life he succumbed to a tragic confusion: rather than dedicating himself to the glory of *Engelland*—the 'land of the Angels'—he devoted himself entirely to furthering the glory of *England*, an impulse that was also at work in Queen Elizabeth. The directing impulse of the fifth post-Atlantean epoch, that of conquering for human consciousness the realm of the angels, was redirected through John Dee (as also through Queen Elizabeth) toward conquering new lands for England. An *expansion of consciousness* was supplanted by an *expansion of empire*. But this does help bring to light a very significant event in world history: the connection between a certain occultism and the geopolitics of England during the Elizabethan era.

If we ask how this geopolitical goal was to be achieved, we may find the answer in a being who accompanied John Dee throughout his tragic life, a being who worked invisibly at first, but later through the sinister figure of Bartlett Greene, a deceased soul that had remained behind after death in the earthly sphere. Working from the unseen world, this Bartlett Greene spun around Dee an imperceptible web whose threads drew him on throughout his long life. It was as though he were a marionette directed by an unseen hand. Only in old age, broken in body and spirit, did Dee finally see the web of deception for what it was; and, as he lay dying, he turned *toward the East*.

In this picture Gustav Meyrink indicates the location and the method of a certain western occult stream. Moreover, he also shows how, after having first fallen to the impulse for earthly power, this stream—depicted here in the figure of John Dee—falls further into error. For ceremonial magic was practised at the séances John Dee hosted. At these séances appeared the surpassingly beautiful figure of the Green Angel ('of the western window') who communicated guidance of various kinds. This 'angelic' guidance led to journeys—for instance, to the Bohemian court of the Emperor—and also provided means to secure funds adequate for such purposes. The directives of this angel (and its designated agent, a charlatan) were implemented with great homage and total psychic dependency—in the spirit, that is, of true 'strict observance'. And so things remained until at the end of his life Dee finally understood that this 'angel' was in fact a demonic being—and that behind all these doings stood Bartlett Greene, a departed soul wandering the Earth, and that behind Bartlett Greene stood a secret brotherhood whose intentions the latter brought to pass.

John Dee died in abject poverty, forsaken by all, having been for a lifetime an instrument to realize the aims of a secret brotherhood that abandoned him to his hard fate when they had no further use for him.

There is still *more* in this story of great significance to anyone seeking concrete insight into certain ideologies, methods, and means quite well suited to providing deep insight into the human subconscious. But it would be impossible even to briefly touch on such things in this short review. We can only hope that what has been offered here regarding Meyrink's book will be taken as a *key* to open many another concealed truth.

Review of *The Hieroglyphic Monad*, by John Dee of London (current English edition, Samuel Weiser, York, ME, 2001)

IN 1564 John Dee of London published (in Antwerp) a book of twenty-four theorems, dedicating it to Emperor Maximilian, who ascended the throne that same year. The book consists of two parts: an introduction addressed to the Emperor, followed by the twenty-four theorems on the 'hieroglyphic monad'. In his introduction, Dee seeks to enlist the Emperor's favor, while at the same time pointing out in carefully chosen words how the book might also lead its reader astray. He describes how after infancy (*infantia*), childhood (*pueritia*), and youth (*adolescentia*)—and already during the course of the latter— comes the age of choice (*optio*), at which time one can choose either of two paths: that of worldliness or that of wisdom. Dee sums this up in the following diagram:

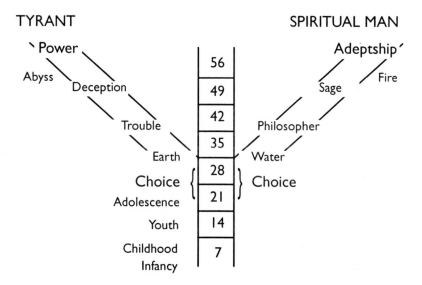

The first path leads through trouble and deception to power, and ends in the Abyss; the second leads through philosophy, wisdom, and adeptship to Fire. At the end of the first path stands the this-worldly human being, the despot or tyrant; at the end of the second stands the spiritual human being, the philosopher, or *pneumatikos*. This diagram establishes beyond doubt that Dee possessed true knowledge regarding human life—such for example as the significance of the seven-year cycles, which Rudolf Steiner has more recently described.

As regards the second part—the actual content of the twenty-four theorems—it consists of a detailed treatment of the symbolic value and amplitude of the following symbol:

This symbol is essentially the sign of Mercury, to which has been added that of Aries. Dee calls this symbol (further combined with the signs of Moon, Sun, Cross, Four Elements, and Aries) the 'hieroglyphic monad', and in the course of his twenty-four theorems describes how not only the signs of the planets, but also the letters of the alphabet can be derived from various elements of this symbol. Furthermore, Dee draws from this symbol extensive geometric and arithmetic relationships. What all this leads to is the realization that the *same* ordering principle at work in the macrocosm (astrology and alchemy) is evident also in the lines and forms of the 'hieroglyphic monad'. In fact he states that just as by taking account of Fire (Υ) the Sun's relationship to the Moon can be understood in terms of the Four Elements, and by taking account of Warmth gold's relationship to silver can be understood in terms of the four conditions, so also by taking account of the fiery power of Love, the Heart can be related to the four ethers.

Nowhere in this text, however, does Dee employ *concepts*. Throughout he speaks in symbols, but in such a way that the *relationships* established among the symbols lead to concepts. So that we cannot say the content is *concealed* behind the symbols, but rather that the symbols *reveal* the content. They do so, however, not directly, but only through establishing symbolic relationships. By way of example we might consider how a staircase on the one hand separates us from the level above in that it must be ascended, while on the other it connects us to that higher level in that it can lead us there. Just so can Dee's symbolism be taken either as separating or as connecting. On the book's title page we find written: 'Let those who lack understanding be silent, or else learn.' And in fact the reader has no other choice, for what the book has to say is not immediately evident. It must be sought for, so that we may rightly liken the search to 'ascending a staircase', for it amounts to developing the reader's thinking. It is in fact a school. And if the reader presses on, it will be precisely *through* this overcoming of initial difficulties that the content can become accessible to *living* experience and be properly valued—that is, not be taken in a merely *mechanical* sense. The symbolism protects it from *Ahriman*. Symbolism is a refuge from Ahriman—this is a truth we may experience intensely when we 'read' the 'hieroglyphic monad' of John Dee of London.

But in our present time such protection no longer suffices. Today the content must protect itself. Truth protects itself by its own power. This indeed is the 'esoteric' in the Esoteric Science of the age of the consciousness soul.

MIDNIGHT SUN:
A CHRISTMAS MEDITATION

WHEN DAYLIGHT has vanished away, when shimmer of eve has dissolved into darkness of night, when the midnight hour resounds, then a great stillness comes over the wakeful soul.

Whatever I must do, I will do it tomorrow. Whatever I have done, I have done yesterday. And whatever will happen to me, may it happen. I, however, immerse myself in the boundless ocean of midnight stillness.

For stillness is great like the ocean. It streams into my soul; it fills my body; it flows through the whole of my being; and its majestic wave-beat washes upon the shores of the world, there where the primeval might of Saturn's world-earnestness reigns. The stillness flows through the world. It weaves from star to star. It permeates all cosmic space.

The waves of world-stillness rise and fall. My soul breathes them. My soul surges with silent world-inwardness. My soul is the world.

And the world is unending stillness. And deep. My soul grows deep. Deeper still. No thought, no memory, no desire. Stillness. . .

Primal-power filled is the world-might, strongly it sustains the world within. Powerfully it flows through my body. World-awake it holds my soul.

> The world is mighty.
> World might fills my soul.
>
> The world speaks.
> My soul is all-listening.

The breath of the ancient-world-ground fills my soul with un-speakable splendor. Bright resounding blissfulness streams through my soul. Sublime presence bestows joy upon my soul.

The world is good.

Goodness breathes on my soul from the ground of the world.

My soul is wholly primeval world-intention streamed through by primal feeling. The world past arises before my soul in primal feeling. My soul senses the world-stream of will, which streams out of the world-past into the world-future.

My soul flows in the stream of world-will. And the world-will is the fire of midnight. . .

In the depth of the midnight hour, arises before the soul, awake in still solitude, the red orb of the Fire-Sun in the dark space of world-silence.

World stillness breathes in the darkness. In the silent darkness of world space, arises before the soul, the fount of her fiery power. Out of it, ancient feelings sound forth; from it, ancient will streams forth.

At the midnight hour, the soul celebrates the primeval festival *of facing the World Sun.*

In outer life at this time, Christmas is celebrated.

PART TWO

Russian Spirituality & The East

ANTHROPOSOPHY IN THE EAST

THE QUESTION OF how to present Anthroposophy in the East has for some time occupied the minds of a growing number of people who have a lively interest in the future of the Anthroposophical Movement. In considering this question, it is obvious that it is not a matter of somehow bending and remolding Rudolf Steiner's Anthroposophy so that it may become, for example, Russian. Rudolf Steiner's communications, whether about the great cosmic relationships or about the intimate depths of human existence, are so comprehensive that people of every land and of every folk can learn from them. No, there is quite another purpose for this question. It is not the *content* of Anthroposophy that is in question, but the *manner* in which it is presented. For Anthroposophy cannot simply be presented as it is: a completed whole, a foreign body imposed upon East European culture. It cannot break in as a complete spirit-complex that has grown in another place and then stand there demanding that one somehow come to terms with it.

Rather, Anthroposophy must be represented within any culture in such a way that those belonging to that culture are given the possibility to participate in *building it up, in helping it to grow.* All peoples must be allowed the chance to rediscover Anthroposophy by their own efforts. And that is possible with the aid of deeply progressive forces that work behind any given culture. There are such forces in every people. They are described in spiritual science as the Folk Spirit, or the Archangel, of the given people. And one must make an alliance with this Archangel if one wishes to place Anthroposophy rightly into the cultural life of another folk. Rudolf Steiner described the forming of such an alliance with the Folk Spirit as the necessity that the *new* be linked on to *what is already there.* Rudolf Steiner himself gave abundant examples of *how* this linking should be handled. He linked Anthroposophy to various things; the most important linkage, though, was to *Goethe.* Rudolf Steiner showed how the impulse that worked in Goethe, carried further, becomes spiritual science.

Now the impulse that inspired Goethe was directed toward grasping nature in its *process of becoming*: the development of the nature of light in his *Theory of Color*, the nature of plants in his *Metamorphosis of*

Plants, the nature of animals in his *Metamorphosis of Animals*, and the nature of human development in his *Faust*—the drama that could also have been entitled 'Metamorphosis of the Human Being'. Goethe's aim in all these works was to show how *one* basic force, *one* essential being, streams through diverse forms. Thereby the individual forms, which the being temporarily takes on in its metamorphosis, are merely *stages* which *tell* about the nature of the being itself. Just as *one* basic force reveals itself in root, stem, leaf, flower, and fruit of the plant, streaming through the sequence of its manifestations, so also does the being of Faust stream through various forms of consciousness, revealing itself in stages.

This essence of Goetheanistic striving—to recognize in visible forms the manifestation of invisible being—is the impulse that Rudolf Steiner connected with. And this connection is noted not only through the fact that he shed light from various sides on the lifework of Goethe, but also through the fact that the actual practice of the Goethean approach toward nature was placed at the beginning of the path of knowledge in his book *Knowledge of the Higher Worlds and its Attainment* as a sequence of inner exercises. For example, the exercise of repeatedly directing one's attention to the plant processes of germination, sprouting, growing, blossoming, withering, and dying, described in *How to Know Higher Worlds*, is actually the training in the soul of a sense for the invisible being that streams through the metamorphosing forms. It is a practical exercise in a Goetheanistic attitude of soul toward nature.

Goethe progressed on his path of experienced knowledge through the different realms of nature as far as an inner meeting with the Christ impulse. This meeting he describes in a grand manner in the last act of the *Faust* drama. But it was not possible for him to move on from a general recognition of the Christ impulse to a concrete comprehension of the revelation of this impulse in the historical figure of Christ Jesus. The greatness, the nobility of the Christ *impulse* he could appreciate; the mystery of the Christ *Being* becoming Man lived no doubt in his soul as *effect*, but not as knowledge.

Another important personality was in a diametrically opposite situation toward the end of his earthly life. Vladimir Sergeyevich Solovyov (d. 1900) had, toward the end of his life, reached a deep knowledge of the Being of Christ. Not only did he bear in his soul a living consciousness of the working of the Christ Being—that is, of the Christ impulse in general—but also of the Christ Being, Himself. It is important to stress that Solovyov had not only reverence for Christ, faith in Christ, but also understanding of Christ. The historical figure of Christ Jesus, the Mystery of the God-Man in whom the divine and the human were united in a new Covenant—this he understood to a very high degree. And he understood this Mystery of the God-Man in the sense that he beheld in it the fulfillment of two archetypal cosmic yearnings: the yearning of everything perishable to take part in the immortality of spirit, and the yearning of the eternal spirit for complete revelation in matter.

The Resurrection of Christ is the moment in cosmic evolution when these two yearnings—of matter and of spirit—celebrated their fulfillment; for there the body was made spirit and the spirit was made body. It is not a 'subjugation' of matter by spirit, not a 'freeing' of the spirit from the 'bonds of matter', but is a reconciliation (Versöhnung) eternally longed for by both beings. And in this 'reconciliation' Solovyov beheld the revelation of the eternal Son.

The most essential thing that can be said in a short characterization of the spiritual value of Solovyov's work is to stress the fact that he possessed an understanding of the Son as a Being distinct from both the Father and the Spirit. In the Resurrection was the most perfect revelation of the reconciling Son. His Body, having gone through the greatest possible self-renunciation and given over to death, became a revelation of the Father's Will; and the Spirit, having bent down deeply into earthly darkness, united itself with Earth's mortal destiny.

Solovyov had a living Christological knowledge that was central to his world view. Around this center were grouped all his other views— beginning with the history of humankind, and ending with nature. When one inwardly views Solovyov's whole world-conception, one has the impression that the center is tremendously luminous and alive, whereas the surrounding spheres—the further they recede from the center and the nearer they approach the periphery—become ever more abstract and thin. A living, shining Christology stands in the center of Solovyov's world picture; next to it is ranged the sphere of historical considerations still wholly irradiated by the living Christ knowledge; and last comes the sphere of natural philosophy, described exactly and meaningfully, indeed, but admittedly abstract. The concrete, living perception of the God-Man, whose *moral* resplendence enlightens the *general* sense of world history and of natural life, could not be far enough extended by Solovyov as to provide him with an equally concrete and living *view of nature*. For natural science, Solovyov had only just enough cognitional force remaining so as to grasp it with grand and meaningful ideas. These ideas were nonetheless abstract—unable to go into concrete particulars. A living Christ perception and an abstract view of nature—this could be a short characterization of Solovyov's world picture.

Now this world picture can in a way be regarded as a polarity to *Goethe's* picture of the world. For Goethe strove toward a detailed, concrete, living, spirit-filled view of nature. It was possible for him to partake with his consciousness in nature's *process of becoming*, whereas he could only penetrate to the general effects of the Christ Being; not far enough, however, for a comprehension of the Being Himself. But it was this incomplete world image of Goethe's, precisely this nature-view, that Rudolf Steiner connected to and completed with his tableau of the cosmic development of humanity, out of which the Christ Being becomes comprehensible. Thus we can say: the further development of Goethe's view of nature leads to spirit-perception that has its center in Christ cognition. It is possible, however, to reach the same spirit vision, not by linking on to the organic nature-view of Goethe, but by linking on to the moral Christ-cognition of Solovyov.

Just as one can extend Goethe's incomplete view of nature so that it comprises the spirit worlds and Christ Jesus, so can the incomplete spirit vision of Solovyov be extended, through a perception of the spirit *worlds*, to make possible the concrete penetration of nature. And this is possible when, linking on to the Christological visions of Solovyov, one shows how this Christology gains immensely from the light shed by a deeper knowledge of cosmic facts and the being of man. It is indeed possible to show how the moral forces, concentrated in Christ Jesus as in a focal point, worked *cosmically* through the earlier incarnations of the earth; and how the realms of nature that surround us today are reminiscences of those earlier conditions. Thereby, by means of the cosmic, a bridge is built from Christ cognition to nature cognition. And it becomes clear that as one can proceed from a true knowledge of nature by means of cosmic spirit vision to a comprehension of Christ, so can one proceed from a true Christ comprehension along the path of cosmic spirit vision to a true knowledge of nature. It is possible, therefore, to link on to Solovyov, as well as to Goethe, in order to reach Anthroposophy, which is a Christianized knowledge of the World Spirit working in human beings and in nature.

Schematically we could summarize the above as follows:

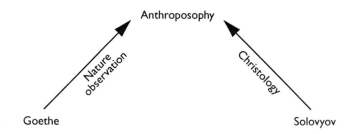

If then one wishes to present Anthroposophy in Russia—or to Russian people anywhere—one *can* link on to a spirituality born of the deeper forces of *that* land and people. In Solovyov's life-work are expressed to a great extent the deeper forces of the Russian Folk Spirit. By connecting with Goethe, Anthroposophy has united itself with the deepest essence of Middle Europe. Likewise, it can unite itself with the deepest essence of East Europe by connecting with Solovyov.

Through this connection, indeed, the *right* presentation of Anthroposophy to the European East is made possible. For it is not right to present Anthroposophy merely as a finished whole, without considering what in the way of folk character is there to receive it. By connecting to Vladimir Solovyov, Anthroposophy can be taken up by the East European people with the participation of their own fundamental, individual soul forces. Otherwise such a participation would be greatly impeded.

It should perhaps be added that what has now been said in the form of a general consideration is wholly and completely substantiated by experiences one has when representing Anthroposophy to people who belong to the East European culture. Experience has shown that the *Christian* aspect of Anthroposophy, above all, finds receptive ears there, and then the general world-conception can, by means of inner participation, be accepted on the groundwork of the Christ comprehension. Not until one has begun to feel, to a certain degree, the *goodness* of the cosmos, can there arise a striving after the *truth* of this goodness. After cosmic moral greatness has been experienced *through the direct breath of the Christ Deed*, there can arise a deep moral need to understand how the cosmos is fashioned in its being and becoming so that such an exalted greatness is possible.

Reverence for the cosmos, which was the scene in which the deeds of Christ could unfold, is the beginning of the path of knowledge for the East European soul. Then the first verses of St John's Gospel could be found to be the most suitable soul exercises on this path. And if we have called 'Goethean' the soul attitude that seeks to grasp the invisible streaming through the changing forms of nature, then we may attach the name of *Solovyov* to the soul attitude that we have described above. For the necessity for linking with the individual essence of a folk character when presenting Anthroposophy extends right into the region of intimate soul exercises.

CHRISTIANITY IN RUSSIA

ACCORDING TO HISTORICAL TRADITION it was in the tenth century that Christianity became predominant in Russia. At that time the Grand Duke Vladimir ruled in Kiev. Clearly sensing the inadequacy of the old pagan tradition and conscious that the stream of human evolution had progressed further, the Grand Duke made the decision to allow the most progressive spiritual stream of the time to flow into his land. He sent forth trusted ambassadors to bring back reports of what great movements the world had to offer.

The result was that *three* spiritual movements were presented for his consideration: the Judaism of the Chosars, the Islamism of the Arabs, and the Christianity of the Greeks. Christianity was chosen, for both the Torah and the Shariah were experienced as not having enough free radiance, and having too much compelling authority. About Christianity, on the other hand, the ambassadors reported: 'During the liturgical ritual we experienced this world as if it were the world of spirit.' ('We felt ourselves as if in Paradise,' according to the words of the old chronicle.)

So Christianity was chosen *as the result of a ritual experience.* Neither the Christian world-conception nor a preached sermon was decisive for the acceptance of Christianity in Russia, but rather the experience of the Eastern Christian liturgy, the Mass.

Now the essential factor in an experience of the liturgy is the effect it has on the participants. It allows them to live consciously in the ether body rather than the physical. The liturgy is actually the creation of powerful effects on the surroundings, which can be experienced as though they were etheric. It is an image of the etheric imaginative world—not of the *objective* etheric world outside man, but of the *subjective* etheric world within man. The *inner* processes of the ether body when penetrated by the Christ-power—that is the actual essence of the Eastern Christian liturgy. It is not the *beholding of cosmic* expanses. It is an inner, heart-warming experience, enlivened through taking place in the ether body instead of in the muffling, obtuse physical body.

This experience, then, was decisive on the world historic occasion of the Christianizing of Russia. Christianity reached Russia not through people being convinced of the *truth* of Christianity as a world-conception, but through the enlivening breath of the Christian cult. And this predominance of the significance of cult over world-conception has been retained through the ten centuries of its existence in Russia. In fact, up to the last third of the nineteenth century, a lack of interest in the life of thought was characteristic of the whole life of the Church of Russia; not that thinking was suppressed, it was just not cultivated.

The development of Christianity in Russia has therefore taken a course that differs considerably from the course of Christian development in the West. It did not take part in the great Western battles of world-conceptions. The whole evolution of Scholasticism, the great conflicts with the Arabistic life of thought, the Reformation, have hardly touched Russian Christianity. Even the separation of the Churches (into the 'Greek schism' and the 'Roman heresy') had no great influence on Russian thought life; for the *ideological* basis of the separation was already in the forming of the Russian Church. At that time these preconceived views were simply taken up, like the tail of a comet, together with the cult.

Even the necessary polemics of the seventeenth and eighteenth centuries around aggressive efforts of Catholicism toward reunification produced virtually nothing original in the life of thought. The Russian apologists merely made use of the arsenal of ready-made Protestant arguments against Catholicism, and of Catholic arguments against Protestantism.

The life of Christianity in Russia, however, was not limited to the cult, for alongside the cult—experienced and fostered by the people in general—were *individual* strivings. What the cult offered to all the people in general at special and specific times, these individuals attempted to acquire as a constant possession through their own individual efforts. Now, what was offered by the cult at these special times was 'life' in the etheric body. And to attain this life as a permanent possession was the striving of the disciples of those mystical schools which, up to the end of the nineteenth century, formed around individual leading personalities. These leading personalities gave instructions as to how, through exercises, one can cause both the awakening and the continuous state of remaining awake in the etheric, or life body. They were prayer exercises which—together with a certain way of life and with the help of certain other aids— awakened to activity the center of the life body that is found in the heart region.

The course of this awakening was not pursued such that first a center was created in the head, which then was brought down into the region of the larynx, in order, *lastly*, to be transposed into the heart. On the contrary, it was *begun* directly with the center in the heart, or in some cases out of necessity with the larynx center. In this way the development of the *head* center was excluded.

This is as much as to say, if we regard the *inner* aspect of this objective fact, that the development of *thinking* did not come into consideration on this path. It was an intensive training of feeling, right down into the will. It was not a striving for knowledge of the *cosmos* outside of the human being, but rather it was a striving for a heightened experience of the hidden essence of *human* nature. This path did not lead out into the cosmos, but led into the inner human being.

From the foregoing one can see that in Russia, Christianity, which really was bearer of the Christ impulse, was not able to take hold of the life of thought—neither in public life, nor in more intimate strivings. It penetrated deeply into the *subconsciousness* of the people. On the higher levels of consciousness, however, it did not show itself capable of forming world-conceptions. The formulations of seven Ecumenical Councils contained in essence immobile thought pictures that rode upon the waves of the Christian life of feeling and persisted through the centuries. They stood there, not as riddles spurring one on to a solution, but as a final *answer*, as the content of a revelation making all further questioning superfluous.

Thereby arose an inner discrepancy in the historical development of the Eastern European culture: this profound heart culture could hold its own less and less with every passing century. The need was growing to be nourished from the *head*; for the spirit of the times, coming more and more to expression, caused such changes in the human being that progressively the leading role tended to be assumed by the head. In the East, the head had, however, only been able to develop its own primitive life of thinking. Thus the life of thinking—now required gradually to take over the leadership in the human being—was inadequate.

At the turn of the seventeenth century, Peter the Great, the first Tsar of Russia, had a lively feeling in his soul for this situation. Just as the Grand Duke Vladimir had felt the inadequacy of the old pagan conceptions and turned to Byzantium in order to receive Christianity from there, so did Peter the Great, seven centuries later, turn to the West, namely to Holland, in order from there to receive the head culture. In so doing, Peter the Great opened the door into Russia for the stream of intellectualism. This stream was intended to fill the vacuum that had arisen through the one-sided development of East European spiritual life. But the ideas that now reached Russia in this way had no relation to the foregoing centuries of Christian heart culture. They were not suited for the task of building a world-conception that could bind head and heart into a *unity*. The two streams continued to run parallel without joining together—the stream of heartless intellectualism and the stream of thoughtless Christianity.

However, as intellectualism tended progressively toward materialism, the two streams could not move along in parallel for long. There arose a battle, described in all its psychological drama in the works of Dostoevsky. The last stage of this historic drama is the extreme form of Russian Bolshevism.

How is this battle waged?

On the one hand, everything is gathered which makes Christianity appear nonsensical—as stupidity made into a principle. The Church had nothing with which to counter this stream of destructive cleverness except the effect of its cult on the heart, and the fact that the heart feels everything that the materialism of Bolshevism has to offer as empty and flat. Materialism cannot counter the criticism of the heart, nor can the Christianity of the Church counter the criticism of the intellect. So at present in Russia there is on one side a tremendous devastation of the heart, and on the other an ever-growing antipathy toward—actually a horror of—any life of thought. Thinking as such seems to an increasing number of people not suited for playing a role at all in world-conceptual questions. There arises the horribly fallacious equation: thinking = materialism.

On the other hand, the conviction that the heart cannot be oriented toward the truth, that there can be no objectivity in the life of the heart, becomes ever more firmly rooted. So arises the other horrible equation: heart = error.

These two attitudes surge up against and repulse each other. The possibility of reconciliation between these polarities does not exist in the present-day configuration of forces in Russia. Out of her own forces no relief can be found for the tension that grinds down the soul. It is impossible for a stream of spirituality—powerful in thought—to arise there, which could bind thinking and heart into a unity.

Since the fourteenth year of Bolshevism has begun, one can no longer speak of the possibility of a world-conception arising in Russia that might include cognition of the Christ impulse, as once the cult was received as a heart-penetrating force. A world-conception is needed today, however, in which the *life of thought* could accord with the old heart inwardness, but this life of thought cannot be created in Russia. In the past, creative activity was directed toward the life of the heart. Today it is crippled by the shattering battle of antitheses. A thought life that meets the above requirement does, however, exist in middle Europe. It is the spiritual science of Rudolf Steiner.

The future of the spiritual life of Eastern Europe depends on the answer life will give to the question: will the people of Russia be capable once again of receiving something great from outside—this time for their redemption—as twice before in the past Russia took up foreign spiritual substance? Will it be able to develop sufficient devotion to take up the Anthroposophy fostered in Middle Europe, as it took up the Christianity of the East and the intellectualism of the West?

The destiny of Russia is dependent on whether—after it has taken up the science-less spirituality of the East and the materialistic science of the West—it will also take up the *spiritual science* of the Center.

THE MISSION OF EAST EUROPE
IN RELATION TO THE MISSION OF THE WEST

IN THE ESSAY ENTITLED 'Christianity in Russia', the view was expressed that an important factor of Russian spiritual life is to develop devotion for what comes to it from without. And in the near future the task will be to take up Anthroposophy in the same way as the Eastern Christian ritual was taken up in the tenth century, and Western intellectualism was taken up in the eighteenth century.

Now, however, the question arises: if the European East has to take up what has arisen in the West, what significance does this reception of what has arisen in the West have for the West itself? In other words, what does East European spiritual life have to *give*?

In order to be able to answer this question, it is necessary to regard the scene of this 'give and take' from a certain aspect of human nature.

Within the inner life of human beings two poles work together: that pole of the inner life where the tendency toward immobility, toward stiffness, predominates; and that pole where the inner life itself as a driving force prevails. The form-building activity of thinking and the formless sheer impulsivity—these are the two polar faculties of human soul-life. Thanks to the first, human beings are in the position to have an ordered inner life. They can form their soul-life according to definite intentions. What otherwise would just flit through them leaving no trace, is here held fast and so structured that it becomes accessible to the inner eye of consciousness. *Conceptions* (world-conceptions too) are possible in human life because human beings are endowed with a capacity to think systematically.

Thanks to the other faculty, the human being not only thinks but has also the inner *strength* for striving. For human beings are only *complete* when, *beside* their sure, dependable, and clearly-formed conceptions, they have a flaming *fire* of enthusiasm, a flame-nature that cannot be tamed by any form. And for us human beings are *great*, not only because of their valuable insights, but also for the amount of fire their souls are capable of generating. It would truly be *narrow-minded* of us if we would admire a Giordano Bruno *only* on account of his thoughts. Does not his greatness lie, rather, in the mighty flame that was his noble soul, that which also prepared the way for his destiny of death by fire?

Or do we judge Leo Tolstoi, who died twenty years ago, to be great because of his insights? Are not his ideas (for example on the Gospels) actually what is of least value in him, while his mighty strength of striving, his holy earnestness of seeking, is what forces us to look up with reverence to the bearded old man from Jasnaja Poljana?

Surely, world history is not only an organic process of the growing, thriving, withering, and dying of world-conceptions, communities, and cultures, but also a *burning* on the earth's surface in the bodies of human beings. Have not entire peoples often burst into flame, either in outbreaks of destructive earth-fire—followed by annihilation, revolt, revolution—or else in the fire descending from heaven—from which arise religions, great ideas, new cultures? The world-historic figure, for instance, of the Maid of Orleans, whose *ideas* were those of a Lorraine peasant girl, is only comprehensible when we know that she was filled with a heavenly fire that descended on her, giving another direction to the historic course of European peoples.

Now when we return to our question of the significance of the European East with regard to the European West, then it can be said on the basis of the foregoing: just as the Maid of Orleans attained world-historic significance, not through her ideas, but through the fiery *impulse* of her soul, so the significance of Russia for the West lies not in new insights, ideas, etc., which may have arisen there, but in the *flaming power of her soul*. The whole past history of East European culture shows us clearly *what* talents for spiritual life Russia has. Great *new* ideas and world-conceptions have not arisen in Russia; in the realm of *thought life* the European East has produced very little. And the thought life which—apart from a few exceptions—devel-oped there had a character that strongly deviated from the Western concep-tion of 'philosophical thinking'. It moves, not along a chain of reason-ing to a conclusion, but in single thrusts. It is aphoristic through and through. Between each single complex of thoughts there are dark, thought-less abysses. Their relation must be sought in the depths of the subconscious outside the thought element. It is subjective. Thereby also its negative side is characterized. Just as the objective, formulated thinking of the West has the drawback that it can easily become *cold*, so the subjective, unformed thinking of the East has the drawback that it easily takes on the character of an *inflammatory process*. And this inflamed, feverish thinking is not suited for creating large, coherent world-conceptions. Like sheet lighting in the night sky, there can be unexpected, surprising glimpses and insights, but—in comparison with the grandiose achievements in thought, for instance, of the German idealists, who let flow into humanity a mighty stream of sharply contoured, clear ideas, producing health and strength and educating human beings—it is really an inadequate groping. It has impulsive strength, but is lacking in a clearly con-scious strength of formulation. It happens mostly in flashes.

Thus we have seen that in the past the productive, creative signifi-cance of East European spiritual life was not directed toward the *thought* element; it did not allow a world-conception to arise which could make its way through humankind. The creative forces of its spiritual life proceeded in a different manner. They did not work in a *form-building*, idea-forming way; they tended to *fire* enthusiasm, to enliven forms, to intensify conceptions. For as the Christian ritual, entering into Russia in the tenth century, became intensively inward—an inwardness which the decadent Byzantine spiritual life was no longer capable of maintaining—so did the materialism com-ing into Russia from the West become intensively inward. And the Bolshevism of today [1930] is the inwardly intensified materialism of the West. For what in the West was a conception, or a thought picture, became in Russia a life-filled reality. Russian Bolshevism is the materialism of the West inflamed in its practical solution for human moral social life.

In looking at Bolshevism, it must be admitted one is motivated to ask all materialists to come forward immediately and tell, in truth, *why* they do not take the side of Bolshevism. A strange answer would emerge: what the Communists say about the driving impulses of the *materialistically-minded* bourgeoisie *is true*, and equally true is what the latter say about the driving impulses of Communists. Both sides, being equally materialistic, recognize their own kind.

The greatness of East European spiritual life has always been that— receptive as it is regarding the *forms*—it possesses the high *talent for firing enthusiasm*. And in human history this gift relates to the talent for form-building in the same way as in the super-human cosmos the hierarchy of the Spirits of Form, the Exusiai, relate to the hierarchy of the Spirits of Movement, the Dynamis. For just as the Form Powers build the world substances into a cosmos and the Movement Powers make the world forms inwardly mobile—so out of East Europe there flows (and will increasingly flow in the future) a stream of mobility into the forms of the West.

The form-transforming West—this applies *also* to the thought life—can be permeated by a stream of profound inward intensity coming from the East. This would happen when the latter accepts the kind of forms from the West that allow an inward intensification to occur without any danger to human development. If European spiritual life finds the strength to permeate itself as much with *spiritual-scientific* insights as it has with natural scientific insights, then it will be able to offer the East what is needed to awaken to its deeper levels of being.

What this awakening can signify we will show by an example. There are those who often, and to a certain extent rightly, point to the *weakness of will* in East Europeans. They say—also rightly—that they are passive, that they do not actually oppose anything, and do not with all their strength of being desire anything. They are not striving, but contented people. They are not of a fighting nature, but rather sufferers, resigned to their destiny. Now in response to this widely-held opinion, two things can be said: firstly, we can admit its relative correctness; then we can ask *why* is this so? Could it be for the reason that *that* which should be willed has not yet made its appearance? Are East Europeans 'lacking in will' because their will despises everything that has as yet been offered to them? Does not this sleeping will wait for a *goal* that could awaken it?

It is possible to be convinced—and to have good *objective* grounds for this—that East Europe, now weak of will, shall in the future be described and admired as 'the land of tremendous strength of will'. There will be a time when spiritual-scientific insights will flow from Europe into Russia (even if by means of inspiration from the dead) and will give birth there to a culture that, as regards inner intensity and intimate sympathy of soul, will surpass much of what we were accustomed to deem great. Spiritual science can awaken the sleeping will of East Europe by placing before it goals that can set it into motion.

That it is the mission of spiritual science, among other things, to fructify East Europe, this we have attempted to show in earlier essays. Here we have to answer the question: what can the suggested awakening of the East signify for the *West*? There must be a possibility for *spiritual science* to permeate *life*, especially social life, as strongly as materialistic natural science. It should just as *radically* take hold of life as materialism is striving to do in present-day Bolshevism. And as an idea is first *grasped* by the head and then lived through descending into the heart, so shall spiritual science, *if* its truth has been sufficiently perceived in Europe, be able to enter the *life* of East Europe. And as, on the other hand, the heart that has been fructified by thinking in accord with spirit can return the gift back to the head as riches of the soul-life, so can the West (if it has fulfilled its mission) thanks to an inwardly intense raying-back from the East, be tremendously enriched. The soul-life of the West, withering ever further, can receive a mighty influx of inner intensification of the soul through the awakening of the East here described.

Through *conceptions in accord with spirit* the West can awaken the East: the awakened East can give the West *life in accord with spirit*.

MOVEMENTS OPPOSING
SPIRITUAL SCIENCE IN THE EAST

IN THE ESSAY ENTITLED, 'The Mission of East Europe in Relation to the Mission of the West', we spoke of the 'firing with enthusiasm' which Western culture can receive from the European East when it has been awakened by spiritual science.

Now, powerful hindrances have first to be overcome before East Europe can be awakened by means of spiritual science. Strong streams of opposition exist in both the West and the East. The aims of these streams are quite *other* than an awakening of East Europe by means of spiritual science. The Bolshevism at present ruling in Russia merely represents the finger tips of a hand that is stretched out from the West. Here is *one* example (there are others) that illustrates this: in the year 1893, a certain C.G. Harrison held a series of lectures in London before the 'Berean Society'.[†] In these lectures he gave a thorough critique of the life-work of Madame Blavatsky and the Theosophical Society from the point of view of a Western occultist. He was also successful in showing that there exists in the West an established knowledge of occultism. In this connection he spoke too of the future of the European East, stating:

> The Russian empire must die so that the Russian folk may live. Huge social-political experiments would be made in Russia which, thanks to the character of the Russian people, would be possible there, but would meet with insurmountable difficulties if carried out in the West.

Well, the 'huge social-political experiments' of which Harrison spoke 37 years ago [i.e., 1893], have actually been carried out. In Russian Bolshevism we have an illustration of these experiments, which decades before were *known about* in the West. Now the essence of Bolshevism in its effect on the human soul is that it strives to drive

---

† These lectures were published in 1893 under the title *The Transcendental Universe: Six Lectures on Occult Science, Theosophy, and the Catholic Faith: Delivered Before the Berean Society*. A new edition with an extended editor's introduction was published by Lindisfarne Books in 1993. ED

spirituality out of the realm of consciousness. It is a movement that wills to eliminate any prospect for spiritual science. It wants to exclude a spiritual world-conception—a prerequisite for spiritual science—from human *consciousness*. This is the *one* opposing movement instilled from the West.

In order to take a look at the other opposing movement—which is the actual intention of this essay—we must first point to a few phenomena that can be taken as precursors of the *second* major stream of opposition; namely, the Eastern stream. These phenomena are the *moods* that increasingly assert themselves in the non-Bolshevik-minded part of East European humanity. The more aggressively the 'ecclesia militans' of materialism, the Communist Party, behaves, the stronger—in the souls of non-materialistically-minded people of the European East—these moods become. They can be more or less characterized in the following words: We have put great trust in Europe. We have honestly valued European culture. But we have been *deceived*. Instead of bread we have received stones, and instead of fish we were offered snakes. *Poison*, the soul-poison of materialism, Europe has given us. Indeed, trains are running, airplanes flying, factories clattering in our land—but the peal of Easter bells has ceased. There exists, however, the age-old East, the folk-sea of Asia, whose peoples quietly worship their gods. The East is *unaggressive*. It lives for spirituality. Therefore we have misjudged the East and have preferred the aggressive West to it—the West which lives for materiality. *We have erred in turning for centuries toward the West.* The time has now come to make the great turn-about. The *material civilization* of the West we have received; now we should turn to the East in order to receive from there a *spiritual culture*. Living together with the West has brought us Bolshevism—living together with the East would never have done so.

This mood of disappointment with regard to the West and the yearning for a change of orientation toward the East grow each year and take hold gradually—more or less unconsciously—of ever wider circles, especially of the kind of people progressively inclined, striving toward the future.

To such moods can be traced two streams of Russian spiritual life that have arisen during the last decade and have major *symptomatic* significance: *Eurasianism*, as a social-political-religious stream, and the

occult, mystical stream inaugurated by the artist *Nicholas Roerich*.[†]
These represent the two symptoms pointing to the fact that at the
present time a strong impulse exists in the souls of Russians to turn
toward the Asian East.

The representatives of Eurasianism say essentially the following
about their intentions: Russia is neither Europe nor Asia. It is its own
sphere of culture. It can be regarded as having equal ties to the Asian
as well as to the European spheres of culture. It is, in tendency, *Eur-
asian*. Now the East is theocratic, the West democratic. Russia, however, cannot adopt the democracy of the West, devoid of ideas or
world-conceptions; for that it is too 'Asian'. Nor can it adopt the
unquestioning religious theocracy of the East; for that it is too 'European'. It must become *ideocratic*, it must become a 'world-conception-
state'. Neither gods nor the masses of the people shall rule in this
state, but *ideas*.

That would be the *program* of Eurasians.

With regard to this program, however, two things can be said: on
the one hand, the ideas that could take the helm in a future Russia are
lacking to the present-day representatives of Eurasianism; on the
other hand, the mood of this program is the expression of the feeling:
the time has come for us to turn away from the West toward the East.
And the above program of the eastward-directed stream, at the cross-
ing point from a preponderance of Western influence to a preponderance of Eastern influence, is only an incomplete picture. It is merely a
manifestation of *one* particular *stage* of the new orientation of mood.
The streaming change of direction cannot remain at this stage; it
flows on further.

The movement proceeding from the well-known Russian painter,
Nicholas Roerich, can serve as a symptom of this 'streaming on further'.
This movement aims to be a channel of influence on humanity—and
especially on Russia—from a trans-Himalayan spiritual center. Those
who belong to this movement are enthused by the thought that a
content from Inner Asia can be poured into the *cup* of Western civilization. They are convinced that the values which will replace the Russian spiritual culture destroyed by Bolshevism are being preserved in

† Nicholas Roerich (1874–1947) was a Russian painter and spiritual teacher. ED

central Asia, and only wait for the right moment to flow into the cultural 'vacuum' that Russia has become. And this 'vacuum' in Russian spiritual life, that is, the annihilation of traditional Christian spiritual life, is, in those circles and from *this* point of view, *welcomed*. These circles look upon the Bolshevists as unconscious *co-workers*. This may be the reason why *Roerich* was recently refused entry into India on the grounds that he is in contact with the Russian Communists. The *Roerich* Movement actually has, as yet, very little clarity of contour. Its task seems to be to create and spread the mood: out of Asia will come a mighty stream of spiritual life, which is greatly yearned for. The terrible vacuum that has arisen *will* be filled. Look toward the East, whence comes true salvation.

As Eurasianism signifies *a turning away* from the West, so does the *Roerich* Movement signify a *turning toward* the East. These two streams are symptoms of the dangerous mood that can lead Russia to take the attitude toward Europe of throwing out the baby with the bathwater; that is, that through an antagonistic attitude toward Europe they will repulse spiritual science also. On the other hand, these two movements are symptoms of the fact that the attraction of Asian spiritual life, which bears a hidden danger, is growing.

Every culture is a definite relationship between humanity and the cosmos. Only the conscious understanding of this particular relation of the spirit in humanity to the spirit in the universe—of which a culture consists—makes human beings into intelligent *bearers* of this culture. Now there are cultures that are great in their comprehension of the universal spirit, and others that are great in their comprehension of the human spirit, that is, of the *personality*. In general one can say that there are cultures in which the *personality* stands in the foreground and the cosmic spirit is felt to be merely a background for the personality; and there are others in which the universal World Spirit stands in the foreground and the personality recedes into the background. The West has a de-spiritualized dark world picture, but has a sense for the human personality. For the Westerner, the personality *as such* is valuable. The East relates differently to the personality. There the personality has value only to the extent that the cosmos endows it with content, for the essential element of existence is the universal World Spirit on which the personality, too, depends. A spirit-filled world picture with the personality as a part of it—that is characteristic of Eastern cultures.

The West bears within as its greatest treasure the *Mystery of the Personality*. Through thousands of years it has struggled to comprehend how World Spirit (*pleroma*) became personality; namely, Christ Jesus. In contrast, the East bears as its greatest treasure the *Mystery of the Cosmic Spirit*. Through thousands of years it has striven to follow the call of Gautama Buddha, whose personality had for ever passed into the Spirit of the Cosmos. Just as the becoming flesh—the *coming into visibility*—of the Cosmic Spirit through thousands of years moved hearts in Western lands, so did the never-to-return—the becoming *invisible* of a human soul—move the hearts of the East.

So there stand today (considering all aspects) two life-pictures juxtaposed: one is the picture of the spirit-filled personality on the background of a world void of spirit; the other is a picture of an impersonal World Spirit of which personality is the mere appearance.

Should the Asian spiritual life stream into East Europe, then the evolution of East European spiritual life would take a direction that would *not* result in development of the free human personality. Ideas, moods, and strivings would spread which would, in spite of their greatness, *pass by* the significance of the human personality. These ideas, moods, and strivings would not be adequate to understand the cosmically historic mystery of personality, the Mystery of Golgotha. Although East Europe would receive a spiritual world-conception, it would at the same time lose, in the deepest sense of the word, its Christianity. Thus, too, it would be unable to unfold the greatest treasure of human history, the *personality*. For just as a plant cannot flower without sunlight, so the *personality* cannot unfold within a culture that deprives it of the light of conscious comprehension of the Mystery of Golgotha.

Rudolf Steiner's spiritual science gives both a world picture in accordance with the spirit and also a comprehension of the significance of the personality. It could give *everything* that the Asian East can give, and more: a comprehension for the mission of personality that the East cannot give.

Spiritual science *can* satisfy the deepest yearning of the European East. But it is in danger of being misjudged as a result of the general rejection of European spiritual life and the expectant attitude (fostered consciously in the European East) toward the Asian East. For a lack of interest in European spiritual life, coupled with a yearning devotion toward Asian spiritual life, can mean the greatest possible hindrance for the fulfillment of the true mission of the European East.

THE SPIRITUAL LIFE OF ASIA

IN THE ESSAY ENTITLED 'Movements Opposing Spiritual Science in the East', we pointed to the subtle temptation that approaches East European spiritual life; namely, the temptation to turn its back on Europe and to take up Asian spirituality.

Now the question arises: What is the inner configuration of Asian spiritual life?

If we wish to focus more closely on the inner configuration of the streams forming Asian spiritual life, we must ignore many, many things. For instance, we must ignore Islam, which is not a *present* consideration in this question.

What is a primary consideration, however, is the great antithesis between the two Asian cultures, the Indian and the Chinese.

India and China are actually two poles of Asian spiritual life. They confront each other in the greatest imaginable contrast. Through many thousand years of history, India has followed the behest of destiny to take in and preserve *all* the world's streams of culture—it makes a place for all of them within the country's magnificent spiritual life. China, on the other hand, was surrounded by a wall as a sign of being closed off to everything that happened outside. India was *open*. It took in all religions (Christianity also had already been taken in during the first centuries of our era, Christianity in India being no less ancient than it is in Great Britain) and preserved them (including the primeval religions: Brahmanism, Zoroastrianism, Buddhism, Islam, as well as a number of transitional religions). China, however, was *closed*; and although breaches were made in the Great Wall, it was only a matter of time before that which had broken in was assimilated into the *monotone* of Chinese spiritual life.

The basic mood of Indian spiritual life could be expressed in the following words: The highest wisdom of the Primal Being of the world has been revealed to us and has been ever and again newly proclaimed. This wisdom is the highest. There is enough room under the heavenly vault of this wisdom for all insights, all cults, all rituals and arts. For whether you think or pray, whether you act or meditate, in the end what is essential is that the core of the human being be united with the divine. Everything in life can be oriented toward this primal truth; in relation to it everything has its place. No religion is so untrue that it could not contain something of the truth of that Primal Being which rays into human nature; no outer form of religion is so true that it could encompass that endless Primal Being. There is nothing to be feared. India is strong enough in its consciousness of All-Oneness to allow all the spirituality that lives in the world to flow in. For as the ocean can absorb all rivers into itself, so the wisdom of India is all-encompassing—all the spiritual streams of the world can be taken into her.

So there lives in India the proud consciousness of possessing a synthetic culture; that is, a culture that includes *side by side* all the stages of the past, from the primitive Dravidian, through the Vedic culture, Persian Zoroastrianism, Buddhism, Alexander's Greek culture, the Arabism of the Caliphs, Mongolianism, and the modern civilization of the English. Also, space is made for all views and directions of present-day spiritual life. For instance, orthodox Brahmanism equally recognizes *six* philosophic world-conceptions.

This characteristic of Indian spiritual life is the after-effect of the primal impulse of Indian culture: the cooperation of the seven-rayed wisdom of the seven Rishis. Through this cooperation of the Rishis in the Indian soul arose the deep-seated predisposition for *synthesis*, for making do without form or specialization.

And thereby the *other* predisposition of Indian spiritual life is indicated; namely, the feeling that regards the outer world as Maya, illusion. Not only are the things perceptible to the five senses felt to be illusory, but so also is *form* as such. Everything particular is felt to be Maya. This synthesis is possible, for everything particular is *disregarded* as being Maya, illusory. Religions can all exist side by side for the reason that their differences, their special qualities, although necessary, are not essential. Everything particular is *only* form, and form is Maya—but essence is always the same.

In bold contrast to the basic temper of Indian culture is the temper that lies at the basis of Chinese culture. The Chinese would say: What people believe in, the *content* of their views, does not interest me; what is important is the *form*. The views of human beings are subjective; their form however is for all equally binding, for that is what is social. In social life form becomes *order*, and what is most important in the end is order. Insofar as Buddhism, Islam, and Ancestor worship conform to *order*, they are equally tolerated. Insofar as they foster order, they are welcome; but insofar as they disturb order, they are enemies of the people. That is to say, *because* they are anti-social, *they are untrue*.

What is of highest value for the Indian in his culture is formlessness, while the highest value for the Chinese lies in the *form*. Form is that which stands in opposition to all that is subjective. While India was cultivating the highest degree of subjectivity, of inwardness, China was striving to eliminate all subjectivity. In India and China, *Aryan* and *Atlantean* primary impulses confront each other. For the Indian wisdom is actually the *wisdom of the* 'I'. The basic mood of the Indian culture is the feeling: the '"I" is divine'; the 'I' must not be sought in what is earthly, for it is rooted in the divine.

While the Indian wisdom is the wisdom of the 'I', true Christianity is the *reality of the* 'I'. It was reserved for a later time and for another culture to experience the content of the Indian *wisdom* as *reality* in the earthly. Thus Indian wisdom is actually the primal impulse for the whole of the post-Atlantean Epoch and also of Christian evolution: the impulse for a *self-conscious* 'I'.

In contrast to this, China preserves the basic Atlantean impulse. There it is not a question of cultivating the 'I'—of developing self-consciousness—but rather of fostering the group 'I', the group order. For when the Indian says 'know in thyself the divine Self,' the Chinese would say 'we conform to the divine Self working through order.' Chinese wisdom is not an 'I-wisdom', it is a 'we-wisdom'. Its content appeals only to the 'we', to the group; not to the 'I', to the self-consciousness of the individual.

An argument can be brought against what has been said here about form and group with regard to Chinese spiritual life. Does it tally with the powerful manifestation of the stream of *Taoism* originating from Lao Tzu? Is the content of the teaching of Lao Tzu, as described in his *Tao Te Ching*, not an *individual* mysticism where the sage in solitude inwardly experiences the formless *Tao*? In reply we must say: if we *carefully* read the *Tao Te Ching* (which is difficult, for *one* translation into *one* language is already a limitation, and we are dependent on various translations into different European languages), we find that Taoism does not contradict what we have said above at all. The experience of the *Tao* as described is such that one can say: The *Tao* reveals itself to the 'I' of the knower not from the 'inner' but from the 'outer' side. It is not an object of *cognition* but a way to be *followed*. It does not reveal itself as *content*, but as a determining effect. The following diagram can help show this more clearly:

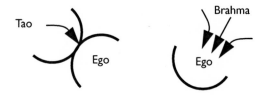

The first sketch shows how the *Tao* relates itself to the 'I'—it does not unite with it inwardly, but impels it to deeds and insights. The second sketch shows the relation of the 'I' and Brahma in *Indian* experience—where Brahma streams *inwardly* into the 'I' as content (however, it does not happen with the fully incarnated 'I'). Actually, the difference between the two great primal impulses can be seen in these sketches. The primal impulse of *Atlantis* (the 'pushed' 'I') and the primal impulse of *Asia* (the 'waxing' 'I').

We can therefore say that the *Tao* of Lao Tzu is actually experienced as *form*, as supersensible world form, which brings world order into existence; and the social order should be an image of this world order. So it is that Lao Tzu's book (*Ching*) has *two* parts: the cosmic-spiritual (*Tao*) and the human-social (*Te*). It is not an 'individual mysticism' as it might appear to the superficial glance of the Western reader; rather it contains *political wisdom* founded, however, on universal order.

But the contrast between India and China does not remain unmediated. There developed a third Asian culture, providing a kind of bridge between the contrasts of India and China. On the high plateau of Tibet a spiritual life arose which links the spiritual dispositions of India and China. Within this spiritual life is to be found the *center of* the whole spiritual life of Asia from the aspect of both India and China. Deep in Tibet there is a place where a wisdom is cultivated which is the final synthesis of the *entire* Asian wisdom.

Now, when considering the Tibetan spiritual life more closely, we have to take into account the effect of the unique Tibetan landscape on human souls. The desert highlands of Tibet are especially suited to foster development of a particular characteristic of the human soul; namely, a *tremendous capacity for abstraction.* Abstraction in the human soul thrives in these desert highlands. It is hard in the West to form an idea of this capacity for abstraction, for in the West this capacity is limited mainly to the realm of thinking, the life of ideas. Feelings and will impulses are for the European *intensely* experienced. Compare, for instance, how on the one hand suffering and joy, sympathy and antipathy, are experienced, and how on the other, a concept is experienced. Consider how much more a person is involved in a feeling or wish than in a 'mere concept'.

If we try to imagine a soul-life in which feelings and will impulses are experienced in the same way as the European experiences abstract thoughts, then we can form a picture of the particular quality of the soul-life that flourishes in Tibet. *It is a capacity for abstraction reaching into the life of feeling and will.* Those people who have developed this capacity to a certain extent in themselves can be called 'human beings who are dead to life'. This is how Madame Blavatsky, among others, designated those who belong to Tibetan wisdom centers. Such 'dead' human beings are, however, especially qualified to unite within themselves the wisdom of India and China. For both the synthesizing spirit of India and the form-creating spirit of China are unified in the capacity for abstraction we have described. With its help, the linking of the greatest syncretism with the most impersonal form is possible.

In Tibet the 'I-wisdom' of India is amalgamated with the 'we-wisdom' of China into an 'it-wisdom'. The sense for the 'it', the impersonal, existing beyond the 'I' and 'we', has ripened in Tibet in close relation with *Buddhism.*

And the posture of Tibetan spiritual life in relation to India and

China can be seen through the traditional story of *how* Buddhism came to Tibet. For when the ruler of Tibet, Songtsän Gampo in the year AD 610, decided, under the influence of his two wives—an *Indian* princess and a *Chinese* princess—to import Buddhism into Tibet, he sent ambassadors simultaneously to India *and* to China in order to bring in books and teachers from those lands.

This story typifies the situation of Tibet in relation to the whole of Asian spiritual life, the place where Indian and Chinese spiritual life are brought together. But this union is no mere side-by-side existence; there arises out of this union a third element. Out of the union of 'I-wisdom' of India with 'we-wisdom' of China the 'it-wisdom' of Tibet arises.

This configuration of Asian spiritual life is a major concern for European humanity; for if the Europeans, especially the English, have to begin to come to terms with *Indian* spiritual life, so Russia has to begin to come to terms with *Chinese* and *Tibetan* spiritual life. This coming to terms must be taken up in all seriousness because what Communism, now ruling Russia, brings with it is preparation of the ground for the absorption of the Chinese 'we-wisdom'. Meanwhile, within the intelligentsia, a mood is growing that could cause people to look with yearning expectation toward the inner-Asian highlands.

What is this preparation of souls for Chinese spirituality by Communism, and how can we understand Eastern European spiritual life coming to terms with inner-Asian wisdom? These questions shall be considered more closely in the next essay.

CHINA AND EAST EUROPE

THE SPIRITUAL STREAM working in Chinese spiritual life was described in the essay 'The Spiritual Life of Asia' as the 'we-wisdom', in contradistinction to the 'I-wisdom' of India and to the 'it-wisdom' of Tibet. This description was intended to express the basic character of Chinese spiritual life; namely, that its nature is non-individualistic, and that it appeals to group consciousness.

When we compare the basic mood of the Chinese with that of Europeans, the difference between them, to which Vladimir Solovyov also pointed, is conspicuous. Whereas the European basically believes in progress—that the future, *as such*, has an advantage over the past—the attitude of the Chinese is the opposite. They have the deeply-rooted conviction that the past, *as such*, has an advantage over the future. The Chinese cultured person feels that the 'original' of all values in culture lies in the past. The present and the future are merely copies, or copies of copies, of the originals. Perhaps something new might come about through the process of copying, or even much could be distorted, but the fact remains that what is culturally valuable has *already been produced*, and now the task is to protect it from deterioration.

This basic feeling as borne by Chinese culture with regard to time explains (among other things) the tendency of Chinese art and science to preserve modes of thought and style, and to limit creativity and novelty to the elaboration of detail. In art, one may only *execute*; in philosophy, *make commentaries*; in science, *elaborate details*. Thus arises the minuteness in Chinese art and the enormous commentative literature in which—from a Western point of view—the splitting of already split hairs is pursued with astonishing success. For where there is no striving for what is essentially new, creative activity is directed toward the details of execution, and so the 'ancients', that is, the great leaders of Chinese spiritual life, worked by reminding people from time to time of the great *Originals*. In this sense, the mission of Lao Tzu in Chinese spiritual life can be understood. He called up memories of the great things 'which the ancients knew'.

For the conscious bearer of Chinese culture, the progressively inclined European appears to be an uncultured person, a barbarian. For only someone who does not know what is truly already there of value within culture would wish to create anything 'new'. Such people, then, do not possess what is old. They have no culture. And it is true that within Chinese cultural life the representatives of those tendencies that find expression in modern Chinese 'Republicanism', those, that is, who wish to destroy the old order, are actually uncultured. For China, it is absolutely correct to say: either tradition or barbarism. The various 'generals' who today [1931] rule over 'the land of four oceans' are not representatives of culture, but rather of anti-culture.

This traditionalism of Chinese spiritual life has a definite result. It brings with it a diminution of the value of the individual personality. For if what is most valuable is already present, if what is most significant must be sought for in the past, then nothing essential is expected as fount of creativity from the personality. One no longer has the attitude toward the individual personality: what does this person bear in the way of new creativity that through him or her can reach humanity? Instead one has the feeling: to what extent is this person a bearer of what has been preserved? Personalities are not valued for what they are in themselves, but only insofar as they are permeated by the generally accepted *forms* (forms of behavior, art forms, forms of thought, etc.). The individual personality becomes merely part of a whole. The value of this part depends on how completely it is expressedly representative of the whole.

Traditionalism and group consciousness are, therefore, the basic characteristics of the Chinese.[†] But the important factor to be considered is that the Chinese people are not, by nature, materialistic. For both the Chinese tradition and their social sense of unity are not materialistically oriented. That which one calls in China 'education' does not make people into materialists —on the contrary, education and a certain spiritualization have the same meaning in China.

Even the learning of the ideographic characters of the writing is in itself an intensive exercise of spiritual faculties, for the use of these characters brings with it a far greater inner activity than the use, for instance, of the Latin alphabet. While with the Latin alphabet it is an almost mechanical process to read the written word that is merely put together out of letters, the 'reading' of Chinese writing is an inner process whereby one sees in the signs not letters but thoughts. Through Chinese writing, thoughts, not just letters, are made visible. Therefore reading is already a kind of meditation, an effort in which the ether body is intensively active as well. And this accompanying

---

[†] Against this proposition it could be argued that in the history of China—especially in recent times—there are plenty of examples of both things: strivings for modernization, and the special prominence of and reverence for individual personalities. It is well known to the writer of these essays that not only are there innovative efforts in China, but that these strivings have achieved recently a decisive victory over the Hanlin Movement, which was working for a return to the pure principles of Confucianism. He is conscious, too, of the role played by individual personalities in these events.

movement of the ether body is what works against materialism, which is itself a complete anchoring in the physical body.

Now this living in the ether body, which is the essential quality of Chinese culture, has the characteristic that human beings do not feel themselves alone but feel themselves to be members of a whole. On this rests both ancestor worship and also Chinese national consciousness. For national consciousness is very much alive in China. It differs quite significantly from the modern European national consciousness. It is *moral*—which the Western State consciousness no longer is. For us today, it is a matter of course that politics—that is, the behavior of States—is amoral. The individual English man or woman, for example, is on the average a decent person; that is, they are themselves neither blackmailers nor burglars. But the State, which comprises millions of such decent people, wages the Opium War in China or the Boer War in South Africa. The State, that which must lift itself above individuals and demand self-sacrifice from them, is, from a moral perspective, inferior to the individual. The State in Europe is not a *superhuman*, but rather a *subhuman* organism. And to this subhuman entity the individual has to submit.

The Chinese national consciousness, however, is the opposite of this. There the State is a living being that embraces the individual not only dynamically but morally. It is not only a power, but also has spiritual and moral greatness. From the moral perspective, it stands above the individual.

The Chinese say to themselves: The State does not rule over me, but rather I serve it. I serve it, however, not because it is more powerful than I am, but because it is *greater* than I. Therefore I shall become morally more perfect when I take part in its life. For the State is a sublime moral being, higher than the individual. There are robbers within the State, but the State itself cannot be a robber. Therefore the Middle Kingdom did not strive to conquer other lands. This land grew larger by spiritual and moral means—not by use of force. For it 'conquered' other lands through being conquered. The Mongolians conquered the Kingdom—so Mongolia became a part of the Kingdom. The Manchurians conquered the Kingdom—so Manchuria became a part of the Kingdom. Beware, Europeans, of conquering us by outer force—your land can also become a part of the Kingdom.

So it is somewhat in this manner that the feeling of a representative of Chinese culture toward the 'Kingdom', and toward foreigners, could be expressed. Out of this feeling, for example, the book *China's Defence Against European Ideas*, by Ku Hung-Ming,[†] was written. This significant representative of high Chinese culture wishes to state in his book that the Chinese conception of the State is a more spiritual one than that of the West. He clearly allows the tone of the final sentence of the above monologue to pervade his whole book: Beware, Europeans, of conquering us by *outer* force—your land can also become a part of the Kingdom—by the *inner* force of our culture.

At present this threat is aimed especially at China's neighbor, the Union of the Soviet Socialist Republics; for Bolshevism, which rules there, has penetrated deeply into the inner life of China. It has broken through the 'Great Wall', like the Mongolians, like the Manchurians. It has broken into China. Now a conflict begins between Bolshevism and Chinese culture.

From the other side, from the Pacific, the mercantilism of the Western bourgeoisie broke into China, poisoned it with opium, and exploited, and still exploits it in the most scandalous manner.

So now China, guarding the ancient Atlantean tradition, stands between two worlds that threaten its existence—Western Commercialism and Russian Bolshevism. These two streams are actually the two *last* consequences of materialism. The clashing with China of the most arrant materialism in its double form—the most resolute Proletarianism and the crassest Bourgeoisism—is a modern event of tremendously tragic significance for all humankind. Like an embodied thesis and antithesis—with the greatest possible tension and contradiction between them—stands China, the oldest humanity, confronting the most recent humanity in the form of the crassest materialism.

Describing the mood of the 'great sages' of China in the second half of the last [nineteenth] century, Ku Hung-Ming writes:

When the great Chinese sages had overcome the Taiping rebellion, there remained two difficult problems for them to solve.

---

† *Chinas Verteidigung gegen europäische Ideen. Kritische Aufsätze* (Jena: Eugen Diederichs, 1917). This book has not been translated into English. ED.

The first was the work of rebuilding: the practical problem of the reconstruction of society and government administration. The second problem was the measures to be taken to counter the influx of Europeans with the destructive forces of their modern, utterly materialistic culture.

The first problem was then solved in an exemplary fashion.

In their struggle with the other problem, on the contrary, the problem of how to counter the destructive forces of modern European civilization, the great Chinese sages met with a complete failure. The Chinese sages, in confronting the destructive forces of modern materialistic European civilization...were helpless.

Ku-Hung-Ming sees the cause of this failure in the fact that the Chinese sages had no knowledge of Europeanism. But he solved the problem successfully in his own destiny by taking up Western spiritual life while remaining within the Chinese spirit. He says wholeheartedly:

I have taken Europeanism into my soul—but behold, the Chinese in me is victor! Just as *within me* the struggle of China with Europe ended with the victory of the former, so can the struggle of humanity within the world—of China with the West—lead to the victory of China.

So this is the solution of the Europe-China problem from the Chinese point of view. And it must be admitted: Europe, *without* the spiritual science inaugurated by Rudolf Steiner, is just as little a match, *spiritually*, for China, as China is a match for Europe in technical civilization. Without the fructification of European culture by spiritual science, Ku-Hung Ming's solution will be *the* solution of the Europe-China problem. Then the Chinese will travel on European railways, and the thinking of Europeans will move on the 'tracks' of Chinese thinking.

The conflict we have described above concerns especially the wave of European bourgeois ideology penetrating into China from the direction of the Pacific. However, since Ku-Hung-Ming wrote the above book, there has been a significant change in the situation.

From the Western direction, the wave of Russian Bolshevism has come right up to the boundaries of China and even partially penetrated it. For the Chinese sages there arose a new task: the struggle between the Chinese *social* view of life and the Russian materialistic socialism.

What, then, is the balance of forces on both sides in this conflict? What are the prospects for the future of this culture war?

Communism in Russia strives for the collectivization of all spheres of life. Its aim is to organize all spheres of life in such a way that a mechanically comprehensible and controllable whole is constructed. To achieve this, people must be suitably re-educated. They must be so educated that they relinquish in themselves any inclination toward individualism while at the same time developing the faculty for 'keeping step' in mass movements. The sense for being and living within *organizations* must be developed. The 'I-consciousness' must give way to the 'we-consciousness', and the whole of life must be so organized that it is an expression of this 'we-consciousness'.

Now what is significant is that the materialistic 'we-consciousness' of Communism runs up against the age-old Atlantean 'we-wisdom' of China. It is characteristic of this meeting that Communism strives to take on the role of teacher, of 'savior'. But just as little as Russian Communism has anything new to say to Western Europe on the subject of world-conceptions, so little has it anything new to say to East Asia in the social realm. For as the West is in advance of Bolshevism in materialistic theory, so China is ahead of it in social *praxis*.

To subsume all life into organizations and to train men and women into being 'organization-people'—this *ideal* of Bolshevism has been long since realized in China. For instance, Dr. MacGowan[†] states the following about the broad mass of Chinese people:

> If one were to place the poorest and most uneducated of these people on a solitary island in the ocean, they would get together into a political organization just as quickly as would people who have passed a lifetime under the protection of a reasonable democracy.

† John Macgowan (d. 1922), author of thirteen works on China. ED

The Chinese are born 'organization-people'—they have a sense for collective labor and collective action at a level that must really appear as an ideal to Russian Communism. Yes, even the economic form of Communism belongs to a certain degree to China's past. China has already passed through a kind of Communism. During the reign of the Emperor Shen Tsun (1068–1085), the great sage Wan Senshi, invoking the 'ancients', realized a kind of Communism which, however, was dissolved after the Emperor's death.

Thus Russian Communism shows to the Chinese the distorted image of their Chinese attitude of soul: the feeling for an organic 'belonging-together' appears now in the form of mechanical collectivism; the view of the State as a moral being becomes a Class-State; the ideal of loyalty becomes Party-dictatorship; and ancestor-worship becomes class-consciousness.

But on the other hand, if the Chinese confront a materialistic *distortion* of their ideology in Bolshevism, so do the Russians, who have been schooled in Bolshevism confront a spiritual *archetype* of their ideology in Chinese life. In the previous article we saw the effect of Bolshevism on the human soul, which expresses itself first in a strengthening of the conviction that the 'we-attitude' is superior to the 'I-attitude', and second in the growth of a yearning for a *more spiritual* lifestyle than shallow Marxism allows. In light of the above, we can now see how Bolshevism provides the most suitable possible preparation for an influx of Chinese ideology—the Atlantean 'we-wisdom'—into East Europe. Bolshevism creates the striving toward collective spirituality, and it is exactly this *collective spirituality*, from out of the far distant past and carried on through the ages, that China bears.

MONGOLIANISM AND EAST EUROPE

IN THE PREVIOUS ESSAY regarding the Chinese in relationship to modern Eastern Europe, the attempt was made to show how the present conditions in Russia are especially favorable for the Chinese way of thought to influence East European spiritual life. In order to understand what this influence could mean in the whole stream of East Europe's historical evolution, it would be important to direct

our gaze once more into the East European past to shed light from a
new aspect onto the interplay of forces in its historical development.
Earlier we considered the East European past from one point of view:
the history of Christianity (see 'Christianity in Russia'). However, the
Christianity that came from Byzantium to Russia is not the only
thing that has a fundamental significance for the history of Eastern
Europe. The migration of Norsemen from the north-west was equally
important for its development. For in the ninth century of our era,
Norsemen came into Russia, becoming there the ruling class until—
through the mixing of blood—they disappeared among the Slavs.
What does this fact signify?

The legends of tradition describe this event in the following way:
The Slavic tribes lived scattered over the measureless expanses of Eastern Europe. But they were scattered over the expanses with nothing
to unite them. So the elders held council and sent messengers to the
Norsemen, 'Come to us and rule over us, for our land is vast and rich,
but there is not the strength in it to inwardly hold it together.' This
approximately was the content or the gist of the message. So the
Norsemen came and became leaders of the Slavs.

This saga reveals the essence of what happened at the time of the
Norse immigration into Russia. The Slavic soul-life had, it is true,
breadth and fullness, but it lacked an inner mainstay, a soul backbone. The Slavic soul was large and delicate, but it threatened to drift
far afield if the cohesive strength of the strong 'I'-impulse of the Norsemen did not enter from the opposite pole. That is the inner meaning
of the message sent to the Norse princes as quoted from the old
chronicle: 'Come to us and rule over us, for our land is wide and rich,
but there is no order in it.' It is truly hard to imagine that the Slavs
were actually complaining of possessing too much land and riches
and that foreigners must come and 'make order'.

From the mixture of Slavs with Norsemen arose the Russian folk
('Ruots' means in the Finnish language 'Swede'). This folk received
Byzantine Christianity, and thus there arose Russian culture in the
form it took during the first historic period of the Russian empire, the
epoch of Kiev. During this period the effect of the Norse impulse
showed itself clearly. It was the impulse for self-assertion in the physical world, the impulse for a strong consciousness of the self in the

earthly realm. This characteristic was lacking to the Slavs of the ninth century (*before* the Norse immigration), but in the thirteenth century (*after* the Norse immigration), it began to develop in a too strongly one-sided manner.

Toward the end of the twelfth century, the Grand Duchy of Kiev dissolved into a number of small states with independent princes continually quarreling with each other. The extreme of *particularism* gradually held sway, like a hypertrophy of the Norse impulse. And while this extreme power of divisive particularism dominated the upper classes and threatened to give a direction to the whole of Eastern Europe, *not* in consonance with the true mission of the Russian people, an extraordinary thing happened. Like a terrible antithesis to this particularism, there appeared before the gates of the frontier towns of the empire the *Mongolian Hordes*.

The old chronicles give us a picture of the feelings awakened by the appearance of the hordes (*Orda*). Like a horrible force of nature resembling a cloud of locusts, they inspired an unearthly terror. Their horror consisted in their *unity* and *uniformity*. Hundreds of thousands of riders on low-backed horses, all armed in the same way, followed by a baggage train of wagons on which they carried their worldly goods, all animated by *one* incomprehensible enthusiasm, all driven by *one* unintelligible urge, but at the same time all in strictest order as if a higher power of organization worked through them all—such was the outer aspect of the 'horde'. But *behind* this outer aspect was a power that the Russians no longer had. It was the power of a *group consciousness* that had become aggressive. It was this power which at that time was called the 'Orda'. The word 'Orda' means neither army, nor folk, nor state, but a 'compact and movable mass that is directed by a group consciousness.' That, more or less, is the way in which one could describe the content of this appellation.

In the first half of the thirteenth century, the collision took place between the particularizing individualism of the Russians and the 'Orda', the tremendously powerful group impulse of the Mongolians. And through the interworking of these two polar attitudes of mind, there arose in the course of centuries the Moscovite empire of the Tsars. This was the result of individualism blunted by the effect of Mongolianism.

So we see that the history of Russia resembles a pendulum-swing between two impulses that have streamed in from outside: the *individualism* that had come from the north as an impulse of the Norsemen, and the group nature that had broken in as a Mongolian impulse from the south. This pendulum-swing is one of the true causes of the antithesis between *Moscow* and *Novgorod* right up to the sixteenth century. For in northeast Russia, effected only by a weakened form of Mongolianism, the old 'spirit of the Norsemen' was preserved. Novgorod was a *republic*, which in its constitution guaranteed the highest measure of freedom of the *individual personality*. It was a free democratic community, which as a member of the Hansa Confederacy, opened wide regions of northern Russia to trade. A lively traffic with the West was fostered from Novgorod.

In polar opposition to this home of the impulses of personality stood mighty Moscow, combining the group impulse of Mongolianism with the Byzantine ideology of rulership. In their battle (between Moscow and Novgorod), which came to an end in the sixteenth century, Moscow remained victor. However, after some time, the pendulum changed direction. Its swing began to go toward the side of 'Norsemanism'. And the time when this change of direction happened is called in history 'the time of confusion' (end of the sixteenth and beginning of the seventeenth centuries). It was the time when the Tartar *Godunov*, representing 'Mongolianism', fought against the *Pseudo-Demetrius*, representing individualistic tendencies. This battle was no mere battle of personalities, rather it was a battle of forces working through the respective personalities. The pseudo-Demetrius, coming from the West, was for the people the one who would bring freedom, incorporating the culture of personality in the struggle against group-consciousness represented by Boris Godunov.

The swing of the pendulum in the direction of 'Norsemanism' (that is, of the earthly impulse of personality) led then, at the beginning of the eighteenth century, to the reforms of Peter the Great, and the foundation of *Petersburg*. Petersburg, as the new capital city of the empire, was to be the place where the personality culture of the West should be fostered. On the one hand it was to be the new Novgorod, on the other it was to carry on the Byzantine ideology of Moscow. As the Moscovite rulers, particularly *Ivan the Terrible*, strove for an association between 'Mongolianism' and the Byzantine ideology of rulership stemming from the Emperor Justinian, so did the Petersburg rulers, primarily Peter the Great, strive for an association between 'Norsemanism' and the same Byzantine ideology.

But this 'Norsemanism' went its own way and came ever more strongly into contradiction with Byzantianism. This contradiction came to a head in the 1905 and February 1917 Russian revolutions. The second revolution provided a clear victory for individualism, and 'pseudo-Demetrius', this time representing pseudo-individualism in the figure of Kerensky, ascended the throne.

The mood that prevailed in Russia during the first months after the February revolution (1917) could be described as 'intoxicated individualism'. It actually was the time when, after the Tsar had been overthrown, everyone felt himself to be Tsar. But a tragic end awaited this individualism-gone-mad. In the night of October 25th (by the old Julian calendar) the dark lightning of Bolshevism struck into a Russia drunk with freedom. With monstrous speed it took possession of all spheres of life.

After this individualism-gone-mad, there followed its extreme opposite, the group-nature-gone-mad—Communism. The pendulum swung in the opposite direction—in the direction of Mongolianism. For although Bolshevism strove to bring to realization Western Marxist theories, nevertheless it called to the surface in Russia the Mongolian 'Orda', the horde, which lived in the depths of the subconscious.

And as in old times the masses of men from the steppes, filled with hatred, attacked towns and assaulted walls (which had made possible a secluded inner life within the towns)—so there now began a horrible exhibition of organized hatred by the mass-man against individualities. Countless members of the intelligentsia were executed for infringing the new highest commandment, which says: 'thou shalt have no inner life of thine own.' Hatred of the inner life, of the personality, that is the central nerve of the Bolshevist terror. In contrast, the French Revolution sought to destroy the 'tyrants'; that is, the *suppressors* of the personality.

At present the *greatest* sin against the basic principle of Soviet culture is a *meditation* carried through in silent seclusion. And all life in the Soviet Union is so arranged that in its style, in its content, in its rhythm, it is as opposed to meditation as possible. It is intended that people shall *not* come to self-knowledge there. They shall continuously—even in sleep—be guided by waves of suggestion directed from the center. And these waves of suggestion are truly powerful. For the daily distributed avalanche of grey newspaper in which one thing is continuously repeated in a hundred forms each day *through the years*; the cinema hypnotizing the thoughtless audience, repeating *one same thing* in endless variations through the years; the daily radio broadcasts; the speeches in clubs; resolutions at mass meetings; mass proclamations on the streets with placard slogans; posters on the walls; theater; literature—all this is the means of directing a powerful stream of suggestion into the individual soul; a stream that, through the written, shouted, spoken, whispered word, through photographs and drawings, through mass proclamations, says: Thou shalt have no inner life of thine own.

It is not just an analogy, it is *literally true* when we must say: the means and principles of hypnosis and suggestion are consciously used on millions of people in the Soviet Union. And as one can speak of States where power rests on trust, on authority, on religion, etc.— so one can at present speak of a State in which the power of rulership rests on *hypnosis and suggestion*.

This stream of suggestion works on the sub-consciousness. There it calls forth the ghost of the Mongolians. And the Mongolian face of *Lenin*, whose picture in practically every building has taken the place of the Icon, is a revelation in the flesh of the forces represented in Bolshevism.

Naturally, there can be no doubt that the pendulum of history will one day swing back again; that is, that a time for individualism will come in Russia—a time 'when Russia will consist of smaller States at whose head will be poets and philosophers'—but this time can be postponed very far into the future if the following happens: Modern Mongolianism in Russia is materialistic, and actually still barbaric, but it cannot remain so for very long. It must bring forth a culture; that is, a new education, a new kind of religion, philosophy, art. For the Russian folk-soul cannot permanently live merely on the dregs of Western civilization. A spiritual impulse must enter in.

Now it is possible that the unindividual spirituality of China might find congenial soil in unindividualistic Russia. This, however, would retard development for a long time. For there could arise a certain contentment if a balance were established between materialism and spiritualism on an unindividualistic basis. And this contentment would mean a stand-still in development.

It is this stand-still that we had in mind when in the essay 'China and East Europe' we pointed to the Chinese spiritual life as a *danger* to East European spiritual life.

THE FINNISH IMPULSE
IN RUSSIAN SPIRITUAL LIFE

A SEQUENCE OF ESSAYS sketching the structure of forces in the East European spiritual life must be continually supplemented—because *any* point of view is of necessity one-sided—with different aspects of consideration in order to create a balance. With every presentation some subject remains which was not essential from the perspective of *that* particular presentation, but which can be of great importance for some *other* aspect. Such a remaining 'subject' still left after consideration of Christianity in Russia, of Mongolianism, and of Norse impulses, is the question of the significance of the *Finns*, of the Finnish impulse in the East European spiritual life.

It is a fact known to historical research that the greater portion of present-day European Russia, including the region around Moscow, was inhabited in the ninth and tenth centuries by Finnish tribes. This region was gradually colonized by Slavic immigrants coming from the south-west, and these immigrants mixed with the Finns. Out of this mixture arose the Greater Russian people, which at present preponderate over the Little Russians and White Russians. This outer fact—the absorption of a number of Finnish tribes into Slavism—brings up questions about the *deeper* significance of the Finnish influence for the growing culture of Eastern Europe.

When in the ninth century the migration of the Norsemen into Russia took place, the expansion of Slavs into the Finnish territories began simultaneously. Now the immigration of the Norsemen had the deep significance that, with it, the impulse of the 'I' entered into the Slavic nature. The Slavic being had naturally developed an extraordinary breadth of soul-life, but lacked the power of inner cohesion, and this power streamed into the Slavic soul through the Norse impulse.

Besides the extraordinary breadth of soul-life, the Slavic soul had still another peculiarity that one could describe approximately by the word 'subjectivity'. As wide as the life of the soul was, still it projected only *itself* into the expanses. It did not go out of itself.

This subjectivity of the Slavic soul, which shows itself especially clearly in the Polish element, gives on the one hand to every expression of that soul a tinge of warmth, of involvement, but on the other hand brings with it the danger of dimming the vision for realities of the outer world. This subjectivity has the tendency to surround the soul with a kind of soul-mist, which is like a constant intoxication of the soul—with itself and through itself. Sympathy and antipathy, joy and pain, live in the Slavic soul in the finest shades; noble melodies of *all* life's music can come to expression through this soul. This soul is deep and wide: capable of rising to greatest heights of beauty and humaneness, and of falling into the most unspeakable wretchedness of depravity; capable of forgiving and loving without measure; and also of being possessed by the Demon of Hatred itself. And the danger that threatens this soul is that of being seduced by its own self—of succumbing to the unconscious wish to prefer its own riches to the realities that are *outside* the soul. Then it could fall into a kind of *imprisonment*—into the prison of its own self. This imprisonment is all the more dangerous because, for the self-imprisoned soul, there remains hardly any possibility for becoming conscious of its own condition. In order to become so conscious, an objective perception of the self is needed—and just that is here impossible.

This subjectivity can become a great danger when an individualistic impulse of independence is joined with it. The 'I'-impulse, hand in hand with the subjectivity we have described, results in a state of chaotic turbidity which, for instance, in the Times of Confusion (1598–1612), or, too, during the Kerensky time of the Russian revolution of 1917, became symptomatically visible.

But this subjectivity would not just have become a danger—which it now is—but rather could have become a power which, like a force of nature, would have overpowered the souls of Russian people had not another force opposed it. And this other force that flowed into Russia's Slavism, working in opposition to the described subjectivity, was the Finnish impulse that united with Slavism in the formation of the Greater Russian folk.

The Finnish tribes, which about a thousand years ago inhabited the greater part of present European Russia, developed a life of soul that differed so strongly from the Slavic soul-life that it seemed to the latter like a riddle. Ancient Finns appeared to the Slavs as 'amazing people', which was perhaps the inner meaning of the word 'tschudj', the old Slavonic appellation for the Finns. 'Tschudj' has the same stem as the word 'tschudö' (wonder) and the word 'tschudák' (odd person). Thus this word expresses something strange, incomprehensible, and the relationship of the Slavs to the ancient Finns was in accordance with this word. The Finns were regarded as wizards, as knowers of the secret effects of the human inner forces—namely, of the word—on the outer forces of nature. Slavs looked at the Finns and said to themselves: these people have a different relationship to the outer world than we do. What they experience *within themselves* also has a significance for the outer world. Their *inwardness* has *objective* significance, while our inner life does not penetrate out of us into the world. They are magicians.

Objectivity, the basic attitude of the Finnish soul, seemed to the subjective Slavs to be something supernatural, reaching out beyond human nature. Therefore they called the folk who had this peculiar objectivity, 'tschudj'.

Now this appellation was largely justifiable for the reason that the objectivity of the Finns was not simply a quality such as that which we know today, say in the sphere of science. Today we understand by 'objectivity' actually only half of what is meant here; namely, to allow the facts of the world to speak rather than the human soul. But the human soul is not only a *perceiving* being, it is also a being called upon to intervene through *action* in the world process. And as there exists an objectivity of perception, so there exists also an objectivity of *action*. As in objective perception human beings allow the facts of the outer world to speak in the soul, so in objectivity of action they allow the soul to 'speak' out into the world as a *kind of fact*. In the first case one lets the outer world project into the soul. In the second case one lets the soul reach out into the world as a *power of the outer world*. And this reaching of the soul out into the world in an *objective* manner was a basic capacity of the Finnish soul, just as the reaching out of the soul into the world in a *subjective* way was the basic characteristic of the Slavic soul.

The aforementioned 'objectivity of action' of the ancient Finn expressed itself in the spoken or sung *word*. The word had a significance and a power that one can hardly imagine unless one has taken part today (1931) in that culture of the word that is fostered at the Goetheanum in Dornach. For this power did not issue from an experience of what was said—that is, from the soul element—but from the experience of the *participation* in *speaking* by superhuman powers. The ancient Finn felt: my speech is a vessel into which the power of gods streams.

This experience, for example, lies at the basis of the Epic of the Northern Finns, the *Kalevala*. The Kalevala is only comprehensible when one regards, not only its content, but also its *form*—a product of a culture that did not have the power to build temples and towns of stone, but yet, through rhythms and sounds of speech, left behind a monument to the vanishing might of the word.

The Slavs, too, had an intense relationship to the spoken word. But this relationship was the opposite of the Finns'. For the Slavic language was in every sound completely filled with soul, entirely permeated by soul-inwardness. It was an *inward* language which, although in its sound it streamed out *physically*, yet in its *inner* effect was directed *inward*, that is, toward the speaking soul itself. One might say that the Finns sent out nature forces when they spoke, whereas the Slavs, as it were, sucked in the outer world when they spoke. And it is quite justifiable in this connection to speak of the Slavs as a people at the stage of babes or *sucklings*. For this way of speaking—when the soul, as it were, sucks in the outer world—is actually *childish* speech. One can see without difficulty that the Slavs at the time of their fusion with the Finns were at a childish stage of development.

It is not so easy, however, to see upon what level of development the Finns stood at that time; for while the Finnish peoples had on the one hand a so-called 'primitive' culture, on the other their inner soul-attitude was one of great maturity. And *objectivity* as a basic quality of the Finnish people is in itself a quality that belongs to an advanced age in comparison with life stages of a human being. For just as the childishness of the Slavs revealed itself in the 'sucking' subjectivity of the soul, so did the maturity—even old age—of the Finns reveal itself in the soul's capacity to go out of itself and act spiritually in *objectivity*.

In order to present the relationship of the Finnish folk to Slavism in a picture, we can say: in the historical meeting between the Slavs and Finns we have the meeting between the little 'grandson' and his old 'grandfather'. The dying Finns, fostering memories of the age-old past, and the young Slavs, living wholly in dreams of the future; these met together in the wide expanses of the East European plains. And this meeting differed from most of the meetings of peoples in European history, for it was a *peaceful* meeting. The Slavs did indeed fight wars, with Greeks, Chosars, Petshenegs, Tartars, etc. 'Finnish wars', however, do not exist in the history of old Russia. An imperceptible breeze of *love* holds sway over the story of the vanishing of two thirds of the Finnish folk into the Slavic folk. It is like a dialogue between the Archangels of the two folks: the young folk of Slavs with the old folk of Finns. And this dialogue assuaged the one-sided subjectivity of the Slavic soul. Through the peaceful fusion of the two folks, the seed was sown among the Slavs for the objectivity that can balance their subjectivity. So the superhuman wisdom of world history worked, thousands of years in advance, to prepare what will become the future culture of the European East.

Thus the influences of Byzantium, of Norsemen, of Mongolians, and of Finns, as has been sketched in a sequence of essays, worked together to prepare the future of East Europe. But after a picture of these *influences* has been given in broad outline, the question arises: How does the true essence of the Russian people reveal itself, apart from all outer influences? What part do the Russians themselves have in the interplay of the various forces that form the history of the European East?

In the center of all these outer happenings is the Russian folk-soul, but as yet it sleeps. Not yet has it *been able* to reveal its being in the realm of outer historical happenings. It sleeps, and dreams— prophetic dreams of the future. And these dreams can be *interpreted*, for they contain seeds for the future mission of East European culture. Just such a prophetic dream of the Russian folk-soul is the *Saga of the Holy City of Kitezh*. In this Saga the deepest destiny forces of the Russian folk soul are revealed. There the ideal is shown—the ideal which works in the deepest subconscious layers of that soul as archetype of the sixth post-Atlantean culture epoch.

This archetype, as revealed through the *Saga of the Holy City of Kitezh*, shall be our next theme for consideration.

THE SAGA OF THE HOLY CITY OF KITEZH AS REVELATION OF THE ESSENTIAL FORCES OF THE RUSSIAN FOLK-SOUL

IN CONSIDERING THE CULTURE of a people, it is important to distinguish the sheath 'I' from their true 'I'. For the *individuality* of a folk is surrounded, as it were, by a sheath of influences of other peoples; influences which are, however, so deep that they appear to be like characteristics of the folk itself. For instance, in Russia the German has been thought of as the archetype of a philistine. The Russian has the tendency to see the German as a person who pursues trivial things with pedantic exactness. For example, they can visualize a German receiving a Doctor's degree for composing *An Attempt at a Preface to an Outline Description of a Compendium of the History of Luxembourg* (pocket edition, seven volumes).

This picture, need one say, is false. For although there actually is much philistinism within the German life of culture, the German essence does not reveal itself in philistinism but rather in the *combatting* of it. The German being is actually the force within Western culture that *overcomes* philistinism. And whoever disregards this overcoming and sees only the raw material to be overcome, will have a false picture of the German spirit. The philistinism in the German spiritual life does not belong to its true being; it belongs to its 'sheath being'. It comes from the Latin spirit that has flowed into German spiritual life from outside.

When, therefore, one wishes to grasp the German being, one must not seek it in the continuation of Latinism, but rather in the overcoming of it. It is not the figure of Wagner (the pedantic scholar depicted in Goethe's *Faust*) who is representative of the German character, but the figure of Faust. For although Faust, in his capacity of Doctor and possessor of the knowledge of four Faculties, was *ensheathed* in the Wagner element, he was actually the overcomer of that element. Philistinism is related to the German being in the same way as Wagner is to Faust in the *Faust* drama. And if one wishes to get to know the German being in its deepest qualities, one will achieve much more by studying *Faust* than by studying at German universities. This *Faust* drama, based on a folk legend, reveals through its characters the forces that are the destiny of the soul of Central Europe. The legend of Doctor Faust is a prophetic dream of the Central European soul, an expression of the profound forces of its being.

A similar prophetic dream of the East European soul, revealing the forces of its deepest essence, is the *Saga of the Holy City of Kitezh*. As the *Faust* drama reveals the essence of the German folk-spirit, so does the *Kitezh* drama (text by W. Belski, opera by N. Rimski-Korsakoff) reveal the essence, the true being, of the Russian folk-soul. Everything known today as 'Russian culture' is to a large extent the 'sheath being' of Russianism, which consists of the effects of Byzantine, Norse, Tartar, and Finnish impulses. Its real being is hidden behind this sheath. Surrounded by this sheath, it is asleep. But while sleeping it dreams. And a dream of the sleeping Russian folk-soul is the folk saga that arose in the thirteenth century of the invisible city of Kitezh.

The main features of this Saga are as follows:

> Old Prince Jurij built two cities in the Murom forests: one lying more outwardly, on the Volga—the 'lesser Kitezh'; and one lying in the midst of the woods—the 'greater Kitezh'. The people of the lesser Kitezh were known for their hospitality. They took in all strangers graciously. They were great in their capacity for welcoming people. But one day there appeared a power that they could not take in: the horde of Tartars. These destroyed the lesser Kitezh. But they did not know the way to the inner, the greater Kitezh. Now there was a man among the inhabitants of the outer Kitezh, Grishka Kuterjema (which means 'the

confused') who betrayed the path to the inner Kitezh. He laid
the blame for this betrayal upon the childishly innocent maiden
Fevronia, the bride of the heir to the throne, young prince
Vsevolod.

Now when the Tartars reached the city that lay by the forest lake,
Svetlyi Yar, a miracle happened. The prayers and blood-filled
tears of all the inhabitants were heard by the divine Mother. The
town with all its inhabitants became invisible. It rose up into
high heaven, or else, according to another version, it sank into
the depths of Lake Svetlyi Yar (which means the 'brightly shining'). The Tartars fled in terror. The betrayer went crazy. And the
maiden, Fevronia, was led into the invisible city as Princess after
she had earned this rank through *undeserved sufferings* (imprisonment, damnation, death by hunger in the forest).

What does this Saga reveal? In the depths of the Russian folk-soul
lives the image of a *city*; that is, a community. It is not the image of a
hero that incorporates the essence of the ideal of the folk-soul in its
being, but the image of a *social community*. The Saga describes the way
of the city—the destiny of a community—that is threatened by its
counter-image, the Mongolian 'Orda'. The way and goals of *individual*
striving, the problem of an individual path, is not to be found in the
heart of the Saga. For the maiden, Fevronia, too, has no individual
path, has no goal that she is striving to reach. Nor is she significant
through what she *does*, but she has significance in the Saga through
what happens to her. Her *destiny* is the important thing about her. And
this destiny is not a personal one. It is a suffering for the people in general, for the city. This suffering is personally unmerited and without
cause; that is, it has no cause in the *past*. It is a suffering for the sake of
the future—the future of the people in general.

Here a deep characteristic of the essence of the Russian people
reveals itself: its peculiar relationship to suffering, which differs from
that of the European. For while in Europe there is a tendency to
negate suffering—to regard it as something that arises *as a consequence*
of error—in Russia, especially among the common people, suffering is
regarded as something that prepares the glory of the future. There,
suffering is not only a payment for sins, but also a divine privilege.

Suffering is revered; one says *yes* to it in the deepest grounds of the soul. All sufferers—even if they have merited their pain or bear it as a punishment—are revered all the same. Even criminals have always within their merited suffering an element of the unmerited. *Every punishment bears within it an unmerited element.* And unmerited suffering is suffering for all. Every undeserved suffering is a preparation for the future of all humankind. As Christ through his unmerited suffering prepared the future of the world, so can any peasant do something similar when he or she suffers.

The suffering anchored in the depths of the true Russian being is not exhausted with this aspect of significance to the individual 'I'. For the essence of suffering as it is experienced by the Russian people is still not exhausted when men and women suffer because of their 'I'; that is, experience the effects of errors of their 'I' either for instruction or for restoration of balance. In every suffering there hovers above the 'I' a superindividual power. This power hovering above the 'I' bestows a significance of 'humaneness' upon the suffering. The root of suffering is not to be sought in the 'I' alone, but also in a *pain-bringing act of grace* pouring down from above.

Suffering is not only 'law' but also 'grace'. It is not only an expression of the deeds of the 'I', but also an expression of the working dominion of the *spirit self*, of the Holy Spirit in the human being. And the picture of the Ascension of the city of Kitezh, which took place as a result of the unmerited suffering of all for all, is the ideal of the *spirit self*, burning in the depths of the Russian folk-soul.

In the *Faust* drama the problem is handled quite differently. There the question of the striving of a single individual occupies the center of the Saga. This individual, through error and sin, comes to redemption. Faust goes a lonely way. Everything is there for *him*: everything has significance insofar as it is significant for *him*. He is ever striving toward a determined goal that he, for himself and by himself, intends to reach. Gretchen, Helena, and the land that can be retrieved from the sea, are goals which he, without consideration of others, strives toward. They are but stages in his 'I' development.

Faust is actually extremely anti-social in his attitude. And the society that mercifully takes him, the lonely one, into its midst, is the society of the heavenly Powers, within which after his earthly death he can participate. Not until after death does he become a member of a community—during the entire course of his life, he wanders alone.

What, however, is his significance? What is the positive quality that he, as a symbolic figure, brings to expression? The importance of Faust is neither in his moral purity nor in his freedom from error, but in the inner power that was able to withstand the conglomerated forces of the world of appearances without being extinguished. 'He who is ever *striving*—we can redeem.'[†] In these words the heavenly Powers express the positive aspect of Faust. That Faust had *strength* within himself not to drown his consciousness in the ocean of the world, that he could *constantly stand upright with his 'I'*, this was adjudged by the heavenly Powers as of equal value with moral holiness; that is, with childlike innocence, with power of atonement. For this *uprightness of the 'I' alone* gave Faust the possibility of being lifted up into the same realm where the child-like innocence of those born at midnight, and the merit of the penitents, dwelt.

In the saga of the City of Kitezh, the heavenly Powers would actually have to say, 'He who suffers without resistance, him we can redeem.' And there, not the individual, but rather the community is redeemed. For the question that lies at the basis of the Kitezh saga is: How can *we* be redeemed?—whereas the Faust saga answers the question about the redemption of the individual personality.

There is in Goethe's *Faust* no justification of egotism, but rather a description of the path of the human 'I' which, thanks to its inner power, attains to union with the spiritual world *in spite of* all egoism adhering to it. By the same token, there is in the Kitezh saga a justification of passivity and group behavior. For just as the 'I' power of Faust was pronounced holy by heaven, so was the capacity for devotion of the Kitezh people pronounced holy by heaven. There exists a justified egoism, acceptable to heaven; there also exists a justified universality, acceptable to heaven. And as Faust's *activity* opened for him the portal to heaven, so did the *passivity* of the maiden, Fevronia, open the portal to the invisible city of Kitezh.

There exists a justified activity, but it must be directed downward, for then what is above will bend down as grace. There exists also a

† *Faust*, final scene: 'Death of Faust'.

justified passivity which must, however, only be unfolded toward that which is above.

And this justified activity is that in which the German folk-spirit engages in the process of developing the 'I'. Passivity is that in which the Russian soul should engage in order to receive in the future, from above, the *spirit self*.

The Faust saga and the Kitezh saga reveal two significant examples: the impulse of the 'I' and the impulse toward the spirit self as revelations of the essential forces of the German and of the Russian folk.

THE EAST EUROPEAN
CONCEPTION OF SUFFERING

A FEW YEARS AGO a major American film magazine addressed its readers with a call to take part in a competition for new ideas for films. Among the various conditions the applicants had to fulfill, there was especially one which, if not adhered to, would make any idea unusable. This was the stipulation for a 'happy ending'. Every film story had to end happily, otherwise it could not hope for success—it would not suit the taste of an American audience.

Similar requirements for a similar competition were made by another American magazine, only there it was a question of stories, of 'true stories'. And it was not only required that the stories be *true*, but also they must have a 'happy ending', because the American reader cannot bear stories which, although true, have an unhappy ending.

These examples of American tendencies shed light symptomatically on the American's relationship to *suffering*. Suffering is for the American something that actually should not exist in life. It has no right to exist. It should be eliminated from life. And if it continues to be there, if it still haunts all the dark corners of life, that must be because civilization is not yet advanced enough. However, there will come a time when the progress of civilization will put an end to suffering. Human beings will then all be materially secure. They will all be either healthy, or, if they experience illness, will be entirely free of pain by means of anesthetics, narcotics, etc., and will also enjoy a long life. However, as long as this has not yet been achieved, one should be ashamed of pain, as one is ashamed of the necessary lower life processes of the body. For the presence of suffering is an *offence*.

This conception of suffering as something senseless and to be avoided is presented by the American author Mulford,[†] in a form that is the final practical consequence of the denial of suffering. In his two works, The *Scandal of Dying* and The *Scandal of Living*, he postulates in strong, vigorous language the *scandalous* character not only of suffering, but also of the extreme form of suffering, death. And with a strong impulse to concentrate on the 'positive', completely *ignoring* suffering, he saw the possibility of eliminating pain and death.

This willful pursuit of absolute 'positivity' by which suffering shall be eliminated—this is the deeply-seated motivation of Americans: the key to the secrets of America. However, one of the secrets of existence as such is the fact that everything essential has its polarity somewhere. Every being has its antipode, every ideology its counter-ideology, every culture its opposite culture. So also does Americanism have its antipode within humankind. Simultaneously with the arising of American culture, there arose in another place on earth its polarity. This is the culture developing in East Europe.

Russianism and Americanism are polar opposites. And hardly anywhere else does this polarity show itself so clearly as in their conception of *suffering*. For as suffering is *negated* in America, so is it *affirmed* in Russia. We attempted to describe this affirmation of suffering in Russia from one point of view recently in the article, 'The Saga of the Holy City of Kitezh'. We looked at suffering as it came to expression in connection with this legend. But a fuller, more conscious expression of the 'wisdom of suffering' can be found in the works of that excellent representative of Russian spirituality—the fiftieth anniversary of whose death we are at present celebrating—namely, Fyodor Mikhailovich Dostoevsky.

The great literary work of Dostoevsky brings certain views to expression. All his works are means for placing before humankind, vividly and clearly, certain truths that were deeply rooted in his soul.

---

† Prentice Mulford (1834–1891). See *Gift of the Spirit, Selected Essays*, Introduction by A.E. Waite, Ryder, 1930.

And these truths which Dostoevsky had to present to humankind were not merely his personal convictions. Rather he made conscious the wisdom that is anchored in the depths of the Russian folk-soul by putting it into words.

Now these truths consisted in a specific conception of *suffering* and of *guilt*. Suffering is for him something that should not be avoided. It is valuable. And all who suffer gain something from that suffering. It gives one more worth. The Staretz Sossima kneels down before Dimitri *Karamazov* when he realizes what sufferings are in store for Dimitri (*The Brothers Karamazov*). The holy man kneels before the undisciplined, passionate young person because he has reverence for his future suffering. And something further is in this wonderful deed of Sossima's. It contains, in addition, an expression of gratitude on behalf of all people for everything that Dimitri will suffer. For every sufferer—even a criminal—suffers for all. All humanity is sick, and this sickness comes to a crisis in a particular individual, through whom the burden is removed from the others. Just as in an abscess all the poison in the organism is concentrated in *one* place so that the organism as a whole is freed from poison (for through one part of the organism concentrating into itself much poisonous matter, the organism as a whole is benefitted), so every sufferer—yes, even those overcome by the dark forces of evil, those possessed by evil—represent a place within humanity where poison is concentrated for the benefit of all. Therefore the 'kneeling' gratitude of Sossima was appropriate, for in Dimitri, the poison of the Karamasovs was coming to a head.

It is thus with all suffering. Suffering is never merely a 'personal problem' of *one* individual, it is the concern of all humankind.

The first thesis of Dostoevsky's conception of suffering is, then:

Every sufferer suffers for all.

Now there exists a suffering that is deserved: that which is inflicted as punishment, or is the result of aberrations; and there is a suffering that—like birth-pangs—heralds the dawn of something new. People can suffer because of their crimes, or suffer through the greatness of what is passing through their souls. There is a difference between suffering the bitter dregs from the cup of passion, and that pain of sacrificing something lower so that something higher may arise.

Dostoevsky shows how these two types of suffering can become one. He shows how every punishment can actually be transformed into birth pangs of a higher life. Every punishment is unjust, is a martyrdom, so long as the person has not recognized his or her guilt. If it has been recognized, however, it is already an awakening to a higher life, and then the punishment is no longer punishment, but rather the process of birth, in pain, of a higher human being.

Justice can only exist when the guilt has been recognized and the punishment is freely willed. When this happens, however, there intervenes a process of grace from the spiritual world; and then justice becomes irradiated by the light that begins to shine from within the human being. As the moon vanishes by day in the sunlight, so the just reprisal vanishes in the eclipsing light of the sun of grace that always shines in the depths of humaneness.

And so the second thesis could be formulated thus:

> *Every punishment can be transformed into sacrifice, into the birth-pangs of a higher human being.*

Such insights are only possible when one has an intense feeling for the belonging together of all people, the unity of humankind. Out of this feeling another fundamental insight of Dostoevsky's arises: that every crime has in its background many more guilty people than one would think. The whole is responsible for all its parts. So, for instance, all the brothers *Karamazov* were guilty of their father's murder: Dimitri *wanted* to do it (he did not, however, do it); Ivan *knew* of the plan and did not prevent it; and Alyosha *was unable* to prevent it, that was his fault. The murder itself was done by the hand of the lackey, Smerdyackov; but *the forces* that moved his hand belonged to the others.

And so it is in every community. Many are guilty when *one* person sins. In the future development of conscience, it will be necessary to take not only one's own deeds, but also those of others into the sphere of one's conscience. Conscience can extend itself, it can awaken into its *complete* scope when one becomes conscious of this fact: you are a member of the whole. And the vivid experience of this fact leads us to the recognition of the third thesis proposed by Dostoevsky:

> *Of one individual's crime, many are guilty.*

If humanity is a whole, not only physically but also morally, and if it follows that the suffering and guilt of the individual concern the whole, then the question arises: How is it with the light-filled, the good, the true? If the gloom, pain, sin of all are the concern of all, must not the same be true of happiness, blessedness, goodness? Does not the unity of humankind also comprise the unity of everything that prospers?

In putting this question we direct our attention to the most significant, the most central of Dostoevsky's insights. For we are actually asking about the nature of that power which can inwardly transform punishment into sacrifice, which creates the value of suffering, which makes it possible for all to bear the guilt of all.

Now this power is just as much there for all human beings as suffering and guilt are there for them. This power, which makes all suffering holy, which can transform every punishment into sacrifice, which is the sun of the conscience, the light 'which lighteth every man that cometh into the world'—this power is Christ. Christ is for Dostoevsky neither a dogma nor an ideal. He is *actually present* wherever suffering is felt in such a way that one wishes to kneel before it, wherever punishment suddenly, through the miracle of inner transformation, begins to shine as a sacrifice for all humanity. When light falls on hidden tendencies of your own soul that make you co-responsible for things and deeds that you would have otherwise immediately turned away from—then Christ is present. And this is the final and most central thesis of Dostoevsky's 'wisdom of suffering':

All suffering can be experienced as the breath of Christ's spirit in human souls.

Dostoevsky's relationship to suffering is as characteristic of Russia as Mulford's relationship to suffering (as something senseless) is typical of America. For just as it is natural in America to negate suffering, so is it natural in Russia to affirm it. A 'happy ending' is for Russian spiritual life—yes, even for the Russian destiny—just as foreign as the Russian tendency toward 'self-torment' is foreign for the American. Dostoevsky's works have no 'happy ending'; through the clouds of suffering and passion that surround his characters, there often radiates the light of that Being Who is the *key to the secret mystery of the affirmation of suffering.*

THE POSSIBILITIES OF DEVELOPMENT
IN EASTERN CHRISTIANITY

ONE OF THE MOST IMPORTANT EXPERIENCES that can be had among
the peoples of Eastern Europe is that in those countries an intensive
participation of the soul in the life of the Church is no hindrance to the
taking up of Rudolf Steiner's spiritual science. No conflict arises in
the souls of those people who, on the one hand, through destiny and
inner propensity are strongly connected with everything that belongs
to the life of the Eastern Church, and, on the other, have turned with
the same devotion toward Anthroposophical life. It is even possible—
apart from various outer situations—to observe the opposite: Not
only does the coexistence of Anthroposophy with Eastern Christianity not cause any conflict in the souls of honest, unprejudiced people,
but rather it tends to cause an inner security in the whole soul-life of
such people. Out of this there develops a soul-life that combines clarity of thought with warm open-heartedness and a naturalness of the
whole personality.

So we can say that in the *realm of the soul* Anthroposophy is wedded
with the *spirit* of Eastern Christianity. Through this marriage there
arises something just as positive as arises through the marriage of a
truly scientific attitude of mind with Anthroposophy. For just as the
meeting between a scientific outlook and the communications of
spiritual investigation creates no conflict in the soul, so such religious
convictions meeting with Anthroposophical truths create no conflict.

Now a religious conviction of this kind that keeps the heart open
for the truths of spiritual science is, in spite of all, still existent in
Eastern Christianity; for there was in it, up to the very recent times,
always more love of Christ than anything else. The essence of the life
of Eastern Christianity was the inner *communing* of humanity with the
actually present Christ. This communing and this love of Christ was
held to be more significant overall than problems of dogma and organization; for the essential difference between Greek and Roman
Catholicism lies primarily in the fact that dogma and organization
play quite a different role. A fact that can be observed everywhere is
that Greek Christians do not feel themselves bound in their *thinking*

to definite forms; it is no sin for them to think *freely*. The faithful Roman Christian, on the other hand, merely through the fact of belonging to the Roman Church, is duty-bound to a particular kind of thinking laid down by the Church leaders. The thinking of the Catholic has to submit to the orders of the infallible official teaching in Rome.

The *infallibility* dogma, decreed from Rome, is a final break with the free spiritual life.[†] It is no longer compatible to think freely and to be a Catholic. In the Eastern Church it is still compatible. Personalities such as Solovyov and Dostoevsky were free in their thinking, and yet absolutely Orthodox. This was only possible because the dogma was not really grasped intellectually. It hovered in the heights of heaven, high *above* the level of the intellect. And therefore it did not *pressure* the intellect—it is actually more the object of an upward-gazing *contemplation* than an ordinance for thinking. In the East the dogma did not crystallize out as thought *alongside* other thoughts. It remained hovering at a certain supra-thought level, without descending into the realm of intellectual thinking, as if awaiting human beings—with their faculties of comprehension—to grow upwards toward it. The dogma was experienced, for instance by Solovyov, not as an ordinance, but as a goal for thinking. For him the Nicean Creed, for example (which by the way is not spoken in the Church, but *sung*) was not to *prohibit* other modes of thought, but was rather a call to research, a stimulus for independent cognition. And this stimulus, in his case, had the best possible results. For in him we have a man who ascended in his thinking to a *comprehension* of Christianity, without in the process estranging himself from the spirit of the Eastern Church (see, for example, his *Twelve Lectures on Godmanhood*).

Because the dogma in the East was preserved at a certain starry height, it does not work coercively on thinking, as is the case in Catholicism (and also in Protestantism); rather, it leaves a free space

† The Eastern Patriarchs, together with their Bishops, issued in answer to the Encyclical of Pius IX, a solemn Declaration in which is stated that 'infallibility rests purely and solely on the *universality* of the Church, unified through love; and the immutability of dogma, as well as the purity of the Ritual, are not entrusted only to the care of the church hierarchy, but also to that of the whole community of the Church, which is the Body of Christ.' (Chomiakoff, *A Few Words of an Orthodox Christian about the Western Confessions*, 1853.)

for the intellect. During the millennia of its development, the Eastern Church had little interest in the intellectual. It had the feeling that the teachings of Christianity were exalted above human opinions. The source out of which the convincing efficacy of Christian truths should flow into the souls of human beings cannot be sought either in the realm of argument or in authoritative ordinances, but rather in the immediate influence of Christ Himself.

The Church is the place where one communes with Christ. And all human beings have a right to this communing, the laity as well as the Patriarch. No representative of Christ is needed on earth, no 'throne of Peter', because Christ has risen and lives *with us* even until the end of time. And the actually present Christ was loved by many people in the East—not merely believed in, but *loved*. This love has always been the true inner life of Eastern Christianity.

Neither the Bible, nor Church tradition, are the essence upon which Eastern Christianity is based; rather it is based on the love of Christ. And why a free spirit still holds sway there is because nothing in the world can compel one *to love*. Love arises in freedom. The magic breath, the unspeakable beauty of the Christ Figure, is the source from which conviction of the truth of Christianity streams into the souls of human beings. It is this immediate breath that makes up the true life of Eastern Christianity. Moreover, it is also true that in Russia there is no doubting of Christ's existence. He is either loved or hated there. Even the godless Bolshevik movement is, in its true soul depths, far from *doubting* the reality of Christ. What provides the impetus of that movement, what fires its ardor, is certainly not doubt. It is *hatred*—the fiery will to *destroy* this Christ breath. One does not 'doubt' what one hates with all one's soul. One is not 'sceptical' regarding what one is determined to kill.

Now it is nonetheless true that all prominent *representatives* of Russian spiritual life (to the extent that they are truly *representative*) had the consciousness deep in their souls that Christ lives. Not only Dostoevsky, Solovyov, and Tolstoi, but also less significant representatives of Russian spiritual life who live today, each in his or her own way, have a relationship to Christ. Dostoevsky's striving to understand and describe the *battle* of Christ with the dark forces in human beings, Solovyov's striving to foster *knowledge* of Christ through his Sophianic philosophy, Tolstoi's yearning to make outer life an *expression* of Christ—these impulses of the great ones go on working even today, and are elaborated by a whole series of personalities (unfortunately sometimes in a most fruitless direction). What Dostoevsky through his life's work sent flowing into the human *feeling* by violently stirring it and *awakening* it for the task of modern men and women; that to which Solovyov strove to lead *thinking* in free cognition; what Tolstoi (not as thinker, but as a striving person) brought into the world as a mighty impulse for the *will*—this was simply and solely the Christ presence close behind the souls of these three.

And when we ask the question as to the possibilities of the development of Christianity, we must not seek the answer in the abstract, but in real life. And real life gives us in *answer* to our question three life stories of outstanding, characteristically representative personalities of Eastern Christianity. Dostoevsky, Solovyov, and Tolstoi are in fact figures of the greatest possible significance for the development of Eastern Christianity. They are fit to tell us in the *language of reality* what are the paths of thinking, feeling, and willing of a Christianity tested by experience and pursued in the East.

However, before we take up that subject (which we will do in the next essay) we must first direct our attention toward the other essential difference between Eastern Christianity and Catholicism. We have spoken above of *one* difference—the significance of *dogma*. Now it is a question of gaining insight into the difference of their relationships to the realm of *organization*; specifically, Church organization. For as in the East dogma hovers in the heights and religious life consists not in a particular *Creed* but in direct Communion with the *Christ Being*, so also is the *Church* in the East more supersensible than organizational. Its power lies not in its outer organized structure, but in a spiritual being whose name is *Sophia*.

If we would understand the true significance of the 'Church' (as in the East it is more or less clearly grasped), we will have to concern ourselves with things that are very hard to force into sharply outlined concepts. But this much can at least be clearly grasped by thought: that the outer Church is only the *body*, in and above which live both a *soul* and a *spirit*.

The body of the Church is the outer organization that is founded on the threefold basis of the Creed, the Seven Sacraments, and the Hierarchy called to fulfill these Sacraments. This body is fragile and imperfect (not in its *form* as Creed, Sacraments, and Hierarchy, but in its *substance*: the human beings who fill out this form). But there lives in this body its soul, and there works in it its spirit.†

Sophia is the soul of the Church, the Being of Wisdom, who cannot be possessed by a single human being because she can only reveal herself to the *community* of human beings. And *Christ* is the spirit of the Church. Sophia, as the soul of the Church, belongs at the same time to the Being of Christ. She is the breath that goes out from the Being of Christ and is directly received by souls. She is the effective radiance around Christ, the *aura* of his Being. At the same time, however, she is an independent being whose *image* is Mary, the Mother of God.

This conception—that Sophia is on the one hand the aura of Christ, but is on the other hand Mary, an independent being— explains the almost uncomprehended fact that, for instance in icons, both Christ and Mary are represented as Sophia. For they are members of *one* Being.

And a further member of the same Being is also the visible *Community*. But this is a member that belongs to the realm of death and suffering.

So now we might ask: Should not this extended body have to take the *same* path as was taken by the human body of Jesus of Nazareth? Should it not *also* go through suffering and death in order to resurrect as a *new* body, as Spirit body?

Have we—in the case of Eastern Christianity—not only an ideal analogy before us, but also an *analogy of destiny*, a repetition of the *path*? Do we not see that Eastern Christianity, which has remained essentially true to the Spirit of Christianity, is taking a path of suffering that is leading to the *death* of its body, the Church?

And do we not hear out of the *West* how—in a thousand ways—

---

† To avoid misconceptions, readers may be reminded here that the Eastern Church only recognizes *seven* Ecumenical Councils, and therefore the decisions of the *eighth* Council, from which followed the negation of the *Spirit* as an independent principle alongside soul and body, have, for the Eastern Church, not the significance of a dogma, but merely of an 'opinion', with regard to which a person may freely take his or her own stand.

there come cries from those who pass by unconcerned, cries to the crucified Eastern Christianity: 'Save thyself, and come down from the Cross!'?

Yes, and furthermore, already the lots are being cast (by certain 'secret' societies who have their own special plans) for the garments of the not yet dead one.

The *body* of Eastern Christianity is being destroyed. We can expect that it will be destroyed. It is heading for death. But it is not the death of old age, of exhaustion—it is a *martyrdom*. This death is a *path*. And since this path was taken, it will lead to its goal. After suffering and death follows resurrection.

Therein lie the possibilities of development for Eastern Christianity.

SOLOVYOV, DOSTOEVSKY, AND TOLSTOI
REVEAL THE EUROPEAN WAY OF
THINKING, FEELING, AND WILLING

THERE IS A VALUABLE RUSSIAN BOOK that gives a faithful description of the path of development of a Russian peasant in the middle of the nineteenth century. This book, *The Way of a Pilgrim*,[†] contains, among other things, an exact account of how, by means of certain exercises, an 'unceasing' prayer can be achieved; that is, a prayer can be so deeply engraved into the being of a man or woman that he or she prays not only while awake but also while asleep. The process described there is how a specific rhythm can be impressed into the *etheric body*; for through impressing the prayer into the ether body, it becomes independent of the waking consciousness and continues day and night.

'The heart prays in me of itself with every beat,' recounts the pilgrim, 'and I often awoke in the night and heard inwardly how my heart was praying.' He began his exercise by speaking a short prayer-formula, and continued for long enough until a warmth center, which had formed in the larynx, had moved down into the heart.

---

† Most recent edition of English classic translation by R.M. French published by Harper SanFrancisco, 1991. ED

Then the heart began to pray on its own, and spiritual vision opened up.

Here in actuality, concentrated into one individual case, is the whole historical process of Eastern Christianity. For as the *words* of prayer became the heartbeat of the pilgrim, so through the centuries has the ritual of the Eastern Church become a specific *quality of the ether body* for East European people. And although at present the ritual itself is being destroyed, nevertheless what it has caused to happen in the subconsciousness of men and women is still definitely present, and will in the future reveal itself anew.

What is this specific quality of the East European people, and how is it revealed?

In the essay, 'The Possibilities of Development in Eastern Christianity', we pointed to the fact that all prominent representatives of Russian cultural life have an intensive inner relation to Christ. We also spoke of the observation that Eastern Christianity draws its life out of love for Christ. It is really pervaded by a spirit closely resembling that of the *Gospel of St Luke*. There lives in it a Lucan Christianity, a Christianity of shepherd hearts opening toward the light of Christ. This Christianity is not based on the authority of the Church, or on intellectual persuasion, but on an immediate heart-relationship with Christ. Just as one speaks of the sun orientation of certain plants (heliotropism), so one can speak of an almost organic orientation toward Christ by East European people. And this inner orientation toward Christ (which *also* shows itself in the present wave of Christ-hatred) is that quality belonging to the East European people to which the above question refers.

Now this quality *came into being* by means of the Eastern Church specifically by way of its ritual. Having come into existence, it becomes, however, actually independent of the Church. It has become the characteristic of individual human beings, and reveals itself in significant individuals through their transformation from 'consumers' of the Church's spiritual nourishment into 'producers' of spiritual values for all humankind.

There were quite a few such producers of universal human values who arose as a metamorphosis out of the being of Eastern Christianity. Among them the most significant are the *three* personalities: *Vladimir*

Solovyov (d. 1900), *Fyodor Dostoevsky* (d. 1881), and *Leo Tolstoi* (d. 1910), for in their life-works these three personalities reveal the paths of the further development of Christianity in East Europe with great clarity. And in these personalities one can gain insight into three different aspects of the possibilities of development of East European humanity as bearers of a specific mission with regard to all humankind.

Vladimir Solovyov is rightly called the greatest Russian thinker. Neither before nor after him have there been greater achievements in the realm of philosophical speculation in Russia. But although it is right to call him the *greatest* Russian thinker, it is not quite correct to call him only a *thinker*. What distinguishes him from Western philosophers is the *point of departure* of his lines of thought. As point of departure, as 'given', the Western philosophers either take the sense world or the 'I'; but for Solovyov, the point of departure is not the 'I' only, nor the outer world only, but the *Christ* is also 'given'. His entire Gnosis (for it cannot exactly be called a philosophy) is not built on the *duality* 'I'-world, but on a *threefoldness* Christ-'I'-world. For him Christ is just as real as the world and the 'I'. And the contradiction between world and 'I' is there, according to him, so that a third element, the Christ, may ever better be comprehended.

Thus, for him, Christ is not merely the 'content of faith' but the *real* solution to the riddle of existence. He says to himself: The contrast between myself and the world is the *riddle* of existence, but the reality of the living Christ Being is the *solution* to the riddle. And his whole thinking was focused on *this* solution.

Dostoevsky, too, was a man whose life-work was wholly oriented toward the Christ. But his interest was not directed solely toward *knowledge* of the Christ, but primarily upon a condition of soul in which the Christ-Sun could shine brightly. This condition of the soul Dostoevsky seeks by way of describing and living through the utmost battle of contradictions within the human soul. All contrasts of which the human soul is capable—all abysses of passion, of hatred, of cynicism, on the one hand, and the greatest clarity, capacity for love, and refined culture of heart on the other—he seeks out and describes with earth-shattering power. Through the power of contradiction in the elemental soul forces of human beings so well portrayed, he *awakens* the soul of the reader. He can awaken the *feelings* for the archetypal problem of Feeling: how can human beings reach an inner harmony, a *unity* of their whole being, without losing anything of their *powers* that manifest through contradictory human urges?

Two powers meet together in the human breast: the destructive, dark power of evil and the creative, light power of good. This meeting is a ceaseless battle in which first one pole, then the other, conquers.

This battle is an unbearable tragedy—it means terrible suffering for those who are awake to it. What then is the way out? Self-control, the *suppression* of the lower by the higher, is not the answer. No form of self-discipline is—for Dostoevsky—a solution to this problem, for that which is suppressed is still present. It then simply works on in other, invisible, hidden ways (perhaps through *other* people?). The people of the West have self-discipline, but the unity of being that is achieved through it is dearly paid for—the elemental soul forces dry up. There arises the genus of 'head person'. That should not be. Human beings ought not to lose one whit of their heart forces. The right way is to achieve *eternal peace*, not a 'dead restfulness'.

The Power that leads to such a peace manifests in the human soul through making it capable of *affirming* suffering, and allowing the power of love to stream through it. Should the soul have passed through the cleansing fire of suffering and have met with such a Being who awakens the *whole* human soul force to a unified potency of love, then the value of existence would have been found. Thus the wholeness of the human being would be established, not through suppression, as would be the case with discipline, but through love, which can be so great that *all* the forces of the soul can be taken hold of by it.

Does there exist a Being who has the power to kindle such a love? Is there anything in the world worthy of such a love? In answer to this question, Dostoevsky points to the Christ, who was for him a living Presence not only in his own soul but in the souls of others. 'What ye do unto the least of your brethren, ye have done unto Me'—that was the mood that lived in the soul of Dostoevsky as the solution to the archetypal problem of the feeling-life resulting from his orientation toward Christ.

As Solovyov can rightly be called the great Russian man of thought, so Dostoevsky can with no less right be called the great Russian 'man of feeling'. No one has so deeply unveiled the mystery of pain and love as the epileptic convict, Fyodor Dostoevsky. And just as Solovyov allowed the gnostic impulse for cognition of Christ to flow into the spiritual life of Eastern Europe, pointing to future ways of *thinking*, so there flows through Dostoevsky's life-work an impulse for the *future of human feeling*. The *direction* which the *true* development of thinking in Eastern Europe will take is revealed to us in Solovyov; the basis for its future feeling becomes visible to us in Dostoevsky.

Something else is revealed by *Leo Tolstoi*. Neither through his *thinking* (as a philosopher, his views are a last flickering of *old* concepts not significant for the future) nor through his *insights into human nature* as shown in the characters of his novels, is he here of value to us. Strange as it may seem, Tolstoi is important to us neither for his philosophical nor his artistic *achievements*,[†] but rather for the *power in his soul* which burst through him. For there surged through Tolstoi a tremendous power of soul-life that *in itself*—apart from his writings—represents a world-historic event. That a man *motivated purely by inner impulses* can come into such conflict with the surroundings that love and honor him, that an eighty-year-old can still follow the mighty impulse to *begin life anew*—these are symptomatic expressions of a power freed from all prescribed paths, which can bestow on a person the 'eternal youth' of the ability to begin ever anew—however advanced and old he may be.

In Tolstoi lived a faculty for beginning again, for a change in direction, for constant initiative, which points to profound wellsprings of existence. The powerful *impetus* within him is an expression, a premature revelation, of the *power of will* of East European human beings; asleep at present but to awaken in the future. The *will of the future* reveals itself in Tolstoi, just as the thinking and feeling of the future are revealed through Solovyov and Dostoevsky.

And this will was also permeated by the Christ impulse. For it expressed itself—although chaotically—in the elemental desire to transform life—outer life—so that it becomes a revelation of Christ:

[†] It is obvious that we do not here make the assertion that the artistic and philosophic achievements of Tolstoi are *in themselves* valueless. We are only saying that when *seeds for the future* are sought, attention must be directed not toward achievements, but toward that which is hidden behind them.

Life in all its forms must become through and through an expression of the *conscience*. Just as through Solovyov and Dostoevsky there flowed into humankind impulses for the Christianization of thinking and feeling, so through Tolstoi streamed the impulse for the Christianization of the *will*, of the *will* that reveals itself in practical, everyday, and social life.

And so we can see in the personalities of Solovyov, Dostoevsky, and Tolstoi the germinal seeds for thinking, feeling, and willing of the future. The three have in common their devotion to the Christ as the power who guides the thinking, feeling, and willing of the future. And this devotion points to the *fourth germinal seed* for the future, namely, that of the *Christ-permeation of the 'I'*. It is that 'I'-consciousness which the Apostle Paul points to with the words: 'not I, but Christ in me.'

Having directed our attention to the *positive* potentials, we are now faced with the task of sketching as well the *negative* potentials that can hinder development of East European humanity and deflect them from their true goals. This will be the subject of our next consideration.

ANTI-CHRISTIANISM IN THE EUROPEAN EAST

IN THE ESSAYS 'The Possibilities of Development in Eastern Christianity' and 'Solovyov, Dostoevsky and Tolstoi...' the attempt was made to show how the Christ impulse cooperated in the forming of East European humanity in an organic fashion. This *organic* relationship with the Christ impulse can be seen through the fact that the creative thinking, feeling, and willing of representative personalities of East Europe are wholly directed toward an understanding, an experience, and a realization of the Christ impulse. While West European thinking gradually takes on a form that causes even the *question of the* Being of Christ to become ever less important, so that this thinking is in the process of *forgetting* Christ—at the same time the characteristic of East European thinking is that Christ remains *unforgettable*. And this unforgettability of the Christ expresses itself not only in the fact that much love flows toward Christ, but also in the fact that there exists a strong stream, the stream of Christ hatred, which recently has come to the surface.

One does not touch the essence of the present war being waged in the Soviet Union against the spirit by describing it as a wave of scepticism. In this war it is surely not a question of doubt, for those who wage this war are much too intensely involved with their souls for any doubt to be possible for them. It is clear enough from the whole style in which the spirit in any form is fought against in Russia that the spirit that is being combated is felt to be an absolute reality; a reality that must be *destroyed*. It must be rooted out of people's hearts.

To achieve this, it is not enough to show that Christianity is incapable of standing up to critical thinking. The opposition must work at a much deeper level than that which can be achieved simply with the help of thinking. For it is not a question of merely displacing one idea by means of another idea, rather it is a question of annihilating one *power* by means of another power. And so, alongside of criticism, wide use was made of the weapon of *mockery*. Mockery was to affect the heart in the same way as criticism affects the head. It was to make the heart just as empty of Christ as critical materialistic thinking has made the head empty of spirit. Thereby the battle has moved out of the realm of discussion—a fighting with arguments—into the region of direct influence, direct intrusion into the inner life of another in order to destroy portions of the soul. The war is now waged in the sphere of breathing and blood circulation within the human organism; for the power of mockery, the force of cynicism, reaches down into the rhythmic system of the human organization, just as materialistic intellectualism works on the head system.

Cleverness is widely used in present-day Russia to distort the figure of Christ Jesus handed down to us in the Gospels, and to picture it in such a way as to arouse disgust and loathing. (Yes, disgust and loathing!) Using 'quotations from the Gospels', Jesus is described as a cowardly and lying swindler. In order to demonstrate this, in 1924 a rather thick book was written with the title *The Jesus of the Gospels and His Teaching*.[†] This book contains practically everything the human

---

[†] The book was published in 1931 by a professor of the University of Riga. This professor lectures to youthful students in Lithuania on the comparative history of religions

intellect can bring up in the way of trivialities, slander, mockery, and lies aimed *against* the figure of Christ Jesus. The spirit of a cold hatred by which the author is possessed breathes from every line of the book. This hatred merely pretends to pursue the 'objectivity of scientific investigation'—in truth its basic intention is only to hurl blows by all possible means on the figure of Christ Jesus. Through the strictly structured, almost formal paragraphing of the book's text is audible a hidden gnashing of teeth. This book is in actuality a document of Christ hatred. But it certainly is not a document of Christ *doubt*, for the effort behind the book does not attempt to show Christ as an uncertainty, but rather to call up hatred in the soul of the reader toward the Christ. And this hatred was really aroused, for there are in Russia today thousands of people always ready to make great sacrifices whenever there is any opportunity to contribute toward the destruction of Christianity.[†]

Nor were the efforts of these people without success. A large part of the youth has broken from any feeling of inwardly belonging to the Christ impulse. Through this, there is arising in Russia a new type of human being: the 'profane person' who no longer gives the impression that he or she is protected by angel's wings—an impression one always had of the earlier generations. Confronting this new person, one no longer has the feeling: you bear within you a hidden fullness. The new person seems *empty*. And empty they feel themselves to be. There is, gradually growing in them, the oppressive basic feeling of emptiness, of existence without meaning. This basic feeling is also the cause for the continuously increasing prevalence of suicide among the youth, for suicide among communistic youth has today reached alarming proportions.

[Presumably Harold H. Bender (1882–1951), author of academic works concerned with Lithuania. ED]

† The hatred here described is essentially different from the present-day movement (1931) to destroy churches in Spain. When the Russian *people* in the year 1917 experienced several months of untrammeled freedom, they did not show even the slightest tendency to behave antagonistically toward the Church. In Spain we are witnessing today an outbreak of hatred against those places (churches) whence the suppression of the free personality was incited. In Russia, however, this was not the situation.

Now these 'Komsomol'[†] suicides—apart from their purely human tragedy—are significant symptoms for understanding what is really happening. They point to the fact of the *organic relationship* of the East European people with the Christ impulse. The significance of the Christ impulse is for them a motivation for living. It is for the sake of the Christ impulse that it is worthwhile to live. When it is alive in the soul, then life has value. But now there arises a terrible void—*the void of an absence of motivation for living*. And this void, this loss of *courage for life*, follows as the result of that stage of destruction of the soul's relation to the Spirit produced by *mockery*. It follows *without fail*.

Here we touch on an important fact of present-day development; namely, that at present, in the arena of world history, a portion of humanity is experiencing a fate which ordains that its dependence on the Christ impulse for life or death have *visible* effect. In the present European East there is a stream of destiny making visible to all mankind what the *absence* and *presence* of the Christ impulse can signify. The *significance* of the Christ impulse will thereby become visible. This is possible in East Europe because humanity there is not only soul-spiritually, but also organically with their life-forces—that is, *soul-bodily*—dependent on the Christ impulse. Therefore *this* portion of humankind can make *both* sides of the significance of the Christ impulse historically visible. They have the mission to show, as a living experience, both the whole abyss of misery and degradation that threatens a humanity *without* Christ, and also the plenitude of radiant life that stands before humanity *with* Christ.

For the time being, however, *one* side of this mission is being fulfilled, namely, the misery of the falling-away from the Christ impulse. There exists a great deal of misery in the Soviet Union. Not since the time of the Middle Ages have the peoples of the West hungered as people have been hungering there. But that is not the main point. In

† The Komsomol, or Communist Union of Youth, was established in 1918 as the youth wing of the Communist Party of the Soviet Union, its youngest members being fourteen years old, the upper age limit being twenty-eight. Its full designation was All-Union Leninist Young Communist League. Komsomol functionaries played an important role inculcating the values of the Party in the young, and as an organ for introducing them to the political domain. A wave of suicides among young Komsomol members commenced in the mid-1920s. ED

present-day Russia, that the people become so maddened by hunger and need so they shake off the Bolshevik yoke is not so important. No, rather it is a question of having enough bread, and having overcome need, and *yet still hungering*. The *true liberation*, which must happen there, should not come from dissatisfaction of the *stomach*, but from dissatisfaction of the *heart*. The Five Year Plan may succeed. Russia may achieve economically all it intends to achieve. The tremendous *hunger for the spirit* which will then become apparent as a concrete world-historic fact will prove the truth of the words 'Man does not live by bread alone.'

It must be understood that the 'Russian question' is not only a political and economic question, but is in reality a *spiritual* question. For it is not simply a battle of political parties (those have already been swept away), nor simply a battle in the economic sphere; the crucial point of the battle being waged there is centered on the *Spirit*. And the spirit fights against the powers of darkness with two mighty weapons: through the life-giving plenitude of its presence, and through the misery of its absence.

Fyodor Dostoevsky pointed to *three* trials which humanity has to withstand. These are the trials of bread, of authority, and of power. Just as the Son of Man withstood three Temptations in the Wilderness, so the Christ impulse will reveal its might through the fact that humanity must withstand *with Him* the same three Temptations. And one of these three is that of trying to produce, as an aim of existence, a general satisfaction of appetites.

Modern socialism in its various forms is actually that human spiritual stream whose ultimate aim is 'the transformation of stones into bread'. And this socialism in its most extreme form finds the possibility to realize these aims in Russia. The tremendous will energy expended on the realization of the Five Year Plan is essentially nothing other than clear evidence of the suggestion of the Tempter in the Wilderness to transform stones into bread.

But beside this 'yes' will also be heard a definite 'no'. For *alongside* the 'conscious proletariat', the masses deprived of material possessions, there will arise an equally 'conscious proletariat'—people deprived of *spiritual* values. And just as the economic proletariat will direct all their will to the regulation of the possession of material values in a true and just manner—so the 'spiritual proletariat' (of whom the Gospels speak with the words 'blessed are the poor in spirit') will yearn with all the forces of their souls for the *spirit*. There will come a great awakening to *the value of the spirit*. The spirit will be felt as a basic factor necessary in *social life*, as bread is felt now to be. And this will be the *other* answer to the Tempter in the Wilderness, which will sound out with a perceptible clarity from the sorely-tried European East.

Anti-Christianism, therefore, which at present is asserting itself there with the greatest passion, is a portion of that power which exists to make possible the *concrete* revelation of the Christ impulse.

ANTI-CHRISTIANISM SEEN IN RELATION TO THE DESTINY-PATHS OF JUDAS, SAUL, AND PETER

THERE EXISTS A VOLUMINOUS AMOUNT of literature about the essence of Christianity, and yet throughout all its twenty centuries the truth that the essence in Christianity is the Christ Being Himself endures. Neither a new world-conception nor a new system of morals is the main significance. Rather, that which began twenty centuries ago was a new kind of communing between humanity and the Christ Being. From this time on, communing, which in much earlier times took place outside, was transposed into the inner life of earthly human beings. This became possible through the fact that out of cosmic expanses the Christ Being entered into humankind. And at the threshold of the entrance of Christ—from the Cosmos into the stream of destiny called humanity—stands the Cross of Golgotha.

The death on Golgotha was the portal through which Christ, after He had united Himself with the body of *one* man, united Himself with the *whole* of humankind. Just as the actual transition presented itself to human consciousness in the *Easter event*, and the descent into a human body was the *fact of Christmas*, so the event which showed that this transition of Christ had been completed was experienced as *Pentecost*.

Christmas, Easter, and Pentecost (Whitsun) are the three stages of Christ's path from the Sun, to Palestine, and thence into the inner being of humanity. And according to how different groups of people comprehend this tremendous event—this comprehension being mostly one-sided—these individual groups of people will belong to one of the *three basic streams* of Christianity. There exists a Christmas Christianity; that is, a Christianity living wholly in the mood of the descent of the grace of the Heavenly Father: the Father in heaven has revealed Himself on earth through the Son. There exists also an Easter Christianity oriented toward death and resurrection, which is capable of raising itself to the feeling: in the Son's deed of love, death was conquered through death. So also there exists a Whitsun Christianity, which through *the spirit within humanity* strives to unite itself with the further working of Christ.

The Christmas stream of Christianity is that which lives in the moods and thoughts grouped around the word *Grace*. For this Christianity, the primary thing is not so much a personal effort of human forces, but rather the recognition of powers of a higher order than the human. For it, even Christ Jesus is merely an expression of the Father forces. The words 'I and the Father are one' are understood in such a way that the stress is placed upon the word 'Father'. The inner life of this Christianity consists of all that the soul can experience when bowing before a superior power.

In the Easter stream of Christianity, on the other hand, what is primary is the development of the human capacity for love. Instead of the superior Father-God, the Son—the Brother-God—is the center of their striving. Love of Christ is the central nerve of this stream. But here Christ is not merely the fulfiller of the Father's Will, but is also the God-Man, who out of inner freedom entered into death and conquered it. And the members of this stream are people who, to some extent, can take up into their souls an experience of death and resurrection.

Now the two streams we have described are distributed among humankind in such a way that Christmas Christianity is spread chiefly in the West, and Easter Christianity chiefly in the East. It is a generally known fact that Christmas is celebrated much more inwardly in the West, and Easter much more profoundly in the East. But apart from this, the comprehension of the Being of Christ is of a kind in the West that leads people to regard the Father as that in Christ Jesus which—as against His human nature—is of greatest significance. The comprehension of Christ in the East, however, is directed toward the individual Being of the Son. And the Christianity of Grace and the Christianity of Love face each other in this same way also in the forms of Roman and Greek Christianity.

The third Christian stream, however, is more independent of the conditions on the Earth. The Christianity of Whitsun revealed itself through single individualities who have raised themselves above the conditions of culture that surrounded them. These individualities had, along with the consciousness of the guidance of the Father from above and the love from the Son who stands as example, the knowledge of the Spirit.

In history the Wisdom stream of Christianity is most purely represented by true Rosicrucianism and the personalities inspired by it.

The above-mentioned three streams of Christianity stand in the world, ranged in battle against their opponents; for there are forces at work in the world that want to extinguish consciousness of the Father, love of the Son, and knowledge of the Spirit. There exists in the world a 'counter-Christmas', a 'counter-Easter', and a 'counter-Whitsun'. This means that there are powers at work in world history that want to hinder the descent of the Spirit—for example, the slaughter of the innocent children in Bethlehem; that are against the Resurrection—that is, who work against the re-ascent of the bodily nature; and that do not want to allow free knowledge to arise in the inner human being. These three anti-Christian streams must ever and again be brought into the light of consciousness from various sides. Symptoms that lead to a deeper insight into the mysteries of anti-Christianism must repeatedly be considered. And among these symptoms that from a particular angle bring a greater comprehension of anti-Christianism, belong the destiny-paths of three personalities described in the Gospels: Judas Iscariot, Saul-Paul, and Simon Peter.

Judas was one of the twelve chosen disciples of Christ. Therefore, a 'thief' out for the thirty pieces of silver—this he was not. His betrayal cannot be explained in such a convenient manner. The thirty pieces of silver do not lead us to an understanding of his motives. The tragedy of his destiny, ending with suicide, remains incomprehensible if one fails to *take seriously enough* the level from which the inner motives of Judas' soul are working. And one cannot approach such a comprehension by considering this soul's baseness, but only by asking: What depths of spirit worked in his soul at the moment it turned to that which drove it to the terrible deed?

We must keep in mind the fact that the forces that worked themselves out in the betrayal had their origin at the *table of the Last Supper* (John 13:26–30) and that the betrayal itself was carried out by means of a *kiss*. If we wanted to explain the deed of Judas through 'ordinary' motives, such as greed or hatred, how is one to understand that the one filled with hatred would *freely* choose the kiss as the means of betrayal? And how would the fact be explained—without recognition of a deeper process—that after Christ Jesus had dipped the bread and given it to Judas, 'Satan entered into him'? Would Christ Himself let hatred and greed flow into him?

And yet it is precisely the fact of the Judas kiss and the effect of the Last Supper on Judas that brings us to the essence of the Judas drama. For the Judas kiss, together with the words 'Master, rejoice' is neither an expression of the most heinous unscrupulousness nor of a scathing irony, but rather of what Judas actually bore in his soul: *love* for the Master. And Judas did not leave the Last Supper filled with hatred; he left entirely permeated by the yearning *to reveal the glory of the beloved Master in an earthly fashion*. At the moment when Judas, accompanied by the crowd of armed servants with torches, stepped up to the Master with the words: 'Rabbi, rejoice' and kissed him, he was filled with the unshakable faith that now the day had come when the Messiah would openly reveal his power. But when, instead of this, he saw the Master bound, spat upon, scourged, crowned with thorns— he went off and hung himself.

Judas indeed recognized that the Messiah had come. He understood the mystery of the *incarnation*, of descent. He knew that in Jesus of Nazareth the Messiah is active. But he imagined the working of the Messiah to be such that thereby suffering and death would be eliminated. Judas could not see that the Messiah would conquer them by Himself going through suffering and death. He imagined the deed of the Messiah as victorious, *repelling* the attack from the direction of death. He could not grasp the fact that death was to be overcome *through death.* And so on one hand his soul was filled with the glowing conviction that the Messiah had been born, and on the other with the ever growing expectation of His victorious deed. The *Easter Mystery,* the mystery of Death and Resurrection, remained closed to him. An attitude in opposition to the significance of the Mystery of Golgotha lived in his soul. And this attitude of soul was so strong that for him life became worthless when his hope was shattered.

Judas was a man who bore in his soul the striving to draw the spirit down into the earthly realm, visualizing it merely as *power.* And when his ideal showed that it is powerless in an earthly sense, then the meaning of his life was extinguished.

Saul on the other hand denied the reality of the concrete incarnation into a human being of the Cosmic Christ. The hatred that filled him when he was persecuting the sect of Nazarenes sprang from the feeling: The Spirit-Light of the World radiates into the souls of all people throughout the world. It enlightened the Prophets, it enlightened the Initiates in the Mysteries. Now, however, human beings appear who spread the blasphemous teaching that the Cosmic Being of Light incarnated as an earthly personality. They maintain that the Logos was incarnated in the body of a man whose name was such and such and who took food and drink. This teaching is a gross sensualization of the sublime Being of the Light of the World. Directing attention toward a human idol, a false idol, is a deflection from the right human striving after knowledge of the Cosmic Sun Spirit—deceit and poison are the only significance of this sect for humankind.

Such views were active in the soul of Saul as he travelled to Damascus 'breathing hatred and brooding murder.' And what transformed this man full of hatred into the creator of the high song of love (1 Cor. 5:13) was his experience on the road to Damascus. There he saw the Light of the World (whose greatness was such as to make him blind and dumb for three days) in the concrete figure of the Resurrected One. Then he could recognize: The Light of the World *has* become human. Now human beings *can* unite themselves with God, since God was able to unite Himself with a human being. Thus he became *Paul,* the proclaimer of the fact that this is so.

Here we see in Saul an attitude of soul opposite to that of Judas. For while Judas denied the *spiritual effectiveness* of the Golgotha Mystery,

Saul denied the concrete *earthly* incarnation of Christ. There lived in his soul that force which we have called 'counter-Christmas'. The mystery *of Birth*, Saul could not recognize. Saul desired that Christ should not be born; Judas, on the other hand, that He should not die. The one denied the spirit; the other denied the body.

The one as well as the other were present in *Simon Peter*; he bore in himself both Judas and Saul. He was a man continuously struggling for equilibrium, which he often lost. For when the armed crowd broke into the Garden of Gethsemane, he drew his sword and struck at the High Priest's servant, cutting off his right ear. Later, however, he denied, first *to a woman*, that he was a disciple of Him who had been taken prisoner. What does this contradictory behavior of Peter signify?

That it was not merely a question of fear is obvious—for Peter had not feared to draw his sword against a group of armed men. Rather it was a question of a struggle in his soul between *opposing* consider-ations. For when drawing his sword he did not believe in the power of the Messiah, who could use His spiritual might in place of earthly resistance. Jesus was for him merely a man to be protected. And then, when he three times denied the Master, it was not out of fear, but he actually meant what he said: A disciple of this *man*, I am not. As a pupil he broke his connection to his Teacher *because* he could no longer fol-low all that was to come with his understanding. The significance of suffering and death was closed to him. Therefore, speaking *the truth* three times, he denied Him: a disciple of this *man*, I am not.

Just as, by drawing his sword, he denied the incarnated divinity of Christ, so too, during the Passion, he denied the humanity of Christ. A disciple of that *man*, so he said, he was not. Peter's swaying from one extreme to the other is pointed to in St John's Gospel by the mention of the fact that Peter, who had fervently drawn his sword, was *warming* himself in the High Priest's courtyard at a coal fire. Thereby it is sub-tly indicated that he who shortly before was hot, was now cold. Here warmth failed him, as in Gethsemane coolness had failed him.

Peter lacked *knowledge*—an independent, inwardly-radiant know-ledge. The Christ Impulse had not penetrated to his 'I': therefore he lacked the strength, which can only come from the 'I', to keep his bal-ance. Only through the event of *Pentecost* did he gain this knowledge.

So we can see that Peter was lacking in the power of Whitsun, as

Saul lacked comprehension of Christmas, and Judas was remote from the Easter experience.

What is the value, then, of this outline of symptoms for people now?

For us as modern human beings it is a question of recognizing how forces, which in the drama of Palestine were only present in single personalities, are today working in great spiritual movements with a powerful significance for the course of world history. For instance, at present there *exist* streams that represent the Judas ideology, and other streams that have the Saul attitude of mind. These present-day moods can be understood through these figures in the Gospels. For we cannot understand and weigh the anti-Christian attitude of *Eastern* spiritual life if we do not understand what was living in *Saul*. Then again, certain very significant spiritual streams of the *West* remain incomprehensible to us if we have not struggled to comprehend the figure of *Judas*. And lastly, it is important for the Central European to know how the path of destiny of *Simon Peter*—of the disciple who vacillated between hot and cold until, through the event of Pentecost, he achieved the inner security of spiritual knowledge—sheds light on the path of spiritual development of Central Europe.

What has here been stated in just a few sentences will be the subject of more extensive considerations later when we will attempt to show the significance of the Judas, Saul, and Peter ideologies in the present world-historic constellation.

ANTI-CHRISTIANISM IN EAST AND WEST

IN THE ESSAY 'Anti-Christianism Seen in Relation to the Destiny-Paths of Judas, Saul, and Peter', what was attempted was to show how the three anti-Christian attitudes of soul made visible in these three figures have a significance for all of humanity. On the one hand, there exists the belief that the spirit has to assert itself through *force* instead of through purely spiritual means; then again there is the conviction that the spirit can only be exalted and pure insofar as it is untouched by the earthly; and lastly we have the inner disequilibrium, the vacillating between the two extremes. These are the three standpoints we find in Judas, Saul, and Peter, and they are at the same time forces that reveal themselves as mighty streams within human culture. They appear in manifold ways in the spiritual life of Asia, Europe, and America.

For instance, it is naiveté on the part of Protestant missionaries to believe that the Chinese and Indians do not become Christians only for the reason that Christianity has not yet been convincingly presented to them. In their view, should anyone succeed in presenting it to them, they will surely recognize its advantages over being 'heathen'.

Now this opinion is contradicted by the fact that there are many educated Asians who 'know' about Christianity. They could easily recount all that the missionaries have to say, but yet they do not even consider *embracing* Christianity. This opinion of missionaries *in partibus infidelium*[†] is also contradicted by the fact that in Europe itself, where the Christian teaching is 'known' to all, Christianity has not prevailed. Actually, this last fact is often used by Asians as a reproach to Christian preachers. The embarrassing question put to them is why do they go to so much trouble in Asia, while in Europe itself they have hardly achieved anything. But the polemic between missionaries and representatives of Asian spiritual life is not presently our concern, as we are trying to understand the deeper reasons for an anti-Christian attitude on the part of leading personalities of Asia. For just as you cannot know Christianity itself in its true depths from the sermons of missionaries, so little can you comprehend the depth of that against which Christianity has to fight in Asia from the replies Asians give to missionaries. This must be sought elsewhere, and it shows itself most clearly not where Christianity is rejected, but where it is *affirmed*. And the *manner* of its affirmation in Asia is tremendously revealing.

The fact is that during the last century, in the most important centers of spiritual life in Asia, a Christianity has been taught in much the same way as, say, Platonism is taught in Europe. The figure of Christ Jesus, together with his life-story as described in the Gospels, *occupies* the minds of leading personalities in Asia. And the result of this study is not at all a rejection of the contents of the Gospels as being untrue; on the contrary, it is an acceptance of them as a truth.

---

† *In partibus infidelium* is a Latin phrase meaning 'in the lands of unbelievers', words once added to the name of the See conferred on non-residential or titular Roman Catholic bishops. ED

But this truth of Christianity, which flows ever more strongly into Asian spiritual life, has undergone a peculiar metamorphosis. It has actually become *Asian*; that is, Christianity has been taken into the pantheon of Asia. This 'becoming Asian' of Christianity expresses itself primarily in the fact that an essentially different significance is given to the Being of Christ Jesus than in the West. In the West the standpoint is taken that a divine Being descended into a human body in order to go through death. For the West it was vital that a God had experienced human death so that in the future it would be possible for humanity to experience the God's Resurrection. Through the fact that a God united Himself with the deepest bitterness of human destiny, humankind could be united with the highest beatitude of the Divine lot. *Into* the realm of death flowed life when the Being itself from whom life springs entered into the realm of death. A God *has* died and *is* risen—that is the most important truth which the West, through its highest representatives, has still preserved.

Now in the East, Christianity has been so transformed that Christ Jesus is recognized there as a high teacher, an *Avatar* of the divine world. Yet this divine being did not go through death, and therefore did not achieve resurrection. That a God could die is a contradiction in terms. 'A God *cannot die*, so long as he is God. However, if he dies, then he is *not God*.' This was explained to the writer by a personality who is strongly rooted in Asian spiritual life.

But this explanation is only a logical *expression* of something else, much deeper, that lives in the souls of Eastern people. A basic feeling for the direction in which souls should strive lives there, and works in opposition to the Mystery of Golgotha. This basic feeling could be characterized in the following way: The world is a combination of spirit light and material darkness. A human being is *one* particular type of this combination. When darkness forms a sheath around the light, an individual being arises. The sheaths are that which make up the particular individual. Now the important aim is to free the light from its separate existence, that is, from the sheath nature; and the more this liberation can be achieved, the more perfect is the human being. The high Masters help humankind by ascending up to the spirit. As *such ones* climb upward, a slipstream of souls that are related to them fills the void they leave. When one elevates oneself into the higher worlds there arises a *suctional effect* toward the spirit. Souls are drawn up into the realm of the spirit. And one who is able to develop this force of attraction is a *Guru*, just as one who is drawn upward by a Guru is a *Chela*.

Everything tends in the direction of intensively turning the whole soul-life away from the particularization of the material world and directing it toward the generalization of the spiritual world.

Now this basic feeling differs very significantly from the mood that makes possible an understanding of the Mystery of Golgotha. The *Christian* attitude of soul is such as to be directed wholly toward the *effective power* of the spirit. Here the aim is not to free oneself from the sheath nature but rather to *radiate through* the sheaths, for the Spirit Sun is powerful when it shines into the world of matter. When souls open themselves to this effect, they then play a part in the *spiritualization of the world*. And the more someone consciously cooperates in the radiation of spirit power into material existence, the more perfect that one is. The high Masters help humanity by allowing the stream of spiritual grace to flow down. Thereby an *effectual* spirit *blessing* takes place, manifesting insofar as earthly matter becomes transparent for the spirit. And one who can unfold this blessing and radiant power is a Master, just as those who receive these gifts may be his or her pupils. The most perfect Masters are those who radiate spirit not only into soul substance and not only into life force, but also can irradiate the deepest depths of the material world. The *deeper* their effectiveness, the higher their degree of perfection.

So we see that the two basic attitudes we have described are not only different, but also, in one important aspect, present a contrast. For the Christian, the *streaming-down* of spirit power is, in a *moral* sense, opposite in direction to the *striving-upward* of the Eastern soul. The most powerful cosmic event of the streaming down of the Most High into the deepest depths, the Mystery of Golgotha, meets with no comprehension on the part of people strongly rooted in Asian spiritual life. This is due to the lack of understanding in the attitude of soul we have described.

And it is *this* attitude of soul that works in actual opposition to true Christianity in Asia. We can call this attitude—in the sense of the previous essay—the *Saul attitude*. For as Saul denied that the Christ became man because he saw in that view a materialistic presumption, so the

Eastern soul sees in the traditional Western conception that the Logos experienced death in a human body a materialistic presumption of European humanity. In the view of present-day Asia, Christ Jesus was a high Master who taught and lived Mystery Wisdom, but he was misunderstood by those around him and had therefore to suffer a martyr's death. This conception of Christ lacks an understanding of His *effect* on the life of the earth. This conception of Christ lacks insight into the powerful effect of the sacred Magic entering into the earthly realm through the Mystery of Golgotha.

In the West on the other hand there was an intense feeling for the fact that a flow of spiritual *force* entered into earthly events. Indeed, Western souls had an intense feeling that the might of spirit descended into the deepest abyss to win a *victory* over sin, suffering, and death. But while *living* in the strong mood of spirit-*victory*, they gradually lost an understanding for *spiritual* victory. By *spiritual* means they preserved the ideal of *victory*, but they lost the spirituality of that ideal. Thereby arose a Christianity oriented toward *rulership* of the earth. Earthly *rulership* became more and more the aim of those powerful communities that worked through Western *Churches* and *Lodges*.

These communities are fired by the will to embrace all humankind, one day, under one organization and rulership. They know that there is a world of spirit in which spirit laws prevail, and that below that spirit world the other world of matter exists. This material world has *its* laws, just as the spirit world has *its* laws. Now the laws of the spirit world are *moral* laws; the laws of the material world are *amoral*.

It is necessary, however (according to the philosophy of these communities), that a unification of the two worlds shall one day be realized. Thereby the lower world must be subject to the higher. It must learn, as it were, to be obedient to the upper world. In order to achieve this, the lower world—to which humanity also belongs—must be so organized that the amoral laws of the lower world serve the higher aims of the upper world. The laws of the lower world remain valid within their own realm, but they must be subjugated to the higher world. The higher world must *rule* the lower: the lower world remains, it is true, such as it is, but it must *obey* the higher world.

This relationship of *rulership* to *obedience* must be built into the organization of humanity in such a way that, between the lowest obeyer and the highest ruler, a graduated hierarchical ladder shall be instituted. And *one* Being of the higher world, to whom all shall owe obedience, will rule over this earth-embracing human organization. To this Being is given the name Jesus Christ.

The lower world is however not only amoral, it is also the scene of the activity of evil. Now this evil can also serve the higher. It can be subjugated and can then render true service, for the picture of Satan 'writhing' beneath the feet of Christ is not only a *position*, but also an area of *effectiveness*. Satan can render service to Christ. The Satanic forces within human nature, hidden deep within the physical body, can be awakened and can, when awake, render tremendous service in the work of conquering the world. They can also set evil in motion so that thereby the victory of the higher can be served. Evil is then the *means* to a good end.

These or similar views have taken root very deeply in the West. Brotherhoods and Orders exist that by various methods cause the *separation of means and ends*, and this enters right into the realm of the instinctive feeling-life of European humanity. This signifies, however, nothing less than the opposite of that which has been presented as the intended purpose, for while lower forces are set in motion for a higher aim, the higher aim serves instead the lower forces. The goal is then, so to speak, an opening, and through this opening it is possible for the lower forces to draw down spiritual life out of the spirit world into their own realm. Wherever the motto rules, 'the ends justify the means', there comes into being *a suctional effect* on the spirit world from the material world. Spirit powers are spellbound into matter and become dependent on it.

Thus 'the ends justify the means' by bringing the higher into dependence on the lower. And this domination by the lower used (or misused) as a means for higher goals through the centuries, resulting from the separation of means from aims mentioned above, is the tragedy of the history of the West. For that which the Ecclesia militans[†] allowed as a means for its higher aims has today come into power.

The history of the West teaches us with great clarity that *the means are not justified by the ends*. This same insight may have flashed up in the soul of Judas Iscariot when, after making use of the terrible means of betrayal for the higher aim of revealing the glory of the Messiah, he took his own life. For the Judas *attitude*, of which we spoke in the previous essay, is a mighty world-historic factor in the history of the West. The West has taken up much—very much—of the Judas spirit in striving after the ideal of realizing the *earthly rule* of Christ. Judas, too, wanted that, but events went otherwise—the Messiah was crucified.

But would some *other being* perhaps have acted *differently*? Is there, perhaps, some other 'Messiah' who could, indeed, reveal himself as a *power*, but would not let himself be crucified?

That is *the* question, which takes us very close to the mystery of European anti-Christianism. Even in the West, anti-Christianism is not merely an 'error' in the trivial sense of the word, but bears within it the mystery of belief that rulership of the world by a Being is *possible*. And this belief is not based on phrases, but on an *actual sensing* of superhuman forces that are striving to achieve this aim; forces, however, that work essentially in such a manner that they suck the spirit down into earthly realms.

Thus the anti-Christianism of the West stands in opposition to that of the East—for *there* we have to do with a suctional effect of the *spirit* on earthly things.

By these considerations we have tried to show the blessing-bestowing effects of true Christianity standing between the suctional effects of the earthly in the West, and of the spiritual in the East.

POSSESSION AND ENLIGHTENMENT
SEEN IN RELATION TO THE DESTINY-PATHS
OF JUDAS AND PAUL

IN PREVIOUS CONSIDERATIONS the attempt was made to characterize the figures of Judas and Saul in such a way that they served as a kind

---

† The Church is traditionally divided into the Church Militant (*Ecclesia militans*), comprising Christians who are living; the Church Triumphant (*Ecclesia triumphans*), comprising those who are in Heaven; and the Church Suffering (*Ecclesia penitens*) or Church Expectant (*Ecclesia expectans*), comprising those presently in Purgatory. The Latin *militans* has a primary meaning of 'serving as a soldier, military', but acquired a secondary meaning of 'to struggle', which is the intended sense here in connection with means and ends. ED

of door leading to a deeper understanding of anti-Christianity in the West and East. The cognitional value of these figures is really inexhaustible; but the most essential thing they can teach us is not merely what is shown in those essays, but rather a particular aspect of *self-knowledge*. For if concrete individuals lead us out into the expanses of world history, the world-historical perspectives then lead us back again to ourselves. These *individuals* point to forces that we can find working in world history. When these forces are once found, however, we as people of the present-day can discover them *in ourselves*.

So, when we take this path starting from the *figure of Judas*, we reach first of all the powerful Western spiritual stream, with its many branches, in which a *moral distinction* is permitted between ends and means. It is typical of this stream to use forces of evil consciously in order by their use to produce fruits that are good. Their world is divided into two parts: the world of means and the world of ends. The world of means exists so that through *its* laws—separated as they are from the world of ends, the world of the spirit—the ends of the higher world can be attained.

In reality, however, the world is a whole. This partition can only be a delusion. And yet there are many people who cling to this delusion—people who are at the same time leading personalities. *Why*, we may ask, is this delusion dear to these people. *By what means* does it attract the human soul?

In order to approach inwardly nearer to a concrete answer to this question, let us turn our gaze once more toward the figure of Judas Iscariot. St John's Gospel tells us that the force at work in the deed of Judas took possession of the soul of Judas during the Last Supper:

> And after He had dipped the bread, He gave it to Judas, the son of Simon, the Iscariot. And after the bread, Satan entered into him. Then said Jesus unto him: That thou doest, do quickly.... He then having received the bread went immediately out: and it was night. (John 13:26–7)

In these few words of St John's Gospel the mystery of Judas is expressed. In these words is indicated the actual process that took place in the soul-bodily organization of Judas. What process was this?

The sacrament of the Last Supper is not simply a symbolic ritual expressing a religious and moral content; rather, it is a real process having profound effects within the human organization. The result of these effects is primarily that the body becomes *spiritualized*. In the body an inner change takes place, bringing it nearer to the moral spiritual world. By means of a sacred use of nourishment in the Last Supper, the metabolic processes of the body are spiritualized. This works against the hardening of the body. The body becomes inwardly more mobile, transparent to spirit.

We could also say: through matter from the outer world, the human body becomes material; by its own *structure* it is not so, but this nonmaterial body structure as an invisible form is materialized in that it is filled out with matter from the outer world. This happens through food. Food is the door through which the material outer world penetrates into the human organism to stimulate it to material activity. If, however, a substance were to enter through the same door that would stimulate it not to material but to *spiritual* activity, then we would have the process of the Last Supper. There, subconscious will processes instead of metabolic processes are activated; or more exactly, the effect of the Last Supper is the transformation of metabolic processes into will processes. In nutrition the projection of the material part of the outer world into the human being takes place. Through the effect of the Last Supper, however, the union—the communion—of the subconscious human will with the *spirit-being* of the outer world takes place. Spiritual being enters into man during Communion.

Now in the world there exists nothing unspiritual. Matter itself is only the outer face of something spiritual; but it can be an expression of either a super- or sub-material spirituality. In itself, matter is neutral; but it stands between two intelligent spiritual activities. It is like the surface of water. The surface is not real, for it is neither air nor water, but an expression of processes in both air and water. It is merely a 'mimic' for the interaction of water with air.

The outer material world is similar to the water surface. It, also, is merely the *surface* of two *realities*; and these realities are of a spiritual nature. Therefore one can speak of a *super*-material and a *sub*-material spirituality. The Gospel speaks of these two spiritual realities when it tells of the *Logos* who was made flesh on the one hand, and of *Satan*, the Prince of this world, on the other.

The divine Fullness, working above the material 'water surface', lived in the Christ. The spirit of the abyss, working below the 'water surface', was called Satan.

When we now in light of this consider the relationship of human metabolism to the world, we find three relationships: it can be spiritual-divine as in the case of the Last Supper; it can be amoral-neutral as in the case of ordinary eating; and it can be spiritual-satanic, *as in the case of the effect of the communion bread on Judas Iscariot.*

That everything has to have its polar opposite is an actual fact for a world view fitting to reality. This is also true of the sacrament of the Last Supper. There exists an *anti-Last Supper* (as, indeed, there exist seven anti-sacraments) whose effect is just as *real* as the effect of the Last Supper itself. It, too, is a kind of Communion; that is, the entrance of an extra-human spirituality into the human being—only this spirit stems not from above the natural, but from below. This spirit ('Satan') entered into Judas. There took place in him a change of consciousness that was the polar opposite from that state of consciousness that can be described as 'Not I, but Christ in me.' In this latter state we have to do with an entering of the Christ Being into the human 'I'-organization. The 'I' is not thereby suppressed, but is, rather, irradiated by the Christ light. The 'I' partakes of true *enlightenment.*

The polar opposite to enlightenment is the process of *possession.* Here the 'I' is pushed out of the human 'I'-organization. The 'I' is suppressed by the entrance of a foreign power. And this power makes use of what now belongs to it as an instrument for its own intentions.

From the above, a conception can be formed of how, because of his inner attitude of soul, the effect of the Last Supper turned into its opposite in Judas Iscariot—how it led, instead of to *enlightenment,* to *possession.* His consciousness of self was darkened ('he then, having received the bread, went immediately out: *and it was night*') and through him the night of the darkness brought on what followed.

Now one might think that no reasonable person could ever willingly surrender to being possessed, as it means, indeed, a darkening of self-consciousness and an annihilation of human freedom. But the opposite of this is true, for there are actually many who *yearn* to be possessed. And many are possessed. *Just because* of this, they have wielded a great influence on the course of world history.

Why does this yearning exist? How can a human soul reach the point of wishing to be possessed?

When we look at a human being's ordinary consciousness, his or her knowledge and capacity, we must admit that at first it usually commands very little force. It moves almost exclusively in the abstract—in abstract thoughts and ideas, in subjective feelings, in personal wishes. It is excluded from the workings of the forces of world existence; that is to say the nature forces as well as creative spirit powers work outside human consciousness. Human consciousness can well *use* the forces of the outer world, but it cannot *take them into itself*. So it must, in spite of all technical achievements, admit that it is *powerless*.

So people yearn for a way out of this powerlessness. They would like to enter into the power-being of the world itself. For then they would lose the homunculus glass walls that separate them from the world of powerful being, then they would share in the world-power.

Human beings at present have arrived at the zero point of consciousness—all has become abstract in them. And just as on *one side* of zero the sequence of positive numbers is found, and on the *other side* the sequence of negative numbers, so *above* human abstraction the concrete *super-human* spirit world is found, and *below* abstraction, the concrete *sub-natural* world.

Once it has stepped over the boundary of abstraction, the actual entry of human consciousness into the power sphere of the world of gods—or else of anti-gods—can happen either through enlightenment or through possession. In both cases human consciousness attains the quality it had yearned for; namely *power*, which it previously lacked. But only in the first case is this power bestowed on the 'I'; in the second case the 'I' becomes the slave of a foreign power.

Human beings are only *weak* so long as they remains in themselves; whenever they step out of themselves, cross the boundary of their personalities, they get strong through the cosmic forces that surround them. For this strength they can thank the generous powers of heaven—or else the suctional forces of the inner earth. Either way, power enters into them. Before, as people of the earth's surface, participating neither in the life of heaven nor that of earth, they did not have this power.

The yearning for being possessed is, then, the striving for strength—this is the 'will to power', for power, however, which one prefers not to climb up to, but rather to slide down to.

This sliding-down is an attitude of Western spiritual life that has, since the fading of the Medieval era, actually increased in ever greater measure. It was to counteract this sliding down into the realm of sub-nature that Rudolf Steiner inaugurated the spiritual movement that these articles strive to serve. Anthroposophy is not meant to satisfy a few non-conformists, as is thought among 'tolerant' people in the world; it is an urgent measure of aid for humanity that is sliding down into the abyss of subhumanness. For modern human beings, having come to an amoral world-conception, are threatened by the grave danger of sliding down into an anti-moral world.

Humanity cannot permanently remain at the zero point of amorality. The mood of moral indifference (which reigns today in most modern manifestations of culture, as it does in science, politics, and economics) can be nothing more than a transition. Amorality slides over into antimorality. This transition can be clearly observed in science, politics, and economics, for they increasingly sever their connection from the oft-mentioned 'moral prejudices of an outmoded world-conception.' Thereby, however, they become paths that can lead to possession. Two possibilities face humanity standing at the zero point: either to take the way toward being possessed, or the way toward enlightenment.

Rudolf Steiner's spiritual science points the way to that state of human consciousness called' 'enlightenment', which in the sense of the above considerations is the opposite pole to 'possession'. As the sliding-down through materialism breaks through the boundary of abstract present-day consciousness into a sub-material world found beneath this boundary, so enlightenment can lead human consciousness over and beyond this boundary of abstract present-day consciousness into the world of spirit. Spiritual science leads to an experience of real—that is, active—spirit. Through this experience the abstraction of present-day consciousness is overcome. The yearning for spirit life thus finds its fulfillment.

As we can recognize in the figure of Judas the concentrated workings of those forces desiring to make human beings possessed and allowing modern humanity to slide down into sub-nature, so we can see in the figure of Paul, in the Damascus experience of Paul, the working of that force which strives to effect the enlightenment of humankind.

The powerful light experience that Paul had on the way to Damascus was not merely a vision and comprehension, it was at the same time a *communion*; that is, the entering of a real power into the human organization of Paul. A tremendous *enlivening* of his whole being took place through this experience. This enlivening is a process as real as the process in Judas that led him to *death*.

Enlightenment and *possession* are not only moral contrasts in the sense that the former happens in freedom and the latter in unfreedom, but they also differ through the fact that they signify, respectively, *life* and *death*. And as Judas reaped death through suicide, so Paul inherited life. How can one then visualize the enlivening that was effected in Paul through the enlightenment on the way to Damascus?

Above we spoke of a certain moral indifference that is spreading gradually over humanity. This indifference expresses itself, too, in the realm of cognition and—gradually—also in the realm of art. The inner *life* of the human soul dwindles. This dwindling happens because the forces of the soul are too strongly taxed by the body. The soul and its forces have been too strongly sucked into the body to have much left over for that which is not of the body.

However, it is possible for the inner life to become more enlivened. Just as one who is uneducated can become knowledgeable, so one who is unalive can become very much alive. The inner life can be tremendously intensified. One *can* become more and more filled with life. This can happen through the soul-life drawing away from the body so that the soul frees itself. Then it lives more in the *life body* than in the physical body. Thereby it becomes *alive*.

As the physical body lames the soul forces, so does the life body enliven them. It was such an enlivening of the soul forces through the life body that happened to Paul on the way to Damascus. He became *enlightened*.

Spiritual science *can* cause such an enlivening of the soul forces. For spiritual science too—when it is not a theory or simply bringing comfort through its content—frees the soul from the body. Spiritual science can make the soul so strong that it can withstand the 'suctional effect' of the physical body, so that it is able to experience itself as living in the life body. Thereby the above-mentioned indifference vanishes—the indifference toward truth, beauty, and goodness. The soul again has strength, a great deal of strength, which it can turn toward that which is outside the body. It regains a sense for all that is great, all that is profoundly moving in the life of cognition, in the life of art, and in the life of religion. It becomes *alive*.

Human beings of today are facing a decision: whether to slide down the path to possession, or to ascend on the path offered to them by Anthroposophy to enlightenment.

THE ANTICHRIST IN THE
VIEW OF VLADIMIR SOLOVYOV

THE QUESTION CONSIDERED in the essay 'Possession and Enlightenment Seen in Relation to the Destiny-Paths of Judas and Paul' can reveal new depths if we now immerse ourselves in what *Vladimir Solovyov* has to say about it. For what one finds in the life-work of Solovyov is that he was able to penetrate far—much farther than his contemporaries—into *two* special realms of knowledge. On the one hand, he unlocked to a great extent the Godmanhood of Christ Jesus for cognitive thinking, and on the other he made a significant contribution toward understanding the *opposite* of Godmanhood. The question of anti-Christianism and the figure of the Antichrist, the focal point for all the forces of anti-Christianism, strongly occupied Solovyov's thought, especially in his later years.

Solovyov felt the need to cultivate an *awake* Christianity in his soul. And Christianity is only *awake* insofar as it becomes ever more conscious of that to which historical Christianity points: the *tension* between Christ and Antichrist. The realization concerning this lived intensely in Solovyov's soul. For this reason he—the one who three times experienced a vision of the Heavenly Wisdom, Sophia—

courageously directed his cognitive eye into the abyss of *evil*. What interested him was not the evil that appears outwardly as such—the evil that shows itself, for instance, in all sorts of crime. No, the outcome of evil manifesting in crime was not what he took upon himself to study. Rather, he focused on that kind of evil which has the semblance of goodness, which manifests, that is, not in crime but in *good works*. The subtle, *invisible* evil—invisible even to the intellect—was that to which he ever and again directed his investigative gaze. And the results of this research, formulated shortly before his death, was presented in his book, *Three Conversations.*[†]

This work was written in an very unpretentious form. It is neither a philosophic treatise nor a dramatic work, but rather a sequence of conversations presented in popular journalistic style. They take place during three evenings among four representative personalities: a General, a Politician, a certain Mr. Z, and a Prince. A Lady, too, takes part, but she is only there in order to provide the necessary binding element of friendliness to hold things together. Three of these persons represent in three stages the three justified views of the good. The fourth person—the Prince—represents the disguised evil that hides behind an abstractly moralizing Christianity.

The fact that this work comprises *three* conversations, each of which allows one viewpoint regarding the nature of evil to predominate (either that of the General, the Politician, or Mr. Z), reveals to us the inner composition of the work.

This inner composition reveals, moreover, the actual method of Solovyov's thinking in general. Whatever its *object*, this thinking does not proceed according to a particular *pattern*, but rather to a *rhythm*, the *rhythm of three*. Whatever problem Solovyov approaches, he sees in it a threefoldness and deals with it from three points of view. Thus for him the Eternal is threefold, the Trinity. The human being is a threefold being of body, soul, and spirit. The entire history of humanity is also threefold. It has a first stage in which the Divine operates as the Power that humanity has to obey; then a second stage in which the

---

† Most recent English translation: *War, Progress, and the End of History: Three Conversations, Including a Short Story of the Anti-Christ* (Hudson, NY: Lindisfarne Press, 1990). ED

Divine is grasped as content by means of ideas and is recognized as *Law*; and lastly the third stage, when the Divine no longer reveals itself as outer power or as ideal content, but actually as a *Being*. The *moral* problem, too, Solovyov treats as a threefold one. He sees *one* aspect—the *first* stage of morality—in the clash of the *forces* of good and evil. In the clash of reasoned world viewpoints that can be correct or incorrect, he sees the second stage of morality. And in the pure *being* of spirit—beyond forces and viewpoints—he sees the third and last, the decisive stage of moral life.

He sees the struggle between pure human impulses and animal passions as the first stage, and the struggle between reason and unreason as the second stage, but at the third stage neither any human impulse nor any ideal content has significance. At this stage, righteous indignation, compassion, etc., as well as ideals, principles, etc., cease to play a role as *sources* of morality. Here it is a question of *Beings*. It is a question of direct relationship with supersensible Beings who not only motivate the good or teach the good, but actually *give* the good. In other words, what Solovyov says is that the true essence of the tension between good and evil has a *cosmic* origin. It is a battle that takes place in the world. The human being has a part in it, but 'produces' neither good not evil, for *they* are superhuman. They descend, however, into the inner nature of the human being: and the greatest, most significant descent of the Being of Goodness came about through Christ Jesus. But the deepest descent of the Adversary has not yet [1931] happened. When it does happen, however, how will it appear?

To answer this question is the task of the above-mentioned work. And in answering this question Solovyov proceeds in three stages, which correspond to the three single conversations.

In the first one, the *General* elaborates his standpoint. Here it is shown, in spite of opposition from the Prince (who argues in favor of not combatting evil), that there exists a *natural evil* and an equally *natural good*. And the rightness of the struggle of human nature against inhuman impulses is graphically illustrated by the General's description of the 'greatest experience of his life', when as head of a hundred Kosaks and a Field Battery he slaughtered a band of Bashibazouks who had just tortured—in the most horrible manner—the inhabitants of an Armenian village. 'Divine Springtime was in my soul,' this is how the General describes his soul condition at the moment when he contemplates the corpse-strewn field after the battle.

The General was following neither ideals nor principles when he was faced with the grisly sight of the Bashibazouk deeds of horror. His *human* nature instinctively acted through him to put an end to the excesses of *bestial* nature. The *picture* of the situation itself called forth in the soul of the General an immediate impulse to act. The morality that thus lived in the General is that of the *sentient soul*. It is moral *feeling* that arises in the soul as immediate impulse.

The *Politician*, who holds the floor in the second conversation, represents a *thought-out* moral standpoint. He does not merely act out of his *nature*, he intends to *educate* this nature along the lines of particular principles and ideals. Out of the ideal realm he adds that which he *should be* to that which he *is* by nature of his impulses and instincts. *Nature* is surpassed by the addition of ideas arising out of consciousness. To the natural is added the more purely human. It is the *intellectual soul* language out of which the Politician speaks.

In the third conversation, where Mr. Z (surely Solovyov himself) is the main speaker, a moral problem is elaborated which can be solved neither out of human nature, nor by ideas, but only by means of *supersensible* experience. Moral development—a passing of the moral trials of the *consciousness soul*—is only possible through *cognition* of the actual workings of cosmic good and cosmic evil. Impulse and intellect do not suffice here—a direct cognition of cosmic moral forces and beings is necessary. And the highest requirement for this cognition is to deal with the great trial that humanity must meet—known to tradition as the anticipated appearance of the Antichrist. For this reason the writing under discussion reaches its climax in 'a short narrative of the Antichrist' that Mr. Z received from a monk, now deceased, by the name of Pansophios.

This tale contains the essence of the whole work; namely, a description of the great trial of the consciousness soul facing humanity in the future. This trial is such that all criteria of intellect and feeling fail, for the personality of the Antichrist incorporates in itself that which is perfectly attuned to the feelings and judgements of the age. He is a great philanthropist who leads an irreproachable life. He is an outstanding genius in the realm of thought. His works are read with enthusiasm by the whole world, for they contain the complete sys-temization of the total cultural life of the epoch. Everything is affirmed by this system, everything finds its correct place there. This system is the total summation of the age, the message of peace to the whole world. It contains the possibility of reconciliation in all realms of life: in political, economic, and spiritual spheres.

> And the wonderful author will not only sweep everyone along with him, he will also *please* everyone, so that the words of Christ will come true: 'I have come in the Name of my Father and ye have not accepted me. Yet *another* will come in *his own* name— him ye will *accept*.'

For in order to be accepted one must understand how *to please*.
The personality of 'the coming man' becomes the head of the fed-erated World State. But in the rulership of the world he is not alone, for he has an important helper at his side. This is a 'great magician' from the Far East by the name of Apollonius.

> Half Asian, half European, a Catholic Bishop *in partibus infide-lium*,† he combines in himself in an amazing way mastery of the most recent results and uses of Western scientific technology with knowledge of all those things of solid and significant value that the traditional mysticism of the East contains.

The Ruler of the World solves in a generally satisfactory manner the political problem of the World State and the social problem of universal satisfaction of need. He moves on then to regulate the spiri-tual life. The religions of the world are to be organized in like manner to the states and peoples. And just as he possesses the highest political power, so he wields the highest authority over all religions. He is not only the political but also the spiritual leader of humanity. To bring this to pass a world conference of the representatives of all Christian confessions (the non-Christian religions had already accepted him as their highest authority) is organized in Jeru-salem, at which the Emperor himself presides. But taking part at this conference are three

---

† 'Among the infidels', that is, a Bishop without a Diocese. ED

personalities who frustrate the Emperor's intentions. These are Pope Peter, Father John as representative of Eastern Christianity, and the learned German Theologian Ernst Pauli. From the characterization of these three personalities it is easy to see in them not only representatives of Roman, Greek, and Protestant Christianity, or incorporations of the Petrine, Johannine, and Pauline spirit, but also a Christianized willing, feeling, and thinking of humanity. When they refuse to recognize the Antichrist as spiritual leader (Father John unmasks him as the Antichrist), whereas the other two are killed through the magic power of Apollonius, it is significant that Dr Pauli remains alive. A *cognitive* Christianity is indestructible, even on earth, while both the Christianity of tradition and that of soul warmth can at times disappear.

Between the Antichrist and Apollonius on the one hand, and the three representatives of Christianity on the other, a conflict took place which was not the result of any difference of opinions, or even the result of a disagreement in moral feelings. The origin of the conflict does not lie in the suggestions made by the Antichrist. Those are very fine and are acceptable, but under *one* condition— and that condition is the inner *recognition* of the *Being* of Christ. The three leaders of Christianity are in agreement with all those things that the Antichrist suggests in an organizational direction. The wonderful, resplendent *chalice* he offers they fully respect—*if the content of this chalice is the Christ Being*. And this is just what is impossible for the Emperor. He is preparing this chalice for *another* content. This content consists of the Being by whom he is *possessed*, who entered into him at a particular moment of his life. It is the Being who in one paramount night of his life made an appearance and then vanished *into him*, who whispered to him:

> Do your work in *your own* name and not in *mine!* I shall not be envious of you. I love you and need nothing from you. I ask nothing of you, and will help you. For your own sake, for the sake of your own perfection, and out of my pure and unselfish love for you—I will help you. Receive my spirit! As my spirit once created you in *beauty*, so now it will recreate you in *power*.

At these words the coming man feels 'a sharp, icy stream flowing into him and filling his whole being.'

Now, it was this 'sharp, icy stream' that should, according to the intentions of the Emperor, flow through all humankind. The sphere of action of the Christ would then be taken hold of by Ahriman (called in the Bible, Satan). And to this end a pact was made between Ahriman and Lucifer (called in the Bible, the Devil), shown here in the collaboration between Bishop Apollonius and the Emperor. For Bishop Apollonius, the mystic and magician, is the bearer of the Luciferic principle, as the Emperor is the bearer of the Ahrimanic principle.

Through this pact the strange 'materialistic spiritualism' that is typical of the Antichrist comes into existence. It is not the coarse materialism of the nineteenth century, or the concrete spiritualism of ancient times, but a conception of the spirit that men and women can grasp without effort and with their accustomed ways of thinking in their ordinary frame of mind.

The small group of Christians who are gathered around the three leaders with the concrete revelation of the Divine in the Being of Christ Jesus oppose this 'spiritualism'. Then the separation takes place—called forth neither by differences of opinion nor by anything else human, but solely and singularly on the point of the Being in question. About the 'what' and the 'how' of the Emperor's suggestions, no discussion at all arises—it is only the question of the Who which causes the opposition to appear. And this is the question of the consciousness soul. For in the epoch of the consciousness soul, more and more it is not ideas, intentions, programs, reforms, etc., that are essential, but only who it is from whom these ideas, intentions, programs, etc., proceed. As the essence of Christianity is not its teachings and its churches, but rather the Being of Christ Himself, so the essence of anti-Christianity must also be sought, not only in teachings and organizations, but in the Being who is called 'the Antichrist'.

Accordingly, the fulfillment of the task set by destiny for the three Christian leaders in confrontation with the Antichrist does not lie in a criticism of his views, but in a recognition of the Being who is hidden behind these views.

The work ends with the unmasking of the Antichrist, after which he is plunged into the abyss.

Now there might arise in the soul of a conscientious reader the question: Did then Solovyov really know about the three members of the human soul as here described, and about Lucifer and Ahriman? Or has this all merely been interpreted into it?

Without equivocation we have to reply: Solovyov did not know these things. While writing the *Three Conversations* he did not think with the concepts: sentient soul, intellectual soul, consciousness soul, Ahriman, Lucifer. And yet his considerations, which developed with the help of *other* concepts than these, led him to *realities* that are actually *signified* by these concepts. One discovers these realities when one immerses oneself in this book by Solovyov. So in this case we are not interpreting extraneous things *into* his work, but rather translating into another conceptual language what we have found as realities hidden *behind* this 'mythology' of thinking.

THE DEEPENING OF CONSCIENCE
WHICH RESULTS IN ETHERIC VISION

IN THE PREVIOUS ESSAY, 'The Antichrist in the View of Vladimir Solovyov', it was our intention to show—in the light of Solovyov's work—that the special trial for the consciousness soul demands the capacity to be able to discriminate among *Beings*. Natural sensitivity and intellectual judgment do not suffice for this—a *still higher* faculty is required. In the above essay this faculty was described as the capacity to discern the hidden Being acting behind and through that which initially appears to have been satisfactorily met by one's feeling and intellect. How can this faculty be more closely characterized, and how is it developed?

Every human being is endowed with a capacity that rises above natural feeling and intellectual judgement. This is *conscience*. Conscience is a force that is independent of, and contradicts, ordinary human nature and intellectual judgement. Conscience can reject something in my actions that at first sight seems admirable and good to me. It lifts itself above nature and intellect. But conscience is also not perfect. It also needs, and is capable of, development—for as it is, it is limited. It is in fact, in the first instance, bound to *my* personality. My actions, words, soul expressions are what the judging, testing eye of conscience considers. I feel responsible before my conscience for *my* actions, but not for the actions of other people. For when I make a judgement about other people, I generally, in the first place, use the intellect and not the conscience. My conscience usually has no immediate relation to other people; it is related only to me. It is *subjective*.

But conscience *can* step across the boundaries of subjectivity. It can grow out beyond the boundaries of personality and include *other* men and women and beings in its realm. It can relate itself just as intimately with the souls of other human beings as with its *own* personality. It is possible to feel oneself fully responsible for the free behavior of another, for human souls can be so intimately related that they can recognize each other as members of one organism. It is then that responsibility expands. One is responsible not only for oneself but for others. Then the conscience becomes *objective*.

This 'objective conscience' as a faculty of the soul is expressed in the fact that, to the pangs of conscience caused by our own deeds, other pangs of conscience are added arising from the deeds of others. But more than that, it also represents a *special organ of cognition*. When one takes someone so strongly into the circle of one's soul-interest that they become a matter of conscience, then the being of that person reveals itself to a far greater extent than when one merely stands observing him or her. For as long as one stands opposite another person as an 'objective observer' and makes observations with a lack of concern and a sense of separateness—so long does the deeper being of the other conceal itself.

Lack of concern, sense of separateness as soul attitude, cannot lead one to know another human being. The mood, 'am I my brother's keeper?' does *not* lead to true knowledge of other human souls. A strong relationship to, and interest in, another person leads, on the other hand, deeply into that person's being. For the soul that is experienced as a member of an organism bestows the revelation of its true nature as a radiant *gift* upon those connected to it. And the freely given soul revelation of this kind is infinitely more valuable than the extorted observations of psychoanalysis.

So, for instance, there is more knowledge of the human being in Dostoevsky's novels than in many scientific works devoted to the 'analysis of psychic processes'. For Dostoevsky's knowledge of the human being—though fragmentary and chaotic—was the fruit of an attitude of mind strongly permeated by a consciousness of moral co-responsibility. Dostoevsky, not only in his writings but also in his life, always represented the motto: 'all are responsible together for all.' This was for him no abstract formula, but a basic moral mood of the soul grown out of the painful experience of his life of conscience. This basic mood holds sway—sometimes expressed, sometimes hidden—in all his works. The works of Dostoevsky did not spring from a poetic emphasis, from a flight of enthusiasm for a wealth of colors and figures, or from a love of artful portrayal, but rather from the inner need we could express as follows: *everything* human must be put into the light of conscience.

The writings of Dostoevsky are not just 'psychological novels' in the sense that they describe peculiarities of soul. Rather, they describe the soul qualities *as they relate to conscience*. Also, the central idea of Dostoevsky's writing, the idea of Christianity, is not presented by him as merely true and beautiful, but is made to appear as a *demand of conscience*. Non-Christianity was for him not only untrue and ugly—it was actually lacking in conscience. And the figure of Christ Himself did not mean for him the highest content of faith, but the *highest content of conscience*. Just as a musical person grasps a melody, so does a person gifted with conscience grasp the *reality* of Christianity. Conscience conveys to him *certainty* regarding an objective historical event. It becomes objective. It conveys *knowledge*.

This knowledge, however, is of a higher order. It tells of supersensible things. And one of the fundamental requirements of the path of knowledge of the supersensible is 'to feel oneself as a member of all life.' The feeling of shared responsibility that Dostoevsky's profound insights into the being of Christianity conveyed is also one of the fundamental requirements of that way of knowledge described by Rudolf Steiner in his book *Knowledge of the Higher Worlds*. In the chapter of this book entitled 'The Conditions of Esoteric Training' we read:

> The second condition is to feel oneself *a member* of humanity as a whole. A great deal is included in the fulfilment of this condition. . . . Such an attitude gradually brings about a change in the whole of a person's way of thinking. This holds good in all

things, the smallest and the greatest alike. With this attitude of mind I shall see criminals, for example, differently. I suspend my judgment and say to myself: 'I am a human being just as they are. The education which circumstances made possible for me may alone have saved me from their fate! I shall then certainly arrive at the thought that these human brothers and sisters would have become a different people if the teachers who took pains with me had bestowed the same care upon them. I shall reflect that something was given to me which was withheld from them, that I owe my good fortune to the circumstance that it was withheld from them. And then it will no longer be difficult for me to think that I am only a member of humanity as a whole and *share responsibility* for everything that occurs.'†

Now this feeling of shared responsibility is in reality an expansion of conscience so that it crosses over the boundaries of subjectivity and becomes objective. *Objective conscience* is a requirement for the student of spirit. On the path that leads to knowledge of higher worlds, the development of conscience-objectivity is essential, for it is an organ through which this knowledge is actually mediated. Just as Dostoevsky, in an elemental way, grasped the reality of Christianity by means of conscience, so on a conscious systematic path of spiritual training much can be learned by means of conscience development.

The capacity which thereby arises in the soul is the same as that which we spoke of in the beginning of the above-mentioned essay. There we described the great trial of the consciousness soul to which the *Three Conversations* of Solovyov refer—that is, the capacity to recognize the Antichrist as such. It is not a trial of intellect and feeling, it is a trial of conscience. It is a trial of conscience in the sense that the conscience, having become objective, must recognize the Being who in reality stands behind the grandiose social, political, and spiritual reforms that are there described by Solovyov.

This capacity can also be described from another point of view— now not from that of the inner life, but rather from without. For the

---

† Rudolf Steiner Press, London, 1969, p 108.

question naturally arises as to the relationship of that mentioned above to the precise and concrete descriptions given by Rudolf Steiner of the members of the human being. In other words, how is the 'objective conscience' related to the members of the human being: that is, physical body, life body, astral body, and 'I'?

The normal condition of a modern person in waking consciousness is such that the 'I' and astral body are inside the physical and life bodies, whereby the 'I' is 'at home' in the physical body and the astral body in the life body. The 'I', together with the astral body, leaves the bodies during sleep and lives in the surging ocean of cosmic inspirations. What it can absorb and hold on to of these inspirations becomes, in waking consciousness, conscience. But this conscience becomes subjective insofar as the 'I' primarily exists within the physical body. For the physical body is that which isolates human beings. It is the reason for the fact that one experiences oneself as an individual being, responsible only for oneself. Because the 'I' is bound to the physical body, the attitude of soul arises that can be expressed in the words 'am I my brother's keeper?' The deeper the 'I' descends into the physical body, the more isolated one feels from one's fellow human beings, and the more one feels oneself excluded from humanity's general circle of responsibility.

However, if the 'I' has the power to experience itself within the life body, then its relationship to the surrounding world changes profoundly, for in the life body we no longer feel ourselves to be separate. There, we feel ourselves as members of all life. The life body is something that *unites* rather than separates the soul. Therefore, it is that experience in the life body which is connected with profound moral transformations. For in the life body, one cannot feel such a lack of responsibility for what happens without one's participation as one can feel in the physical body. Thus conscience becomes objective.

So the becoming objective of conscience means at the same time an ascent of the 'I' from experience in the physical body to experience in the life body. However, this ascent means much more. For instance, it means bringing to life 'I'-permeated *thinking*. This thinking is today experienced as a lifeless play of shadows. It is the physical body that makes a thought into a shadow. The resistance of the physical body is too strong to allow *more* of the thought to emerge into ordinary consciousness. But the *life* of the thinker is found in the life body; that is, when the 'I' rises to an experience in the life body, then thinking takes on life. It no longer takes place in the form of faint shadows, but as creative *forces*. Mere ideas become *ideals*.

In the book *Knowledge of the Higher Worlds*, this is also spoken of as a fundamental requirement of spiritual training. 'This truth of spiritual training,' we read there, 'can be summed up in a short sentence: *Every idea that does not become your ideal slays a power in your soul, every idea that becomes an ideal engenders life-forces within you.*'† In other words, the 'I' must be strong enough to *think within the life body*—that is, to create life forces—instead of thinking in the physical body, which lames life forces. For an idea that is torn away from the physical brain through the moral power of the 'I' can be experienced in the life body as an ideal. It is then alive. And its life is a moral one. It is the objectified conscience. Morality and cognition—gnoseology and ethics—join together in the life body to form a unity. For the separation of 'cognitive life' from 'ethics' is only valid in the realm of consciousness that is entirely bound to the physical brain. Conscience becomes cognition, and thinking is inwardly permeated by morality, when the 'I' rises to experience in the life body. Moral cognition and cognitive morality— that is the vital quality of this experience.

When this cognition in the life body is directed toward a process or a being in the outer world, it then becomes what Rudolf Steiner designates as 'etheric vision'. This etheric vision is gradually being prepared in modern humanity. And the trial of the consciousness soul, which is connected with the *concepts* of 'Christ and Antichrist' of which we spoke in the preceding essay, will be successfully withstood by dint of this 'etheric vision'. This vision will be capable of a discrimination between Beings—of which the intellect and the natural feelings alone are not capable. And the expansion of conscience, together with the permeation of thinking by morality, are the precursors of the coming etheric vision: every conscious effort in this direction, moreover, can be a preparing of the way for what is to come.

† Ibid., p31.

SUFFERING AS A
PREPARATION FOR ETHERIC VISION

How does destiny lead human beings to the revelation of the forces of etheric vision? There is an answer to this question which the following considerations will attempt to present.

The development both of single individuals and also of humankind in general is of such a nature that in the process new capacities are produced at the expense of old ones. The appearance of a new faculty is preceded by the inhibition of an old one. For instance, speech became possible through the fact that a part of the forces that were previously used for movement were inhibited, and so were induced to seek *another* channel of activity. Thereby an *inward-turned* movement arose, which was speech; for speech is an inner movement, a gesture turned inward. Through the 'silencing' of outer movement, speaking arose as an *inner* movement. Similarly, thinking is the result of the movement of speech turned inward. Thinking is internalized speaking, just as speaking is internalized movement; for thinking is the life, on a higher level, of the forces that have been taken away from speech. It is born out of silence.

The general tendency of this process of development has been widely used—and misused. Thus there have been—and still are today—individuals and groups of people in Europe and Asia who have tried to develop higher faculties by inhibiting the lower. For instance, the objective of that type of asceticism in which a person freely renounces movement (some have spent years upon a column, a stone, or some other confined space) is the possibility of metamorphosing powers of movement into higher powers. In the same way, to willingly remain silent is a method for transforming lower powers into higher ones. So, for example, Mahatma Gandhi believes that he cannot command the forces necessary to master the demands made upon him by his 'dharma' without devoting one day of the week to silence. He intends, through the suppression of the activity of speech forces, to strengthen his cognitive forces.

Now this practice is subject to a danger. It is possible for the suppression of a power to lead, not to the strengthening of it upon a higher level, but to its degeneration onto a lower level. In other words, the hindered expression of a force can cause the strengthening of a lower instead of a higher force, and a downward metamorphosis can ensue. So, for instance, the suppression of speech forces can lead to a tremendous enhancement of the forces living in the metabolic limb system rather than of the cognitive forces in the head system. And if the life of passions of the person in question has not been purified, then what occurs is an intensification of these unpurified passions. Instead of higher cognitive life of the soul, there can arise an intensification of the instincts and passions, so that the opposite of what is intended can actually happen.

The opposite of what was intended always happens when *one* particular requirement is not fulfilled. That this condition arises is due to the fact that, just as a *small* fire can be extinguished by the same gust of wind that would instead have fanned a *bigger* fire, so within the soul realm, in the event of a suppression of its ordinary outlet of expression, *only the presence of a certain degree of higher activity assures the metamorphosis of a lower into a higher power.* This same fact of soul-spiritual life is referred to where we read in the Gospel that 'to those that have will be given, but from those that have not will be taken away even that which they have.' In other words, those who have developed a strong inner activity will find this latter growing and increasing when the mighty, unavoidable hindrances of the future will have to be met. Those, however, who have only produced a feeble inner activity will be deprived even of that—it will be extinguished.

Not only will it be extinguished in that it will disappear on the level where it was formerly active, but *furthermore*, it will be *transformed* into an activity of a lower nature. For this reason the Apocalypse, when describing the World Crisis (Last Judgement) in mighty pictures, speaks of the formation of *two* humanities: the humanity with the 'sign of the name of the Father and of the Lamb' on their foreheads,[†] and the humanity with the 'sign of the Beast' on their brows. It is not those who lack the 'Sign of the Lamb', but rather those bearing *the other sign*, the 'Sign of the Beast', who *make up* the second race. So the World Crisis will have these two effects: either soul forces are

† See Rev 14:1. ED

heightened above the earthly human level, or they are changed into *bestial* forces that work *below the level* of the human.

This fact of the double metamorphosis of soul forces illustrated in the two preceding examples, the one of asceticism and the other from the Apocalypse, is relevant not only to each individual human being but also to humanity as a whole. If we view it only in its relation to human evolution—to history—we are shown by the course of this history (that is, the *complete* world history as described by Rudolf Steiner) that 'crises' like that described in the Apocalypse have already taken place in the past. There was in very ancient times—according to spiritual scientific investigations—a mighty crisis from which there arose on the one hand an 'I'-endowed humanity, and on the other the animal kingdom. For humanity this crisis signified an *ascent*, for it brought about the development of the organization of self-consciousness; for the animal kingdom, however, it meant a *descent*. From their forebears humankind rose higher—correspondingly higher—as other beings descended, thereby becoming the animals. In the animal kingdom we meet with the results of a powerful metamorphosis *downward* that happened during the 'Lemurian' epoch. But it is the *same* crisis—this time through an *upward* metamorphosis, however—that humanity has to thank for its actual faculty of free self-consciousness. And as the Lemurian crisis produced the differentiation into two realms, the human and the animal, so the human race today confronts an equally mighty crisis that will produce in the future the drastic separation of *a new race* from humanity. This is the meaning of the above-mentioned pictures in the Apocalypse.

Now there are, alongside the mighty crises of all humankind, crises which although they are smaller in scope are precursors of the greater ones. Yes, they even happen within the life of an individual human being, while still exhibiting signs of following this same lawfulness; that is, the law that through suppression a particular force is transformed into another. Had our brain for instance not been hindered in outer movement by the skull bones, had no prison of the brain been produced, it would not have become capable of being the organ of *inner* movement, of thinking. Through being *bound* with respect to outer movement, it was at the same time *freed* for inner movement.

Something similar is true for the soul-life of human beings. The interiorization of soul forces is also produced by way of inhibition. For this reason, *suffering* is the great educator of humanity. The appearance of any new faculty, when developed on a *natural* path, is preceded by a corresponding measure of suffering. Again the Apocalypse points to this basic principle of development by speaking of that part of humanity that bore 'the name of the Father of the Lamb' as consisting of *martyrs*. There it is written, concerning this portion of humanity, that 'they are those who underwent the great tribulation' (Rev 7:14). Suffering raised them up. Through it they could develop forces in themselves that made it possible for them to 'stand before the Throne'. Through tasting the 'enmity of this world', the strong power that is called 'standing before the Throne' arose in them.

Suffering has this significance of course only when one is speaking of so-called 'natural' development, that is, what is caused by destiny. For should one impose human intentions into the sphere of suffering, it can cause the greatest disaster. This is a path that must be left to destiny. Suffering may not be produced willfully. But when the suffering destiny produces is *understood*, it is something that not only can bring comfort, but can even put 'broken' human souls back onto their feet.

And this comfort can also come to those who ask with 'hearts that bleed' about the significance of the tremendous suffering that is at present [1931] borne by Middle and East Europeans—the more so the latter. For this suffering has *one* special quality—the *suppression of all spiritual life* of the human soul. In Middle Europe this is caused by enslavement within the realm of the economy—through economic servitude, spiritual life is inhibited. All attention, all striving, is *forced* to devote itself solely to overcoming economic needs. In East Europe there is not only economic slavery, but also a direct suppression of free spiritual life in any form.

What happens as a result? Just as the wind extinguishes a small fire but strengthens a large one, so through the suppression of European spiritual life there are results. On the one hand there is an actual extinction of that passive, traditional spirituality which has given souls a certain spiritual life up to now. On the other hand, however, there is—in the case of a small number of people—a preparation for the breakthrough of a *new spirituality*.

What the *first* process looks like is known well enough to the world.

But how the second, more profound process happens, that is mentioned hardly at all in public. And yet it is taking place. At first it finds expression in that the soul is filled with a mood of boredom, a mood of desolation in the face of all that is offered by a life devoid of spirit. Then *within* this emptiness arises a mighty *yearning* for the spirit. This yearning is directed, to begin with, toward *other* human beings. It appears as a tremendous hunger and thirst within souls 'to find the other person.' This need—to find, in the life of *loving*, something that may fill the terrible inner emptiness, which may satisfy the thirst for spiritual life—becomes the life-nerve of the soul. And thereby the large measure of selfless interest for the other person necessary for that expansion of conscience spoken of in the previous essay, 'The Deepening of Conscience Which Results in Etheric Vision', is developed. People who feel themselves to be empty can no longer satisfy themselves. The power of their interest is freed from themselves and directed toward others.

Now, through this yearning for the spirit, something else happens. The pain that fills the soul can cause certain half-unconscious efforts of soul forces to arise. These are similar to those of *remembrance*. Only here the whole soul, yes, the whole human being, is harnessed in the effort to 'remember'—not any particular thing—but just to remember, to bring about a particular *state* of soul. This continuous tension of the deepest powers of remembrance can lead to a loosening of consciousness from the body. Consciousness can then experience itself in the life body. And in this experience it can behold that which can quench its thirst for the life of spirit.

Through the *inhibition* of the spiritual life of the soul, an elevation of that soul to experience in the etheric can occur. By going through the school of suffering, there develops in the soul a new, higher faculty. The suffering today laid upon spirit-seeking peoples is a path upon which is awakened a new faculty to be developed—namely, the soul's capacity for having experiences in the life body. And this event will return to human beings the consciousness of things of highest moral significance in the form of experience, things that in tradition have grown ever paler and that eventually could completely disappear from human consciousness.

THE SECRET MOTTO OF BOLSHEVISM

ANTHROPOSOPHY GIVES US the courage to inquire into the true *essence* of life's phenomena once again, as it was possible to do in earlier times. Therefore, in this essay we shall ask the question: What is the *essence*, the essential being, of the will that reveals itself in Bolshevism? We are not asking what *thought* lies behind Bolshevism, nor what surges within it as mood; but rather, what is its deepest impulse? In the following considerations, then, we shall speak of Bolshevism not as it is *thought* or *felt*, but of Bolshevism as it is *willed*.

The essence of Bolshevism can only be grasped through understanding the human being. For what seethes and boils within the depths of a human being surges up to the surface and forms there a stream that creates appropriate ideologies of its own around it. Thus initially we have a process within the human being, and this process can only be understood in relation to the human being.

The bodily life of the human being is a constant balancing of the polarity of the head and the limbs, brought about by the rhythmic system. This is the threefoldness in the life of the human organism: the nervous system centered in the head, the system of metabolism and limbs predominant in the abdomen and legs, and the breathing and blood circulatory systems working chiefly in the region of the chest. These three systems of the human organism are, at the same time, *organs* of the essential human faculties: the nervous system is the organ for reflection of ideas; the rhythmic system is the means for the sustenance of feelings; and the limbs and metabolic system are the region of activity of the will.

Now, this threefold composition of the human being is also at work in three aspects of human *society*. There are people in whom the nervous system predominates, giving them the special faculty of bringing forth *ideas*. These, who are specially gifted for the life of ideas, form that layer of society which is called the 'intelligentsia'.

Then there are people with a poor capacity for idea-life, who let their entire energies flow into work. These people are absorbed in the demands of the physical world, and have little energy remaining for the life of ideas. Their life is limited primarily to the limbs and metabolic system. Actions, not ideas, are the element in which they are at home. And in the third category are people who are neither unintelligent nor passive, but who represent the *life* of the folk-soul. They are those who create and preserve customs, who know how to keep festivals, who cite proverbs and sing old songs, and whose new tunes, if they create them, become folk songs. The special quality, the rhythmic quality, of a folk culture is dependent upon these people.

The Russian revolution is the outer expression in social consequences of a transformation of the relation of the three basic human forces; that is to say, it is the forces of the limbs shooting directly up into the head. It is the rise to ruling positions of those people in whom the metabolic forces predominate. It is the dictatorship of the proletariat.

The intelligentsia were mostly swept away by the Bolshevik revolution. Those who remained were placed in menial positions—as specialists in practical industry. The economic life became all-important: the only realm of life worthy of existence. Thereby the state is felt to be a mighty metabolic process. All spiritual life is then regarded merely as an expression of metabolism, all culture seen as a function of the economic life. The independent life of ideas, the free life of thinking, is not only suppressed—its existence is denied. Philosophy as such no longer exists in Russia. There are no *riddles* of existence to be solved. There are indeed practical *tasks* and *goals*, but no problems. A new 'intelligentsia' is already arising. They are people who do develop a life of thought, but this life of thought is merely an expression of the metabolic forces that surge up from the lower parts of the organism. *Truth*, as such, no longer exists for this type of thinking. Only the best means is sought for. There is only *correctness*.

While the thinking of the old intelligentsia was grounded in itself—that is, formed an element that commanded respect, that rayed in from *above* and was reflected by the brain—so the thinking of the proletarian intelligentsia is so formed that it shoots up into the brain out of the will element, it surges up from *below*. And when *this* thinking denies the independence of the life of thought, it has good reason to do so; namely, that it is *itself not* independent. It is merely the 'how' of wish-fulfillment. It only fulfills wishes.

Yet this kind of thinking projected up from below, this wishful thinking, cannot attain to sole supremacy as long as it meets with resistance on the path it takes through the rhythmic system. The rhythmic system offers resistance to it, and creates its own *independent life* in opposition.

So, too, communism as an ideology, as a way of life, cannot attain to complete supremacy—even after sweeping away the intelligentsia—as long as the rhythms of the *Church* exist. The cultic-folk rhythm of Eastern Christianity stands between the roots of the old thinking and the ideology of violent revolution. In the shadow of this rhythm an ideology in opposition to communist ideology can continue to exist. Protected by the heart rhythm, a space can be preserved in the brain where the thinking 'from above' can be reflected, instead of the thinking 'from below'.

Recognizing this situation, the whole weight of Bolshevist power threw itself upon the task of annihilating the rhythm in the life of the people. In order to see the significance of this fact, we have to consider *what* rhythm means in the life of the folk. Whoever has not experienced the preparatory time for Easter, the great time of fasting, then Maundy Thursday, Good Friday, and Holy Saturday, and finally, Divine Service in the night from Saturday to Easter Sunday, can hardly form a concept of the *mighty* influence of the Easter Festival on Russian souls. A wave of inwardness in the soul streams over the whole land. Nothing—really *nothing*—in the Russian life of culture can compare with the warmth, the inwardness of the yearly Easter experience. One can speak, certainly with justification, of the decadence of the clergy and of the decay of Christian spiritual life, but on the other hand it has to be admitted that in spite of this, every year the souls of thousands upon thousands were gripped by the *mood* that streams out of the truth of Resurrection—a mood in which professors unite with peasants.

The rhythmic course of the year's festivals was oriented toward this yearly Easter experience. Thus the year was not merely a given fact, but a stepwise religious experience. The recurring fifty-one Sundays and Saturdays of the year prepared souls to experience the fifty-second Sunday, Easter Sunday. Through this rhythm of the cultic life, religious life had a *power* that was regarded by Bolshevism as foreign and hostile.

In order to break this power, the rhythm of the religious life had to be destroyed, dismembered, pulverized. For this purpose the work calendar was reformed. Universal Sundays were eliminated. The uninterrupted, five-day, staggered-shift work week was brought in so that every day one-fifth of the individuals are freed from work. So there is no longer any common festival (except for a few State holidays). Thus too, on Easter Sunday, four-fifths of the working population are kept busy. Four-fifths of the workers are thereby prevented from going to Church service. As a substitute for this, amusements are offered.

The possibility for a *shared* religious experience no longer exists. Instead there is the common super-personal life within the economic realm. *There*, community must reign. And religion may at best be reckoned as only an affair of the individual. The words and thoughts directed toward the divine may no longer work for the unity of humankind, only factories and collective enterprises may do so.

Rhythm, as a fount of power for religious experience, is thereby destroyed. Religion, as the heart's own life, is thus eradicated, for this independent life of the heart, this reality of the rhythmic system, hinders the unbounded rulership of the metabolism-transformed-into-thinking. A type of human being is arising consisting only of willing and thinking, and the latter shall serve the former—that is, *a human being without rhythm*, made up only of the faculty of spontaneous decision and deliberation. And Stalin-Dzhugashvili, dictator of Russia today [1930], is a man who comes very close to being just this human type. His tactics are like the spring of a tiger: spontaneous and violent; and each of these 'shock tactics' is draped in an ideology that is subservient to his purpose. His thinking is, in fact, a metabolic thinking. From the lower parts of the organism a powerful impulse shoots up, which is clothed in an appropriate 'truth' by the head.

His rhythmic system has hardly any life left of its own—it is only a bridge between willing and thinking. Feeling has been expunged from the breast region, which is hardly an organ for this any longer. It has become a mere link between commanding will and obedient thinking.

From the above exposition, we can see Bolshevism's *intentions*, and that the question here is of the realization of an ideal human being, stirring in the depths of the will. We have here a grandiose effort to *radically transform human nature*. The aim is to produce a new human being: a human being whose thinking reflects, not heaven, but the interior of the earth, and whose will is not disturbed and weakened by an individual life of feeling. Human beings shall arise who will differ from those preceding them, right down into the physical organization. In them there will be quite another relationship between the three systems of which they are composed. In this relationship the leading role in the organism is conceded to the intelligence of the nerve center of the metabolic system. The nervous activity of the metabolic system is to take over the functions that previously belonged to the upper nervous system: the brain. Then the brain will gradually take up the same relationship to the metabolic nerve activity as the latter previously held to the brain activity.

The heart, however, as the center of the rhythmic system, must have no life of its own. Warmth of heart in the soul-life shall no longer exist. No soul element shall enter heart activity: the heart shall no longer be an organ of the life of the soul. It shall become instead a mere organ of the metabolic system.

Just as religious life, Christianity, shall no longer be permitted to foster community-building in the social organism, so the heart may no longer be an organ for the inner workings of the soul in the human organism. And just as the community-forming activity is given over to the economic life, so the heart becomes merely an organ of the metabolism.

Now we can return to the question formed at the beginning of this essay: What is the essence of that will which lives and holds sway in the striving of Bolshevism? The answer that comes condenses finally into this symbolic physiological image: *The human heart shall become a mere organ of the metabolism.*

COLLECTIVISM AND SOPHIA
(TOLSTOI, LENIN, SOLOVYOV)

IT IS CHARACTERISTIC OF OUR TIME that the working together of many is demanded more and more in all realms of life. For both modern science, which has long since reached a stage where no single individual can master it and which consists of numerous specialized contributions, and socialism in all its forms, are colossal impersonal conglomerations toward which the cognition and action of the present age are oriented. 'Scientific method' and 'cooperation' are the two basic requirements in our age for both knowledge and action. Now 'scientific method' has actual *universal validity* in the realm of knowledge. Only those opinions that everyone can grasp and that all can test are accepted as 'scientific'—everything else is a 'matter of faith'. Cooperation on the other hand is the demand for generalized action. There personal deeds and capacities flow together into a general reservoir of accomplishment. So the present age tends toward an 'everyman's wisdom' in cognition and an 'everyman's capability' in action.

This tendency of modern times—the striving for 'everyman's wisdom' and 'everyman's capability'—is in strict opposition to *mysticism* in cognition and to *individualism* in action. For mystics recognize as true only that which has been revealed to *their own* inner life, whereas individualists act only out of their *own impulses*. Neither of them concern themselves over what people in general might say about a mystic's knowledge or the actions of an individualist. Our time is thus the most *unmystical* and *unindividual* in history: what the individual as such knows and wills is of less and less interest; the individual is only considered as a part of the whole. What our time requires of the single person is roughly this: 'Give up the personal in cognition, for *your* opinions are of no importance to anyone. What *you* believe, what *you* will is of no interest; only that in you which conforms to the requirements of the community—only those of your convictions and viewpoints that are agreed upon by everyone—is significant and acceptable; only those of your actions that are of benefit for all are acceptable.'

So the human soul stares at a merciless, cold *lack of interest for the personal within*. The stern gardener is no longer content with colorful, scented flowers—for the time of blossoms is past—now he or she requires *fruit*. The unfolding of personality, *as such*, was in its time respected and valued; now, however, the times demand of personalities *objective achievements*.

The spirit of the age demands not only objectivity of judgement, but also *objectivity in willing*, objectivity in action. Everyone has the choice of either a cold *sub*-personal objectivity, as of a cog in an enormous machine, or else a warm *super*-personal destiny-reconciling wisdom. But in either case, the human being of the present age *must* learn to eliminate the personal—that is the demand of our time.

This characteristic of the present day is also expressed by the weighty sentence: 'We live in the age of the consciousness soul.' The development of the consciousness soul can, however, proceed in two different directions. After the evolution of the intellectual or mind soul reached a certain completion, human beings have become citizens of the earth. They have, in their descent out of the cosmic womb, reached the earth. They have become personalities. Now, however, the development of the consciousness soul—just beginning—requires human beings to rise above the merely personal. There are two ways of doing this: either by personalizing the impersonal, the objective—that is, by becoming ever *more* a personality—or else by mechanizing their inner life—that is, by becoming ever less a personality. From the personal—the fruit of the intellectual soul age—there proceed two ways toward the objectivity of the consciousness soul age: One is the path to superpersonal objectivity and the other is the path to sub-personal objectivity.

This can be shown by means of the following diagram:

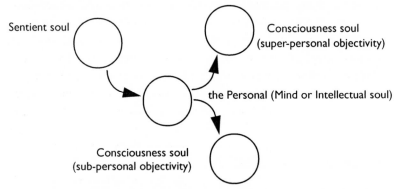

Sentient soul

Consciousness soul
(super-personal objectivity)

the Personal (Mind or Intellectual soul)

Consciousness soul
(sub-personal objectivity)

Nowhere has the contrast between these two paths appeared so blatantly, so vehemently, as in the modern spiritual life of Russia. This spiritual life was still, at the turn of the eighteenth century, a religious sentient soul culture with a tinge of foreign intellectual soul culture at its summit (the language of the upper classes was French).

During the nineteenth century, the culture of the intellectual soul deepened and became independent. It gradually left the mother-sheath of the sentient soul culture that had surrounded and protected it. A wave of criticism and doubt in relation to the values of sentient soul culture poured over the Russian life of the nineteenth century. It took on—because of the fresh youthfulness of this spiritual life—very radical forms. An uncompromising 'either–or' thinking bore down on the traditional values of the sentient soul. Unable to press forward to the inner strength and security of the consciousness soul when it had lost the childish wisdom of the sentient soul, the youthful, radical thinking of Russian intelligence developed a *wavering* tendency. It swung between a deeply rooted ancient religiosity, and a critical, intellectual frame of mind. Incapable of really creating new values, it undermined the old ones. And the most significant representative of this spiritual trend was Leo Tolstoi. In his whole life story can clearly be seen just what paths striving East Europeans must take when they tear themselves away from the spirit-permeated sentient soul element, and seek to attain their own conscious values.

Tolstoi is indeed a thinker who tears himself away from the spiritual life mediated by the sentient soul—not, please note, that he was a thinker freed from traditional religious life, but rather a thinker in the process of freeing himself from it. What is characteristic of him is not freedom from the old, but the process of freeing oneself from the old. And as this freeing of himself took place completely in public, it was eventually sealed by his excommunication from the Church. So now, having failed to appreciate the significance of its ritual, and denying its value; having resigned from traditional mysticism; having at last (through excommunication) completed his break with the old; he stood naked before the great riddles of life and death. He was armed solely with an attenuated moral philosophy, sifted rationally from the Gospels, upon which he honestly strove to model his life.

Indeed, he did free himself from the influence of tradition; he could now freely, as a personality, cultivate self-won values. Two directions were open to him: he could either carry on with the same critical attitude of mind, or else move on to a new creative one. After Tolstoi had put Christianity through the sieve of rationalism, there remained to him a Christianity that essentially represented a system of morals.

However, a system of morals has value only insofar as it is practically realized. So Tolstoi, after he had formed his own unmystical and non-cosmic Christianity, devoted himself totally to the realization of the maxims of Christian morals in practical life. Thus he founded a 'this-worldly' Christianity that does not know the cosmic significance of the Mystery of Golgotha, that does not know the beings and doings of the spiritual Hierarchies, but sees in Christ Jesus merely an exemplary man. For him—and through him for his followers—in place of the cosmic, mystic, cultic aspects of Christianity, the *practical organization of human community living* became of primary importance.

So Tolstoi chose one of the two possible directions; namely, the path to *practical morality devoid of a world-conception*. And because the Christ God became for Tolstoi the Man-Jesus who had founded a new system of morals, Nicholai Lenin (Vladimir Ulvinov) could then pro-claim a teaching that actually did away with the Man-Jesus. For Tols-toi's morality devoid of a world-conception is merely a transitional stage to the kind of this-worldly social arrangement of life that ani-mated Lenin.

Yet it would have been possible for Tolstoi's inner situation (that is, the desire to penetrate Christianity with thinking) to be a transi-tion to quite another impulse. It could have been a transition to the Christian impulse of learning to read the ruling cosmic intentions. Had he taken this path, it would instead have been a bridge to the life-work of *Vladimir Solovyov*.

As a direct path leads from the 'this-worldly' Christianity of Tolstoi to Lenin's Communism, so a direct path could lead from Tolstoi's strongly thought through understanding of Christianity to the Sophianism of Solovyov. As a 'beggar for the spirit', Tolstoi stands at the crossroads between *Collectivism* and *Sophia*. As a *personality* he is free, but he wishes to escape his personality. He seeks the human, the universal. Now there are two different ways universality can be sought; and one is when a *superpersonal* community is formed under the aegis of *Sophia*, Wisdom. Thus to Tolstoi's life-questions, life itself gave two answers. The one answer is the life-work of Vladimir Solovyov (this answer was not, however, recognized as such). The other answer is the life-work of Nicholai Lenin (this answer, indeed, was not antici-pated as such). To the question, 'How can I grow beyond my unsocial, confining personality?' the answer resounds as a strong spiritual message out of Solovyov's life-work: 'Unite yourself with the grace-giving activity of the Cosmic Christ through the power of heavenly Wisdom!' And the opposing answer comes out of Lenin's work: 'Unite yourself in the human masses' own actions through the power of earthly striving.'

Vladimir Solovyov saw the salvation of humanity in a comprehension of Christ as an historical figure, as an impulse for humankind, and as a cosmic Being, so that a *Christosophy* could permeate the social life of human beings. And he devoted his life to working out of such a comprehension of such a Christosophy. Rudolf Steiner indicated that aside from spiritual scientific insights, no more advanced conception of Christ exists at the present time than that of Vladimir Solovyov. For not only does he believe in Christ and worship him, but also he *understands* him. And in order to communicate his understanding to humanity, he strove, armed with the whole conceptuality of nineteenth-century philosophy, to create new concepts worthy of Christ. By aid of these concepts, the relationship to Christ, which was in danger of being lost, might be re-established. Then the understanding of Christ should gradually permeate social life. Then the wonderful and courageous hope of Solovyov would find fulfillment—that *the Christian State* would one day arise. At this time, however, there arose the anti-Christian state of Lenin, which began with raging speed forcibly to impose its ideas, while those of Solovyov, renouncing all use of force, has to wait for recognition in freedom.

Presently [1930], Russia is being collectivized. The intention is to turn it into a mighty mechanism of production. A powerful organization of human beings who are not *permitted* to have any personal views or aims, the Communist Party, rules all the life processes of that land. *Collectivism*, the sub-personal objectivity of the consciousness soul, has assumed control.

And what is the fate of *Sophia*, the heavenly wisdom, whose task it is to permeate the consciousness soul as the power of super-personal objectivity? Did she soar up into imperceptible heights of heaven to vanish into the blue?

While in East Europe *Collectivism* has gained strength, in Middle Europe *Sophia* has found a footing on earthly ground. The impulse that lived in Solovyov, and that through him could find no fuller, more concrete a revelation than in the form of a grandiose philosophical system, floating well above the level of earthly existence—that impulse became mighty on earth, in a form fitting to real life, through the life-work of Rudolf Steiner. Solovyov's semi-incarnated Sophia, soaring above the heads of human beings, became the *Anthropo*-Sophia of Rudolf Steiner, deeply anchored in the *Human Being*. In spite of all outer deceptive appearances, equilibrium is there. If in the battle between Collectivism and Sophia, Collectivism throws up mighty waves of communism, nevertheless, in more intimate ways, Sophia, now become Anthroposophia, makes no less mighty waves in the depths of human souls.

THE SPIRITUAL BASIS OF
THE EAST EUROPEAN TRAGEDY

I

THE MISFORTUNE that has befallen East European humanity is an event in the destiny of humankind which people have met with by and large either by ignoring it with various excuses, or else by completely identifying with it. These latter, who identify with this East European misfortune, become as it were paralyzed in soul; whereas the former, more numerous by far, do not regard it as their concern.

Thus the decades pass by: the misery of East Europe stands there. It remains; it cannot be decreed away—this grey, comfortless, delirious Russia. However, if we regard it not from a political or economic, but from a *human* standpoint, the standpoint of conscience, we cannot avoid facing the question of guilt and expiation. Whoever asks this question has the earnestness necessary to consider—in the light of spiritual science—the events in East Europe as a problem of destiny. For it is not superfluous—indeed, it is only possible against the background of human conscience—to make anthroposophical enquiries into such occurrences in human history.

Let us remind ourselves about what has happened in Russia: not what happened politically or economically, but what happened *mor-*

ally. In order to characterize the upheaval that took place in Russia, let us imagine intelligent, tasteful people who one day begin suddenly to think of nothing but food and the conditions of material life, who regard everything in life only from the angle of its advantage or disadvantage to their digestive system—people who live wholly in the realm of metabolism. So great would be the difference in their whole being that one would hardly recognize such people.

Actually, something similar has happened to the whole of Russian spiritual life. One cannot recognize it any longer. What formerly was first and foremost has become last and least, and what formerly was last and least has become first and foremost. Thoughts of a Dostoevsky, a Solovyov, and a Tolstoi, which have moved generations of men and women, are regarded as archival productions of bourgeois leisure hours. Popular materialistic articles of faith are the framework within which all thinking moves. Instead of interest in world-conceptions, interest in economics holds sway. Capital, production, and consumption take possession of minds in the same measure as had formerly God, conscience, and truth.

Whoever has regarded this upheaval from afar is naturally led to the question: does the true being of East European spiritual life express itself in the idealism of the past, or in the utilitarianism of the present?

If we would answer this question, we must mention a radical fact. We must say: neither the idealism of the past nor the materialism of the present are expressions of the essential being of Russian spiritual life. The one and the other tendency have really nothing to do with Russia's own spiritual life. For if the spiritual life of the *ancien régime* was merely an expression of how individual personalities made use of ideas taken up from the West, so the spiritual life of the Soviet Union is now merely an expression of how the masses make use of ideas that have also been taken up from the West. Both phenomena do not have their roots in the spirit of the European East, but are merely two kinds of reactions to particular ideas stemming from the West. However, there did exist individual phenomena of significance for understanding the truth of Russia's spiritual life, but only of significance for obtaining *knowledge* of it—for as to the *forming* of spiritual life itself, they were of no importance.

The secret of Russian spiritual life is that it is not yet really existent—not that there was and is no life of the spirit in Russia, but that there is no spiritual life arising out of the Russian spirit itself. The exceptions to this rule are of symptomatic significance for the *future*, but not of formative significance for the present. This seems to contradict the opinion, generally held in the West, that the Russians are a richly-endowed people. There has always been great admiration of how easily they orient themselves in all branches of human knowledge and practice, how they can be actively productive in every sphere.

Now this fact in itself is one of the most important symptoms speaking for the truth of the assertion that there as yet exists no spiritual life belonging distinctively to Russia. For the basis of Russian openness and receptivity is the fact that they bear nothing in themselves that could provide resistance to the absorption of what is foreign. They are absorbent because they are empty; they are 'richly-endowed' because they are *beggarly poor* in self-attained spiritual goods.

In order to grasp the reality of the Russian ways—also to see her future—we must first see clearly that Russia is just as poor spiritually as she is materially. She hungers not only in body, but also in spirit. If we penetrate with our gaze through the outer layer of apparent achievements and talent, we find a yawning void behind them. Dostoevsky knew this—that is why he showed princes and clerks, tradesmen and students, all together, standing on the edge of a yawning abyss. Who can read, for instance, The Brothers Karamazov, The Idiot, The Possessed, and not become dizzy? On reading these works we feel that all the characters could at any instant fall into the abyss, that there is no ground underfoot or force of cohesion. Like phantoms they move about—servants and princes, gypsy maidens and highborn ladies— all similar because all of them are mere masks, mere semblances, teetering over the abyss. In pointing to this truth, Dostoevsky showed the two possible alternatives, the two ways for Russia: either this void will be filled by demons, or else Christ will be found. Either possession or enlightenment. These are the two ways Russia can go; a third possibility does not exist.

Yes, one must face the truth: in Russia there is nothing steadfast, nothing secure, nothing upon which a strong living spiritual tradition could be based. Whoever could look into the *heart* of Russia would recoil with horror from the void to be found there: the East can look back on a rich, opulent past and be nourished by it; the West possesses self-made spiritual goods and can view the future with the hope of being able to foster and further develop the best of them; but Russia can look back on nothing in the past as pattern or possession, and has nothing at present that contains potential for the future. How grey is the history of Russia in the past! While high spiritual cultures flourished in Florence, Milan, and Rome, while troubadours in France and minnesänger in Germany offered service to ladies in song and in deed, Russia was the land where barely literate peasant landlords locked their women up in 'terems'† and fought each other with cunning and violence for the sake of a few poor villages, or to gain a more honorable seat at the table of grand dukes, or even to win the graces of the Tartar Khan.

How hopeless are the prospects for Russia's future at present! After Western culture, forcibly imported by Peter the Great, has degenerated as far as Bolshevism, where will this Bolshevism lead Russia in the future? Her spiritual life is without a past and without a future; Russia stands among the nations as a beggar. Only rags and tatters of the past cover her nakedness, only sores and wounds offer the points of departure into the future.

It is hard to admit this truth for a heart that loves the land of its youth, its rich and well-sounding language in which he learned to think, and its fellow countrymen—for we would like to be proud of what we love. Therefore it is little wonder (and still less to be taken amiss) that Russians who have left their own land speak of the 'eternal values of Russian spiritual life that no one can take from us.' We can understand that, standing as homeless beggars at the doors of strangers, they will not admit that they really are beggars—spiritual beggars at that. And as such they speak of a true Christianity which they should possess, and of Russian spiritual treasures which they deem to be only temporarily and superficially hidden from sight. But the truth is that it is only human pride, a national need for admiration, and desire for recognition that motivates them.

---

† The five-storey Terem Palace of the Moscow Kremlin used to be the main residence of the Russian Tsars in the seventeenth century. ED

This is the state of affairs in the eyes of one who looks with interest at the European East in an unbiased way. Now, in recognizing this state of affairs, there arises the task of comprehending its *significance*. For this purpose, ordinary objective judgement does not suffice; we have to use the resources that Rudolf Steiner's spiritual science provides. If we regard the facts we have described with the methods of spiritual science, the following explanation of the spiritual situation in the East of Europe emerges.

If we compare a Russian with a West European, we find a difference in their soul-spiritual constitution, which expresses itself even in the physical body, although it is not obvious. The difference is that the organization of West Europeans is more suited for gathering *experience* than that of East Europeans, whose constitution is more suited for *revelation*. While West Europeans have a constitution oriented toward perceiving and experiencing their objective surroundings (not only of the material outer world, but also of the etheric outer world), East Europeans have an organization oriented toward that which is super- and sub-subjective, not toward that which is objective. The consciousness-bearing organization of East European people is endowed with a strong tendency toward the *vertical* direction— it is like a 'vertical channel'[†] that is open above for the world of the Hierarchies and below for the world of the sub-earthly spheres.

This predominance of the vertical in their orientation is due to what Rudolf Steiner called spirit self or the 'manas-organization' to which he attached a future mission in East Europe. The manas-organization is in essence oriented toward revelation. If it does not remain as potential but develops to a certain degree of maturity, it brings a profound transformation of consciousness, so that the thinking of a person with such a development becomes a process differing significantly from that which results from the development of the consciousness soul. In consciousness soul thinking, knowledge is gained by drawing connecting threads between one phenomenon and another. To have knowledge of something means to have overcome the isolation of this one phenomenon from others. It is quite different

---

† The German word *Rohr*, translated here as 'channel', can denote a hollow object such as a pipe, and is also translated as 'reed' in these essays. ED

for those who make use of a manas-organization. For them the riddle remains unsolved even after they have drawn threads of connection between various phenomena; it is not solved until a thread of knowledge has connected the problematic phenomenon with something essential, that is, with the moral-spiritual level which lies in the spirit world *above* the phenomenon in the world of experience. So for Hegel, world history was a thought process consisting of thesis, antithesis, and synthesis; for Solovyov, who had well mastered the Hegelian technique of thinking, world history was a drama of justice—a cosmic trial between good and evil.

Now vertically-directed thinking is essentially nothing but listening to the spiritual Word—or, when it is directed *down*ward, receiving forced 'impulses' imposed from sub-earthly spheres. The results of this latter process, however, makes people incapable of creating thought content and thought connections *themselves*. Just as students would learn nothing from a professor's lecture if they were themselves speaking instead of listening, or by the most intent listening could learn nothing if the professor were silent, so cognition through the manas-organization depends on the *speaking* and the *silence* of the spiritual world. When the spiritual world thinks in human beings, then they *have* answers to questions, solutions for riddles; but if the spiritual world is silent, then people are empty and poor and cannot do anything but repeat and combine the thoughts of others, or be reduced to ordinary commonplace conversation.

Now the spiritual world only speaks when certain conditions are present. A certain level of purification of the human being—as preparation for a faculty of selfless devotion to the spiritual world—is necessary for even an incomplete manas-revelation. This purification is as much necessitated by the manas-organization as the Kamaloka state is necessitated as a consequence of death. Just as a human being *must* go through a process of purification in the Kamaloka state after death, so a human being, or a group of human beings, or even a people who are karmic bearers of a manas-organization, *must* go through a certain purification. For the manas-organization brings with it the necessity that at a certain point—either in a person's life or in the history of a people—human beings must go through poverty, as beggars for the spirit. This teaches not only the illusory nature of all knowledge, of all capacities not connected with the spirit, but also leads to a cleansing from the Luciferic influence that has been lurking in the human astral body since the Fall. Pride—arrogance—must *die out* in the sphere of spiritual life before the spiritual world will allow revelations to stream down the 'vertical channel' of the manas-organization into the human world.

The process of a painful dying out of pride in a whole people can be observed in the East of Europe. We shall consider in the next essay the nature, the dangers, and the results of this process.

II

In Part I we have shown the connection between the manas-organization (spirit self) and the destiny of the European East. We pointed to the inescapable process of purification that the existence of a manas-organization necessitates, just as the fact of death necessitates the purifying process of Kamaloka. Let us now consider this process of purification more closely.

The power that makes men and women into upright, vertically-oriented beings entered into them following the Fall. In essence it was what today we usually call 'pride'. The Bible shows the nature of this power by the words of the Tempter: 'Ye shall be as Gods.' When pride entered into human nature through the Luciferic impulse, a vertical stream, from below upwards, came into being in the human organization. The physically perceptible expression of this stream is the backbone. What has formed itself physically into the backbone consists astrally of *pretensions of pride*. These pretensions have themselves an object: that they feed on themselves. So arises the upward-streaming swirling movement of the passion of pride. The form of the vertebral column is its physical expression.

Now the basic precondition for the manas-revelation is that a stream must come into being that goes in the opposite direction: from above downward. Regarded *spiritually*, it is the stream of revelation; as *soul* phenomenon, however, it is borne on the *stream of humility*. But opposing it is the pride that lives in all human nature since the Fall. In order to make it possible, then, a purification of human nature must precede the manas-revelation. This purification consists in the dying-out of pride in that part of the astral body required for cognition. Human beings must submit to a process of humiliation that brings the manas-organization to maturity. This humbling is accomplished as follows: those who out of the forces of their consciousness soul have chosen the spirit will be, as it were, imprisoned. On the one hand a protective wall will be erected around them against evil influences; on the other a dome arches over their heads consisting of the *silence of the spiritual world.* Thus arises an empty space where each is quite alone. This space is so empty that even evil cannot enter there. Such people have an opportunity fully to experience their powerlessness and poverty. They also grow fully conscious of the nature of their personal feeling of pride in all its vanity, and the powerlessness of their pretensions.

In this emptiness of soul and silence of the spirit, pride gradually dies away—until one day the decisive hour arrives in which one feels oneself to be a broken hollow reed and finds no more strength in oneself to stand upright in the world. For what has held us upright since time immemorial, the power of our pride, is now broken; the core of life for our personality is wiped out. Then we experience ourselves as *so* empty that there remains only *one thing* to do: to give the last breath of our life of soul to love. When we do this, the walls of our prison vanish and heaven opens above us; the manas-organization has matured. The 'vertebral column', which through the death of pride had become a hollow reed, is filled *from above* with the love-revelation of the spiritual world. So we become again upright beings—but in quite another sense than before. We now stand upright because we knows ourselves to be a connecting link standing between heaven and earth. For the *new* wisdom of world evolution is not heaven's wisdom alone, neither is it earthly wisdom alone; it is their harmony sounded on the strings of the human being who is stretched between heaven and earth.

A similar imprisonment of the human soul also takes place after death. *Kamaloka* is not a world, but a *condition* of the human soul. It is a condition in which the soul is closed off from all that happens in the world. There it goes through the purification brought on by its state of being alone.

Imprisonment takes place not only on the path of cognition and after death, but sometimes in the course of destiny of human individuals on earth. So one will never understand the deeper destiny-tasks of such individualities in the history of humankind as, for instance, Mary Stuart or the Man in the Iron Mask, if one regards their fate merely as 'punishment for the past' and not also as 'preparation for the future'. The *political* reason for Mary Stuart's imprisonment may have been her rivalry with Elizabeth; it may have lain in the birth rights of the one known as the Man in the Iron Mask, who was kept in prison for over forty years—but those are not *spiritual* reasons. The spiritual reason these personalities had to experience and suffer the fate of undeserved prison loneliness is the preparation of a manas-organization.

But the fate of imprisonment as preparation for the manas-revelation is not limited to single individuals. Whole groups of people can undergo this fate—and even entire nations can sometimes be involved. So, for instance, the people of Israel, after they had been led in bondage through humiliation in Egypt, had to wander in the loneliness of the *desert* in order to partake of the *manna*-revelation.

Something similar is taking place today before the eyes of all the world. A great people lives in unfreedom in the East of Europe and is obliged to do compulsory labor for a group of human beings who revere an embalmed corpse—while the desert of spiritual values increases and the wilderness spreads over every realm of their spiritual culture. It is of little importance that today in Russia the labor to which the whole people is enforced does not consist in building pyramids, but rather in socialistic 'industrialization' of the land. It is of little importance that the desert into which the minds of the enslaved people flee is not the physical desert of the Sinai peninsula, but is to be found in universities where there is no philosophy or theology, where law is taught without the supersensible idea of justice, where the history of humankind is taught in disregard of the spiritual formative impulses behind events, where libraries lack the works of Hegel, Fichte, and Schelling, of Spinoza, Plato, and Solovyov, where what is spoken in assemblies has become empty slogan and catchword. In every place, in every institution of life, a desert opens out behind the meaningless forms. The minds of East European people must wander in this desert when they yearn for freedom and the fresh air of spiritual life. They find only emptiness and silence. Thus they are led to the dying out of pride, which has of necessity to reach a certain stage before the first wave of manas-revelation can begin. This is *one* side of the soul-spiritual process that is happening in the East of Europe.

We have characterized one aspect of the transformations of the human consciousness organization, but it has also another aspect that should be considered. The preparation of manas-revelation described in its basic stages above concerns people who *have* made a karmic decision: a decision in favor of the Spirit. The resulting lack of freedom and emptiness arising in the soul creates, through the dying out of pride, an entrance portal for manas-revelation.

But there are *other* people for whom the same situation can call forth quite different results. For them, the silence of the spiritual world and the emptiness taking hold of the soul can cause the soul to turn to the inspiration of evil that flows from the earth's interior. For the soul can be tempted to seek *this other* fulfillment, through surrender to that found not above, but rather *below* the sphere of pride. 'Bolshevism'—not as social-political doctrine, but as psychological phenomenon—is the negation of all that is individual and aristocratic in favor of devoting oneself all the more strongly to a *pride* that is sub-individual and *collectivized*. The pride of the single individual no longer lives—it is mercilessly broken. What lives is the pride, the arrogance of a group consciousness that is morally oriented toward the earth's interior.

In this case, too, vast changes take place in the human organization. When *personal* pride is broken, the flow of pride directed from below upward along the spine is tremendously strengthened; for so long as pride is personal, it stands as a hindrance against the influx of evil from the earth's interior. This influx occurs at the moment a group consciousness opens the door for it. Then a particular mass of people comes into being that is 'fanatically electrified' and thereby capable of accomplishing an enormous amount. *These* people no longer feel emptiness in their souls; they are inwardly filled by an element one cannot describe otherwise than as 'electrified will power'. This expression is meant *literally* and not as a figure of speech—there really is an electric effect from the earth's interior. This inculcates into people that tremendous urge to be active which can be observed in those who are submerged in the group soul.

The sickness of the *positive* stream of destiny in the European East is the absence of the spiritual-scientific life of thought. The *negative* stream of which we spoke in the previous essay does not only find itself in the situation of having to decide in favor of the imported thoughts of materialistic Marxism, but it *too* has succumbed to a particular disease. The people who in Russia have accepted the gospel of class struggle, have done so in the main not out of a healthy cognitional striving but in a state of cognitional stupor. This stupor was prepared long ago, and the means that brought it about were complicated; but what was achieved through these means was a kind of poisoning of the sense organism, which is the basis for forming convictions in those people who have weak cognitional initiative.

The ten senses (or thirteen, when three further ones are developed) as Rudolf Steiner describes them in the second lecture of the cycle *Anthroposophy, Psychosophy, Pneumatosophy*,[†] working together, produce for human beings a *picture* of the world. When their function is disturbed, they produce a *distorted* world picture. So, for instance, pessimism is often an effect of the sickness of the sense organism: the person *sees* all things in a sordid light because his or her senses are poisoned by an etheric substance that is connected with the physical bile. However, if the senses are poisoned by a substance which the ancients described as 'black bile', then a world picture arises that appears to be 'unjust' and 'infuriating'. A person whose eyes, ears, etc., are poisoned by *hatred*—a person, that is, who is not clearly conscious—will also be receptive to a preaching of *class hatred*. Then *everything* that pertains to a person in the hated class will appear in a particular light: all kindness as diplomacy, all generosity as an attempt to bribe, all intelligence as cunning, and all respectable achievements as an expression of lust for power. And further, it will seem, very convincingly, that the ruling class has invented religion, for instance, so that the enslaved and exploited shall not become aware of their true situation. For when people occupy themselves with 'heavenly' things, then, as they are preoccupied, it will not occur to them to want to actively transform earthly matters!

Is this viewpoint illogical? No, it is not. If the experiential premises

† *The Wisdom of Man, of the Soul, and of the Spirit*, Anthroposophical Press, 1971. See p276.

were correct, then the *logic* of this point of view would be ironclad. It *is* logical—but in spite of this it is completely false. It is false because it is based on a *distorted* experience. Where correct logic leads to false views, it is always due to a *distorted image of experience*, which can be traced back to an unhealthy functioning of the sense organism. If, however, the experienced image is distorted, no arguments, no proofs, are of any avail. We can then no longer strive for clarification, but only for *healing*; that is to say for a cleansing of the sense organism. The next essay will be devoted to the question of whether such a cleansing or healing is possible for East Europe, and if so, by what means.

III

Previously we considered the positive preparation as well as the negative preparation of the manas-organization (spirit self) in the East of Europe. This consideration needs to be supplemented because its object was only the *basic characteristics*, such as would appear when one's task is to find and emphasize primarily the *positive* aspects. If we wish, however, to do justice to the *entire* reality, then we must proceed a step *further*. We must fix our attention on those aspects which, with regard to the aforementioned basic characteristics, appear as complications, or even as contradictions. For instance, we can get the impression from the preceding considerations that the events in Eastern Europe signify a path of destiny leading to the manas-revelation in a 'natural' or 'foreordained' manner.

It is certainly true that events in the East of Europe *can* be comprehended as leading to a preparation of that vacuum necessary for manas-revelation. On the other hand, it is also true that here we have not only a *path* of development, but also a *process of disease*; the path is followed in an *unhealthy* manner, whereas it could be followed in a healthy manner. So the essential truth of the *tragedy* of the European East is not that it has to go through a kind of Kamaloka state, but rather that it goes through such a state in an *unhealthy* way.

Let us attempt to clarify the nature, the causes, and the results of that process of disease which accompanies the necessary preconditions for preparing the manas-revelation in East Europe.

Healthy passage through the characterized trials of emptiness and humiliation preceding the unfolding of manas-revelation takes place when one has understood, with certainty of cognition, the meaning and significance of these trials. Then one knows what they are about, and goes through the suffering of the trial not only with level-headed equanimity, but also with the consciousness that what is now on the way to being realized is happening through one's own free choice.

This passing through the 'loneliness of the desert' which precedes spiritual fulfillment is, however, only possible in cases where the person in question has prepared his or her *consciousness soul* for it in a very definite way. Rudolf Steiner stated in connection with remarks about Vladimir Solovyov that the most important cognitional matter of the present day consists in understanding the relation of the consciousness soul to the spirit self. This not only has the greatest significance for understanding the general spiritual events of our time, but has also invaluable *practical* significance for those individuals and groups of people in East, West, and Center for whom this question arises as a *trial of destiny*. Although today the question concerns *every* human being, it becomes one of either health or sickness of the soul for those people who need not only to understand the relation of the consciousness soul to spirit self, but also to put it into practice. So for the European East, this problem is a question of health or sickness. But it was taken up during decisive decades in such a way that *sickness* resulted.

Of what, then, does this question of the relation of the consciousness soul to the spirit self consist? In *practice*, it consists initially of the realization of the basic precondition of spiritual development: to establish and continue that inner balance that was described by Rudolf Steiner in *Knowledge of the Higher Worlds* with the words *working and waiting*. So here it is a question of developing the balance between *courage* and *humility* (Mut and Demut). Courage alone becomes bravado (Übermut) when it is not complimented by humility; yet without courage, no real spiritual work of overcoming is possible. But on the other hand, humility without courage leads to powerlessness, both in the formation of positive karma and in the battle with enemy powers antagonistic to the spiritual progress of humankind.

In the sphere of *cognitive thinking*, it is a question of knowledge of the cooperation of the 'inductive' and 'deductive' methods—a question of the balance between drawing conclusions from experience, and the revealed content of thought-life.

In the *human social* sphere, it is a question of the achievement of cooperation between the two great karmic streams whose representatives—insofar as they partake in the destiny of the anthroposophical movement—have been described by Rudolf Steiner as 'Aristotelians' and 'Platonists'.

In the sphere of *spiritual knowledge*, it is a question of knowing the relationship of the two great streams of esoteric Christianity that are represented in the history of humankind by two spiritual beings: the being of *Michael* and the being of *Sophia*. Ultimately the problem of the relationship of the consciousness soul to the spirit self is the question of the relationship between the *Michael impulse* and the *Sophia impulse* within the comprehensive Christ impulse.

It is not possible here to give a thorough characterization of these two impulses; only a few single traits can be brought forward which are necessary for the theme of this study. So we shall limit ourselves here to characterizing the Michael impulse as that of *thinking permeated by will*, which strives through the great world relationships to understand the Cosmic Christ; while the Sophia impulse can be described here as a *questioning and listening thinking* oriented toward the God-Manhood of Christ Jesus.

Now the Michael impulse is that of the *Spirit of our Time*. This means that every single spiritual striving of the present day that ignores this is either atavistic or superficial and not to be regarded as healthy. So also one can say the following about people who have not yet developed the activity of the Michael impulse: When, in accordance with destiny, they go through the trials belonging to a maturing of the manas-organization, they can indeed experience all the oppressive and painful qualities of this trial, but they will regard it *only* as misfortune and sickness—that is, they cannot endure it courageously and calmly as a trial. The strengthening, even exhilarating consciousness of its significance, they will miss. But further, after going through this preparation of the manas-organization, that which results from it as spirit-fulfillment will leave them just as poor in *knowledge* as they were previously. They will indeed *feel in their souls* the reality of the active spirit, but for their cognition the spirit will remain silent. And it will be silent because no *language* will be available to them which could speak to their understanding. For the *concepts* appropriate to the spirit through the development of the *Michael impulse* are worked out in the consciousness soul and live within it, forming the *vocabulary* of which the manas-revelation makes use. Whoever cannot meet it out of the consciousness soul with actively formed concepts of the spiritual world may enjoy the bliss of spirit light in his or her soul, but for them a knowledge of the destinies of humankind in life and in death is out of the question.

If we now apply this fact of spiritual development to the situation in the European East, then we must admit the hard truth that what takes place there is indeed a preparation of the *organization* necessary for manas-revelation, but that this revelation will have to remain *dumb* for knowledge when the hour arrives. This could only be otherwise if the European East were to take up the Michael impulse of spirit-based concept formation. The *rejection* of the Michael impulse in its decisive years is the tragedy in the destiny of the European East. One way this tragedy can be seen is in the war against Germany [1914–1918].

So it happened. At present in the European East only the *ground* is prepared for the future manas-revelation. In other parts of Europe, for instance, where there are groups of people who have taken up the Michael impulse in the right way—i.e., those people who have prepared themselves properly through a *training* by means of concentration and meditation—not only is the ground prepared, but also the revelation itself can be *consciously* experienced. And it will be *these* people who will be able to bring true help to the Russian East in its desperate state. For they will be in possession of the *word* that mute and suffering Russia lacks and will lack—that word which will signify no less than a *healing* for the consciousness of human beings. But long before this can happen, a living *compassion* and *understanding* for the European East must be consciously *fostered* in those circles of people. For this to happen, however, the unconscious disdain and fear that is often felt toward the European East, even by spiritually oriented Europeans, must vanish.

Neither admiration nor an expectation of wonders is what the writer of these essays wishes to arouse for the mute and empty East, but rather compassion and *understanding* for its tragic situation. It is true, we have *our* worries and *our* trials, but let us not forget that at the eastern door of our house there stand *men and women* in rags with out-stretched hands—and that the time approaches when they will knock! The teachers, doctors, and artists among us are all heavily taxed with their own tasks, but perhaps they could still, now and again, spare a moment as human beings to remember the destiny of the East European portion of humanity. This is necessary so that a stream of conscious sympathy and understanding may be in existence before the hour arrives when the eastern door will be opened.

What happens to the people who succumb to this temptation?

Well, what happens is what can be observed in the European East: a 'people' arises whose conspicuous basic characteristic is *lack of devotion*, an absence of reverence. Instead there develops the urge to criticize everything (often in the most clumsy and narrow-minded way), to judge and to condemn. The 'Movement of the Godless' is not only an effort to spread theoretic reasons for the non-existence of the Divine, but is moreover a movement trying to eliminate all reverence from life. It is the *feeling of reverence* that is being attacked. For this feeling is regarded not only as a weakness, but even as a *betrayal* of the spirit of Bolshevism.

The second characteristic quality of this type of people is their submergence in an unceasing collective activity: meetings, clubs, workers' processions, mass demonstrations, sport clubs—I know not what else; only there is no chance to be alone, not a moment to *stop to think!* Always to be among people, always to be in a group—this is a remarkable mania in these people. If the evolution of human beings in the direction of the Spirit depends on reverence and the need for still moments of peaceful contemplation, two qualities described by Rudolf Steiner as the basis for spiritual development in his book *Knowledge of the Higher Worlds*, then we could contrast this with the psychological phenomenon of Bolshevism, a development that is based on irreverence, mass judgements, and mass thinking.

Now all the above considerations (as also those of the previous essay) can give rise to the following question: Is the manas-revelation, such as it is characterized in these essays, not a kind of mediumism? Does not this characterization give the impression that here is merely passive suffering and waiting until the revelation comes 'of itself' one day?

Before this question can be answered, it is necessary to clarify the concepts of 'passivity' and 'activity' as applied to spiritual life. The ordinary meaning of these concepts is this: 'activity' refers to a consciousness in the state of 'doing', and 'passivity' refers to a consciousness in the state of 'suffering'. This standpoint is entirely justified and useful when one has in mind the *horizontal*, the relationship of the human consciousness to its surroundings. However, if one is considering the *vertical*, that is, the relation of the incarnated human being to the spiritual world, then this standpoint is no longer valid. Then the opposite is true: the receptive attitude toward the spiritual world, the suffering and waiting, is the *active* side of the vertically upright consciousness, while the efforts of the will for the purpose of this or that exercise or task of cognition are the *passive* side. So, for instance, the words Christ Jesus spoke during the hour of Gethsemane: 'Not my will, but Thy will be done,' signify the highest possible activity of the vertically-directed consciousness. But this activity is not visible on the horizontal plane of life; there it appears as passive.

Therefore, the essential requirement for the occurrence of manas-cognition is not the submergence of 'I' consciousness (even in sacrificial devotion), but rather its coordination with the 'higher I'. Unfortunately, there exists much unclarity about the nature of the relationship between the 'higher and lower I'. The 'lower I' is usually imagined as a chalice that is filled from above by the 'higher I'. This may suffice for awhile as a *picture*, but it is not a fitting *concept*. For a moment comes—and it comes when life itself demands clarification in this area—when one cannot do anything with this image.

Another image—although it may at first seem strange—can be very fruitful and helpful in this regard. Consider the relationship of the 'higher I' to the 'ordinary I' as like that of a *pair of eyes*. However, here the eyes are not placed to 'right' and 'left', that is, in the horizontal, but 'above' and 'below', in the vertical. The 'higher I' is the human being's eye in the spiritual world; the 'ordinary I', which is the focal point of the sentient soul, the intellectual soul, and the consciousness soul, is the organ of perception in both the physical world and the elemental world. The true and healthy relation of the two poles of the human being consists in both 'eyes' being coordinated; that is, they must be able to *see together* in just the same way as do the horizontally placed physical eyes. And the functioning of manas-consciousness is essentially nothing other than the fact of the human being's 'upper I' and 'lower I' *seeing in concert*. The line upon which the two 'eyes' are coordinated is actually the manas-organization about which we spoke above, and which, after the purification and transformation of the astral 'vertebral column' of pride, works from above downward as revelation of the spirit self.

If this relationship comes about, then the 'lower I' can learn from the 'higher I', while the higher can also learn from the lower. For only the 'lower I' can have the great experience of *human* love on earth, and only the 'higher I' can endure the experience of the *divine* love of the spiritual world. Further, when divine love is coordinated with human love, then the relationship of the two 'eyes'—of the heavenly and earthly 'eyes'—which was broken by the Fall, is restored again. Then there is the basis for a cognition that has not the remotest resemblance to any form of mediumship, but is the result of the fusion of two experiences: of spiritual and earthly experiences.

This is the task of humanity in general. In the East of Europe, however, it will be achieved by way of the 'lower eye' remaining short-sighted or even blinded, until the awakened 'higher eye' heals it, whereas in the West the other one-sided path is followed.

The description of the condition of the lower consciousness in East Europe as 'short-sighted' or even 'blinded' should not be taken merely as an analogy; these expressions are fairly accurate descriptions of a real stage of the development of an illness presently occurring in Eastern Europe. Let us next consider the development of this illness.[†]

[†] The fourth article never appeared, as publication of *Korrespondenz der Arbeitsgemeinschaft* ceased with the Nazi occupation of Holland. Whether it was ever written is not known. ED

LIST OF ORIGINAL SOURCES

The articles in this collection first appeared in various German journals between the years 1930 and 1938. These journals are listed below, along with the abbreviations used to identify them here. The abbreviation is followed by year of publication and the identifying volume number or date of the particular issue.

Anthroposophie: Wochenschrift für freies Geistesleben [AW]

Das Goetheanum: Internationale Wochenschrift für Anthroposophie und Dreigliederung [G]

Anthroposophie: Monatschrift für freies Geistesleben [AM]

Korrespondenz der anthroposophischen Arbeitsgemeinschaften [K]

Anthroposophische Arbeitsberichte [AA]

PART ONE: EARLY ESSAYS

'The Gospel of St John as a Way Toward Understanding the Spiritual Hierarchies' [AW]: 1930, ns. 9 and 10 (March 2 and 9)

'The Metamorphoses of Logic: The Logic of the Material, Soul, and Spiritual Worlds' [AW]: 1930, n. 12 (March 23)

'The Metamorphosis of Thinking through the Study of Spiritual Science' [AW]: 1930, n. 14 (April 6)

'The Formulation of Meditation in East and West' [AW]: 1930, n. 16 (April 20)

'The Study of Spiritual Science as an Esoteric Schooling' [AW]: 1930, n. 20 (May 18)

'H. P. Blavatsky's *Secret Doctrine* and Rudolf Steiner's *Occult Science*' [AW]: 1930, n. 22 (June 1)

'Western Occultism, Vedanta, and Anthroposophy' [AW]: 1930, n. 33 (August 17)

'The Philosophy of Taking Counsel With Others' [G]: 1930, n.39 (Sept 28)

'The Significance of a Free Anthroposophical Group' [AA]: 1938, n.45 (Jan)

'Resurrection as a Process Within the Human Organism' [AW]: 1931, n.16 (April 19)

'John Dee of London: Two Book Reviews' [AW]: 1930, n. 47 (Nov 23); [AW]: 1931, n. 4 (Jan. 25)

'Midnight Sun: A Christmas Meditation' [AW]: 1931, n.2 (Jan 11)

PART TWO: RUSSIAN SPIRITUALITY & THE EAST

'Anthroposophy in the East' [AW]: 1930, n. 45 (Nov 9)

'Christianity in Russia' [AW]: 1930, n. 47 (Nov 23)

'The Mission of East Europe in Relation to the Mission of the West' [AW]: 1930, n. 50 (Dec 14)

'Movements Opposing Spiritual Science in the East' [AW]: 1930, n. 51 (Dec 21)

'The Spiritual Life of Asia' [AW]: 1931, n.3 (Jan 18)

'China and East Europe' [AW]: 1931, n.7 (Feb 15)

'Mongolianism and East Europe' [AW]: 1931, n.8 (Feb 22)

'The Finnish Impulse in Russian Spiritual Life' [AW]: 1931, n.11 (March 15)

'The Saga of the Holy City of Kitezh as Revelation of the Essential Forces of the Russian Folk-Soul' [AW]: 1931, n.12 (March 22)

'The East European Conception of Suffering' [AW]: 1931, n.15 (April 12)

'The Possibilities of Development in Eastern Christianity' [AW]: 1931, n. 19 (May 10)

'Solovyov, Dostoevsky, and Tolstoi Reveal the European Way of Thinking, Feeling, and Willing' [AW]: 1931, n.22 (May 31)

'Anti-Christianism in the European East' [AW]: 1931, n.23 (June 7)

'Anti-Christianism Seen in Relation to the Destiny-Paths of Judas, Saul, and Peter' [AW]: 1931, n.25 (June 21)

'Anti-Christianism in East and West' [AW]: 1931, n.27 (July 5)

'Possession and Enlightenment Seen in Relation to the Destiny-Paths of Judas and Paul' [AW]: 1931, n. 35 (Aug 30)

'The Antichrist in the View of Vladimir Solovyov' [AW]: 1931, n. 33 (Aug 16)

'The Deepening of Conscience Which Results in Etheric Vision' [AW]: 1931, n. 39 (Sept 27)

'Suffering as a Preparation for Etheric Vision' [AM]: 1931, n. 3 (Dec 11)

'The Secret Motto of Bolshevism' [AW]: 1930, n. 18 (May 4)

'Collectivism and Sophia (Tolstoi, Lenin, and Solovyov)' [AW]: 1930, n. 30 (July 27)

'The Spiritual Basis of the East European Tragedy' [K]: 1935, n. 47 (Sept 12, Oct 1, Nov 2)

FURTHER READING

Christ and Sophia: Anthroposophic Meditations on the Old Testament, New Testament, and Apocalypse (Gt. Barrington, MA: SteinerBooks, 2006). *Christ and Sophia* contains all of Valentin Tomberg's essential anthroposophic works on the Scriptures, providing an invaluable resource for anyone who wishes to gain a deeper understanding of esoteric Christianity, as revealed by a close, meditative reading of the Bible—from *Genesis* to *John's Revelation*. The appendix contains his seven lectures held in Rotterdam in 1939 entitled *The Four Sacrifices of Christ and the Reappearance of Christ in the Etheric World.*

Inner Development, 7 lectures held in Rotterdam in 1938 (Gt. Barrington, MA: Anthroposophic Press, 1992). These talks deal with the spiritual path in its Christian-Rosicrucian aspect, discussing the deeper significance of meditation, the various stages of consciousness (Imagination, Inspiration, and Intuition), the Guardian of the Threshold, and the esoteric trials one encounters along the way, concluding with a description of the life of Rudolf Steiner as the life of a Christian initiate.

Lazarus, Come Forth! Meditations of a Christian Esotericist on the Mysteries of the Raising of Lazarus, the Ten Commandments, the Three Kingdoms & the Breath of Life (Gt. Barrington, MA: Lindisfarne Books, 2006). Drawing on the ancient and often-forgotten sources of esoteric Christianity, Valentin Tomberg reflects on the mysteries of humanity's covenant with God in history. The power of these meditations is that they reflect the author's personal spiritual journey into the depths of God's kingdom within—within the soul, within personal relationships, within nature and the cosmos. A previous edition of this work was titled *Covenant of the Heart.*

Meditations on the Tarot: A Journey into Christian Hermeticism (NY: Putnam/Jeremy P. Tarcher, 2002). This book is one of the true spiritual classics of the twentieth century. Published with an index and Cardinal Hans Urs von Balthasar's Afterword, this publication is one of the most important works of esoteric Christianity. Written anonymously and published posthumously, as was the author's wish, the intention of this work is for the reader to find a relationship with the author in the spiritual dimensions of existence. The author wanted not to be thought of as a personality who lived from 1900 to 1973, but as a friend who is communicating with us from beyond the boundaries of ordinary life. *Meditations on the Tarot* is a timely contribution toward the rediscovery and renewal of the Christian contemplative tradition of the Fathers of the Church and the High Middle Ages.

The Wandering Fool: Love & Its Symbols. Early Studies on the Tarot, with Three Lectures on Christian Hermeticism by Robert Powell (San Rafael, CA: Logo-Sophia Press, 2009). Students of *Meditations on the Tarot* have cause for celebration, for in 2007 a collection of the author's notes was published — preliminary studies of the images of the Tarot cards, illustrating the method he followed This methodology is now revealed for the first time in English translation through the inclusion of material published in Part Two of this volume. Part One comprises three lectures held by Robert Powell, the translator of *Meditations on the Tarot* into English from the original French manuscript. Also included is additional background material from the Luxembourg (Kairos) and German (Achamoth) editions.

Studies on the Foundation Stone Meditation (San Rafael, CA: LogoSophia Press, 2010). A revised translation, with new introduction by Robert Powell, of a fundamental and long out-of-print study of this meditation so central to the life-work of Rudolf Steiner and so pivotal now in this time of the growing realization of the community of the Second Coming of Christ.

The Foundation Stone Meditation in the Sacred Dance of Eurythmy, by Lacquanna Paul and Robert Powell (study material published by the Sophia Foundation of North America).

Rudolf Steiner, *The Philosophy of Freedom: Intuitive Thinking as a Spiritual Path* (Gt. Barrington, MA: SteinerBooks, 1995). Of all of his works, *Philosophy of Freedom* is the one that Steiner himself believed would have the longest life and the greatest spiritual and cultural consequences.

It describes moral intuition as the touchstone for modern human beings on a spiritual path. This seminal work asserts that the ability to think and develop moral intuition is a path for human beings today to gain true knowledge of themselves and of the universe. This is not merely a philosophical volume, but rather a warm, heart-oriented guide to the practice and experience of living spirituality.

LaVergne, TN USA
21 June 2010
186932LV00001B/8/P